A FLAME
CALLED
INDIANA

A FLAME CALLED INDIANA

EDITED BY DOUG PAUL CASE

AN ANTHOLOGY OF CONTEMPORARY HOOSIER WRITING

INDIANA UNIVERSITY PRESS

This book is a publication of

Indiana University Press
Office of Scholarly Publishing
Herman B Wells Library 350
1320 East 10th Street
Bloomington, Indiana 47405 USA

iupress.org

Manufactured in the United States of America

First printing 2023

Cataloging information is available from the Library of Congress.

ISBN 978-0-253-06680-0 (paperback)
ISBN 978-0-253-06682-4 (ebook)

CONTENTS

PART 3: *Fiction*

A FLAME CALLED INDIANA

INTRODUCTION

DOUG PAUL CASE

RE: THE INDIANA IMAGINATION

Almost daily I find myself amused that in the decade I've lived in Indiana no one I've met has been able to definitively tell me where the moniker "Hoosier" originated. Theories abound, of course, and have been cataloged by organizations as disparate as the Indiana Historical Bureau and the United States Forest Service. They include an unusually large woodsman, an unusually adept flatboatman, and an unusually truculent elder militiaman. In almost all the versions I've heard there's a reference to something atypical—if not downright odd!—about the Hoosier, long before comedians and St. Louisans started using it as a pejorative for uncultured people.

These etymological possibilities are at the heart of what I'm talking about when I'm talking about the Indiana imagination because at bottom, "Hoosier" originated wherever the last Hoosier asked said it might have. Indiana is a tall tale type of state. The thrill is in contemplating why each particular story took the direction it did, and what interests me most about these possible first Hoosiers is how they were all in the middle of getting something done. Whatever else Hoosiers have been, we've historically been great doers. As Kurt Vonnegut, our most famous homegrown writer, once remarked, "Wherever you go, there is always a Hoosier doing something important there." And what have we been doing? Painting. Inventing. Racing. Dribbling. Moonwalking. And, of course, writing.

While imaginators everywhere transform *what is* into *what could be*, for many Indiana storytellers the act of developing that *could* seems intimately and situationally tied to their audience. We're not concerned with telling people what they want to hear, but what we hope will expand that audience's perspective.

When the sky is so big and the corn so tall, how could we not want to share that grandness, to enrich our neighbors' inner lives with our dreams, our lyrics, our sagas? Writers in Indiana understand implicitly how narrative shapes perspective, how the more one reads, the more one comes to understand about the world and the incalculable number of varied perspectives living in it. Our state isn't nicknamed "the crossroads" because people are passing through it but because they're stopping on their way, showing and telling. It's true, there's something in the air here, some urge to fill in space with song. There's always room for another writer's tale, always for a new image. I read to learn, to experience the passage of time in new ways, to delight in clever turns of phrase . . . and I get to do all those things with the pieces in this anthology. There is very little as stimulating to a writer as a strong collection of their peer's work; this is what's happening around me, this is with whom I'm conversing! Anthologies like this one are events, celebrations of our imagination and drive.

Historians have previously dubbed the turn of the twentieth century the "golden age" of Indiana literature, when many of the United States's most popular authors, including Booth Tarkington and James Whitcomb Riley, hailed from Indiana. Lew Wallace's 1880 novel *Ben-Hur: A Tale of the Christ* was the best-selling book of the nineteenth century. By numbers alone it would be difficult to assert that we have recently entered a new golden age—there are, of course, a dozen additional states to compete with, and the publishing industry has largely entrenched itself in New York—but in the last one hundred forty years (and doubly in the last twenty!) we've seen a widening of what our writing looks like and what it addresses—a trend I'll happily dub golden. While *Ben-Hur*, for example, chronicled the life of an enslaved Jewish nobleman-turned-charioteer who witnessed the crucifixion, and the most famous of Whitcomb's poems introduced the world to the little orphan Annie, our state's recent writing is more likely to imagine what the world will look like after trudging through the Anthropocene thirty years or to deeply consider the uses of beauty in a time like ours. To use the image of a limestone quarry: our fiction continues to take unusually imaginative leaps, our nonfiction unusually vivid dives, and our poetry unusually full-bodied splashes. While not every piece in this collection is set in Indiana—Buffalo, Puerto Rico, a Pennsylvania train station, a field just over the border in Ohio—all these authors show the commitment to possibility I've come to expect from Hoosier writers. Often all it takes is a few years in a town like Bloomington to appreciate how language's possibilities seem waterborne here and perhaps another to cement that wondrous feeling into your writing.

My hope for this anthology is that it will serve as both a chronicle of where our state's writing is today and a beacon to those who'll take it where it's going next. Somewhere in Kokomo or Gary or Fishers or Hobart, a young writer will catch in these pages the spark of what language can do when you're least expecting it, then pick up their pen or open their notes app to give writing the time-honored Hoosier try.

Bloomington, Indiana
July 2022

RE: SELECTION

In order to submit work to this anthology, writers must have lived in Indiana for at least three years, and the work under consideration could not have been completed earlier than 2010. There is a staggering amount of terrific writing that met these criteria, many of which are listed in the Recommended Reading at the back of this volume. Making selections was a painstaking process, and I had to at minimum answer "yes" to two questions for every piece selected: (1) did this piece teach me something about the Indiana imagination, and (2) could I see this piece inspiring young writers to try something new. This led me primarily to pieces that played with memory or narrative structure, and I'm confident there's something here to spark even the most skeptical of writers.

RE: PROCEEDS

All editor royalties for this anthology will directly fund community writing programs and fellowships for creative writing students at Indiana University Bloomington.

RE: GRATITUDE

I am grateful to several people who made this anthology possible, particularly Dan Crissman at Indiana University Press and Brando Skyhorse, Director of the IU Creative Writing Program, both of whom shouted "yes!" when first hearing this idea. My thanks also to the IU creative writing faculty for their input, especially Catherine Bowman, Ross Gay, and Samrat Upadhyay.

Thank you to Michael Adams, Chair of the IU English Department, for his support and constancy. To Lisa LaPlante for keeping our finances on track. To Jessica Masi and Rose Zinnia for their assistance acquiring permissions and preparing this manuscript. To Bruce Snider for the title(!). To the Case family for cheering on this new Hoosier from Connecticut. And especially to Joe Burns, who sacrificed many a game night so I could keep my nose in a book.

PART 1

NONFICTION

WHAT IT'S LIKE TO SWIM IN THE OCEAN FOR THE FIRST TIME AT TWENTY-EIGHT

ASHLEY C. FORD

IN THE LAST WEEK OF AUGUST, Kelly rolled over in bed and said, "Let's go to the beach." It was a Monday morning, our bodies were damp from an oppressive heat wave, and the far end of Coney Island was certain to be uncrowded. Conditions were perfect for a day by the water. The more he thought about it, the more excited he got. We could get food from Nathan's, people-watch, and swim where the Atlantic touches Brooklyn. "We've never gone swimming in the ocean together," he said. "It'll be a new first." I smiled, nodded, and tried to remember where I'd stuffed my bathing suit. He leaped out of bed to get dressed, but I lay there a bit longer wondering how or if I should tell him our beach day would include more than one first.

The first beach Kelly and I ever visited together was in Santa Monica. This was not a swimming trip, nor was it a day to lie by the water. It was 2013, and we were in Los Angeles for my first Thanksgiving with his family. It was my second visit to the city, the first having been the previous August. I was then twenty-six years old and had the means to travel west of Missouri for the first time in my life. I'd ended my first trip feeling pretty meh, but the second trip—the Thanksgiving trip—made me believe I could live there. The sun seemed warmer, the people seemed more interesting, and I was falling in love.

We rolled up our jeans, took off our shoes, and walked into the Santa Monica surf. He held my hand and told me stories about all of the adventures he'd had at this beach. I closed my eyes and tried to picture them.

My family is made up of working-class Hoosiers; almost all of us live in the same city, and most of us are afraid of driving on highways. On the rare occasion that we traveled out of state, it was in caravans on our way to family reunions; we also took one trip to Pigeon Forge, Tennessee, and a trip to Disney World when I was a toddler.

At Thanksgiving, I learned Kelly's aunt, our host, was a retired president of the Los Angeles County Museum of Art, and that Kelly had spent every summer with her from the time he was seven years old until he was twenty-one. They'd taken boats down the Nile together, ridden bikes around Versailles, and jumped off the back of sailboats in the Pacific Ocean. Quite suddenly, I was embarrassed to admit I hadn't even learned to swim until I was twenty-three, that I had never traveled abroad, that I didn't even have a passport.

Kelly is three years younger than me, and he had seen the world in ways I could only imagine. His family clearly valued the wanderlust I experienced, but I had never had the chance to physically express it. Did they worry about that? They'd deliberately raised a man who prioritized adventure. Did they think I would hold him back? Would I? That night, in bed, I whispered my insecurities. Kelly said, "There's nothing to be embarrassed about. My family loves you. And think of all the things we'll get to do together for the first time."

I did not know how to describe the sadness of knowing they would be firsts for only me, not him, without sounding melodramatic. I kissed him instead. We tried not to keep secrets, but not all secrets are created equal. Some you keep because you don't even know what the truth is or how to tell it just yet. Others, no matter how small, damage the key to whatever binds you together. It's hard to know which is which until after the tides of consequence roll in and the secret, inevitably, rolls out.

—✺—

Now, nearly two years later, we stuffed his backpack with books and my tote with a blanket borrowed from the neighbors, and we set out for Coney Island. Kelly read on the train, and I wrote in my journal about my reluctance to tell him this small truth: I'd never swam in the ocean. I had been to the ocean before, I had even put my feet in the water, but I had never worked up the nerve to dive in and swim. Every time I thought, *I should tell him*, I'd picture him jumping off boats as a ten-year-old, and I'd picture myself in a pool at twenty-three learning how to float. Logic told me there was no reason to be ashamed. The other part of myself fixated on those incompatible images and thought, *This is why you'll never see the world together, and he'll always be showing you where he's already been.*

It wasn't until I had stripped down to my bathing suit and stood at the edge of the ocean that I got nervous about the actual swimming part. Kelly ran into the waves chest first. I went in up to my waist before muttering, "It's too big. I don't know what I thought this was going to be like, but the ocean is too fucking big. I can't do this." Kelly, now farther into the water than I'd ever been, yelled for me to come closer. Finally, I squeezed my eyes shut, dove into a wave, and let it buoy my body forward. I flapped my arms, kicked my legs, and, before I knew it, opened my eyes right in front of him. He wrapped his arms around me and smiled. I licked my salty lips and asked why my eyes didn't hurt. He said, "Well, it's not chlorine." I ducked under his arms and dove back into the water before another wave hit. My body felt powerful, light, and like it had become part of the ocean. Every bit of insecurity floated away. I was swimming in the ocean for the first time, beside my favorite person in the entire world, and I was not embarrassed. I was celebrating.

We splashed around for an hour. I learned that if I jumped into the waves, they wouldn't slam into my body and that, eventually, salt water would burn my eyes too. I was practicing floating when Kelly swam over to me. He gathered me in his arms and asked, "What are you grinning about?" I turned and faced this man who moved from Seattle to live with me in Brooklyn, who makes a point to read everything I've ever written, and who introduced me to his family as the love of his life. I realized he had never thought of me as someone who was catching up with him. He just saw his partner. I pulled him back to the shore and toward our blanket. When we sat down, I took his hand and a deep breath.

"I have something to tell you."

FIFTEEN THINGS I'VE NOTICED WHILE TRYING TO WALK 10,000 STEPS PER DAY

Muncie, Indiana Edition

SILAS HANSEN

1.

On a cold and rainy Sunday afternoon when I didn't want to walk outside: a box proclaiming to be synthetic urine for sale in Nirvana, next to Louie's Tux Shop and across from C. J. Banks in the Muncie Mall, behind the counter where they sell glass pipes blown to resemble tiny carrots and octopi, next to a rack of Rasta wigs.

2.

On my walk between my house and my favorite bar, in the ninety-degree angle created by a lamppost and a banner proclaiming this path to be the Fallen Heroes Memorial Bridge: a gigantic orb-weaver spider and its perfect web that catches the setting sun as I walk by.

3.

On a snowy Friday night in January, on my walk to play euchre with friends: an undergrad standing in the snow, dressed in a pair of gym shorts, snow boots, and a black North Face, holding a PBR tallboy in one hand and a leash in the other, connecting him to a tiny, fluffy white dog, nearly hidden in snow up to its belly.

4.

On the corner of Jackson and High Street, across from the MITS bus station: a single glass jar of Prego tomato sauce—shattered, red splattered across the sidewalk.

5.

The sound of a train whistle off in the distance, announcing itself as it barrels along the railroad tracks that run through and all around the city, sounding eerie and inviting all at once.

6.

A rundown pickup truck full of drunk guys—too old to be called boys, too young yet to be called men—one of whom yells, "I'm going to fuck you up! I'm going to FUCK! YOU! UP!" as they speed by, the others laughing.

7.

A man, standing proudly on his porch at 11:00 p.m. on a Thursday evening while music blasts from inside his house; and then, as I get closer: the stream of urine as he makes eye contact and nods to acknowledge my presence—unashamed, unabashed.

8.

A man in his late fifties or early sixties, dressed like Elvis—rhinestone-studded suit and all—and singing Neil Diamond's "Sweet Caroline" in front of the yoga studio while a group of young women, college-aged, hula hoop around him.

9.

A sign stuck in the grass in front of the Phillips 66 gas station around the corner from my house: yellow corrugated plastic with black sans serif letters: "WALT'S CRAWLERS."

10.

A college student wearing gym shorts, no shirt, and a fuzzy animal head—an otter, perhaps—while skateboarding in the faculty parking lot on a Friday afternoon.

11.

In the parking lot of the liquor store where I buy overpriced, mediocre wine when I don't want to drive to Aldi: an exact replica of the Jurassic Park jeep, windows down, no one inside.

12.

During the monthly art walk through downtown: a man with a face tattoo, advertising his wife's massage business by walking up and down the street in front of the Mexican restaurant, holding a sign advertising $1 massages and "MAGIC FINGERS."

13.
On my way home from trivia on a Tuesday night at about 11:00 p.m.: a thirtysomething man in an Alan Iverson jersey, powerwalking while drinking a bright red slushy.

14.
A squirrel skull and tibia ribs held in a glass case, $30 in the Downtown Flea Market and Oddities Shop.

15.
Two grown men standing in the parking lot in front of Dollar Tree, next to a rundown pickup truck, silently releasing six balloons into the sky, one by one, and watching them float away.

CAVES

RAJPREET HEIR

THERE'S AN UNDERWATER CAVE SYSTEM IN Southern Indiana that contains twenty-one miles of surveyed passages. In 1940, George Colglazier noticed his pond had disappeared overnight in a heavy rain. It had become a sinkhole and entrance to the Bluespring Caverns. Over the course of a million years, pond water had been seeping down through surface soil, reaching the limestone beneath it. The water slowly dissolved small parts of the rock, creating fissures and then cavities. Eventually, the surface level gave way and the pond vanished into the longest known subterranean river in the United States. While the cave system had been discovered in the 1800s, a dam completed in 1913 on the White River closed it off. Colglazier's children were thrilled about the entrance on their property, and the family began welcoming visitors from all around the world to see the caves.

My twin brother, Arjun, and I visited the caves the summer after seventh grade for a YMCA day camp field trip. We used to go to the Y near our house in Lawrence Township, but a brand new one with a larger selection of camps was built in Fishers. Our mom considered the old one "too dingy," so my parents took turns getting up early to make the longer drive for us—a small representation of the way each generation in our family has made sacrifices for the next as they moved from India to England to Indianapolis.

With us that afternoon were twenty other campers, and we were about to be divided into two groups. Half were to wait at the picnic tables, and the other half would take a boat ride through the caves. I got picked for the boat ride; Arjun was not. By that age, Arjun and I didn't talk to each other much at home or around others. Arjun was math and science, left-handed; I was English and

13

art, right-handed. Ordinarily, being on my own wouldn't have bothered me, but he and I were the only non-white campers and all the kids were in the same school system except the two of us. These kids were more attractive and richer than the kids at my middle school. In the first few days of camp, when I felt left out, I'd ask people random questions and write them down in a notebook. This only made everyone nervous around me.

I was happy to see Dan, the cutest boy, in my group. Dan did reckless flips at the pool; he'd leave the diving board while seated in a plastic chair, jump into nests of foam noodles, or attempt somersaults.

Our group talked over the guide as we walked to the caves' entrance. It got colder as we walked lower and lower down a ramp. At the bottom was a semi-rusty deck at the opening of a cave. The dank air smelled of stale blankets, but the coolness was a relief from the sun. In the water was a metal boat, which resembled an elongated version of the pan my mom used to make banana bread, one of the American desserts she liked. A guide helped us step into the boat. Dan was first, and he caused waves to slop onto the deck. Next was Lauren, the prettiest in the group, then several others.

Earlier, while we were at the picnic tables, restless after finishing our lunch, Dan had grabbed Lauren's waist. She let out an effortless shriek as she kicked her legs at him, her hair swishing with sunrays in a way mine refused. My black hair took in all the sun and let none out.

While getting ready a day before, my mom made me change out of my track uniform shorts into a longer pair, even though we were running late. She thought the track shorts were inappropriate. I wore the same longer blue shorts to a family party months later and my grandmother told me to change into pants because she thought *those* shorts were too short. Though my clothing guidelines were different from nearly every girl I went to school with, I was reminded that my mother and her mother had dealt with even stricter rules in their time.

At the picnic tables, Lauren escaped from Dan and did a cartwheel, as girls like her were naturally able to do. As she was suspended in the air, the world held its breath. We were all with her in mid-spin, seeing the flat ground below us and the elusive sky above. Lauren wore an extremely bright, extremely tight, pink tank top and short shorts. Her stomach appeared in a smooth arc of baby softness. She landed laughing.

—⁊⁊—

Trying to maintain balance on the shifting boat as I got in, my legs felt as apprehensive as dismounting a trampoline or bounce house. An obese boy named

Travis was seated in front of me, and Blake was behind me. Concerns about the boat sinking and whether this many people were supposed to be on it were unabashedly voiced by Andy, the most spoiled camper.

Blake was a disabled kid with nearly translucent skin. He was so little that he looked at least five years younger than we did. He never talked. I think one of the counselors said he had Fetal Alcohol Syndrome. Since we were in middle school or on the way into high school, we proudly thought ourselves mature enough to not tease him; no one was mean to Blake, but no one sat next to him either.

The guide instructed us to put our hands on the shoulders of the person in front of us for safety. I wished Dan was in front of me, but it was as if Lauren and Dan knew we'd have permission to touch each other. If we went to a movie, were paired up for square dancing, or needed to learn mouth-to-mouth resuscitation, they'd somehow end up with each other. I considered explaining the directions to Blake, unsure of how much assistance he needed, but then I felt his bony hands hit my shoulder blades. When he sneezed into my hair, I didn't say, "Bless you"—as a non-Christian, saying it always made me feel uncomfortable, traitorous—I just stayed quiet.

Gliding into the cave on ONE OF THE MOST UNIQUE TOURS IN AMERICA, the guide's light at the front of the boat was bright enough that the water's movements and our shadows were illuminated on the textured surfaces. We were on a mile journey through the long, sinuous passages to the heart of the natural world. A skin of moisture glistened on the walls.

The guide, a regular occupant of this underworld, said, "Let's be honest, everyone wants to touch something when they're in a cave, but don't do it. Touching a stalactite or stalagmite can kill it. The oils from your fingers will permanently disrupt the mineral buildup."

I could see why he'd tell kids like us a statement like that early on the tour. I didn't need to read the other campers' minds to know they'd already considered running their hands on the cave walls.

"Ew, something dripped on my head," said Lauren.

"They call that a cave kiss. It's just moisture from the caves," explained the guide.

After showing us formations that resembled an elephant and a pterodactyl, he started talking about the "amblyopsis spelaea," native fish without eyes, fish that can only sense through vibrations, swimming beneath us, and it bothered me how some creatures can adapt to any environment. Losing eyesight to continue living in darkness seemed to go against what I knew of evolution. The fish had been living in Bluespring for thousands of years and could live as long as people. Their main diet consisted of small blind crustaceans called isopods, which live in the water.

"Now I'm going to turn off the light for something we call 'total darkness,'" the guide announced. "The darkness is so absolute that you would go blind if you stayed in here for more than a week."

The darkness seemed to blot away summer. It was not the stillness of peace. I felt nervous to breathe too hard. Suddenly, I felt hands from the darkness run up and down my sides. They could only be Blake's. His fingers moved across my breasts. I couldn't turn to look at him to see if he had done this by accident. Someone touching me in that way could only have been a mistake. Surely disabled kids didn't have those sorts of interests. Then Blake did it again. His hands went up and down my chest, fingertips catching on the soft material of my powder blue shirt. I didn't want to take my hands off Travis's shoulders for fear of losing balance. Any aggressive movement could tip the boat. The guide had said that the water was fifty-four degrees and if you fell in, you'd be dead in under thirty-five minutes. We were one hundred feet below the surface.

For someone so bony, I had developed breasts early. My breasts seemed to dismay my mother, like my growing into a woman was an insult to our family's sensibilities. My mother had probably forced me to dress so modestly to avoid attention. She had never acknowledged why it was so important to cover up, as if I wasn't grown up enough to understand.

Blake grabbed my chest and left his hands there. My growing body—with its creaky joints and skin color deep enough for my brothers to scratch tic-tac-toe boards on my legs during long car trips—was, once more, a problem.

I squeezed the tensed inner parts of my arms, arms that used to throw a football further than many boys, on Blake's bent wrists, but it didn't faze him. Blake drummed his fingers down me and up again like a shiver. Like my ribs were piano keys. I felt repulsed and confused at what he was getting from touching me. Such intimacy with someone who hadn't spoken to me before.

Only the week before, when I was in a different Y camp, Ross, a boy my age, who had buttery rich kid pudge, had pushed me into the shallow end of the indoor pool. I thought he was being playful, so I'd push him back. Then Ross lifted me up and tossed me sideways, and I struggled to stand, catching my breath and blinking away water but he grabbed me before I could catch my breath. As he tossed me sideways, he groped me—me, the only girl my age in a one-piece: a dark blue, snakeskin-patterned Nike one-piece that came up to my neck. The other kids around us, splashes, and the Disney station's music had detracted from my protests and where his hands were. I didn't understand what I had done to him or why he picked me. I certainly wasn't anyone's first-choice crush; he didn't seem nervous around me. His actions were motivated by something new.

A day prior to the pool incident, I had been chasing Ross in capture the flag, and he started to weave in front of me, grinning while glancing back. Even though I didn't play outside with my brothers as I had when I was younger, my competitive spirit still emerged on occasion. I accelerated, my shoes edging into the sweet mud. Then Ross stopped next to some tall grass, turned to face me, and said, "You jiggle."

My face felt as if all the blood had been pushed to the last layer of skin. It was a new brand of teasing that I could not dispute. My breasts seemed so obscene all of a sudden, and I wished I was wearing something even baggier. Though Ross had stopped, tagging him—or any boy—lost its allure.

I didn't tell Arjun about any of this—it never really occurred to me—but I did tell my mom about Ross, and she contacted the Y. She was more about action than talking to me about what happened, but I knew she cared. The afternoon after the pool incident with Ross, a counselor handed me an envelope and inside was a penciled two-sentence apology note on unlined Y stationary paper from Ross. The sentences were formulaic, about how he was sorry he made me uncomfortable and that he would be nicer in the future. It was as if he'd sat in the director's office wondering what to say and the staff gave up and told him what to write.

—m—

With the lights still out, the guide said he was going to slam a seat cushion down on the boat so we could hear the echo. The slam felt sinister, and the echo lasted twenty-five seconds. I counted to distract myself from Blake's hands.

"You guys can talk now if you want. Should I turn the light back on, or do you want me to steer us in the dark for a little bit?" he asked.

"No, let's finish in the dark!" someone said, and everyone seemed to agree. They spoke cautiously at first, then too loudly, as if to see if everything still worked.

"What's Bedford known for?" asked the guide as he steered us back through the way we'd come.

"Limestone!" shouted someone ahead of me.

"That's right. It's the limestone capital of the world. By 1920, 80 percent of limestone buildings in the US were done with Indiana stone. That includes buildings such as the Biltmore, Empire State Building, Pentagon, and DC monuments."

I wanted to listen, but the information wasn't critical to me. The conversation in the boat gave me a chance to speak without calling too much attention to myself. "Stop it. I don't like that," I told Blake. I twisted my head back. I felt his hands move up to my shoulders. Blake said nothing. Whether it was because he didn't want to or couldn't, I didn't know. A couple of minutes later, his hands fluttered on my breasts again.

"No, stop it," I repeated.

Travis half turned, my hands following his swiveled shoulders. "What are you talking about?" he asked.

"Nothing," I replied. Blake continued to rub his hands on me.

Though the cave was not constricted the way throats are, nor the same colors or surface material, I felt like we were inside of one. Moments seemed to move backward in time, as if the world had stopped spinning.

When we were helped out of the boat, out of the dark continent, a shimmer of black dots accumulated before my eyes. We reentered the warm, thick, and heavy air. The smell of the caves would linger deep in my hair roots even after I used handfuls of shampoo later.

—⟋⟍—

Now, years later, it's impossible for me to remember Blake's face. I don't know if Blake had leg braces. Were his eyes halfway shut most of the time? Did he wear light blue a lot or was that someone else? Did he frequently slobber, or do I just want to remember him that way? I never looked at him long enough to really consider him before that day, and I purposefully didn't look at him later.

On the way back from the caves, Lauren and Dan were way at the front of the pack. As we got closer to the picnic tables, I decided I wouldn't tell Arjun about what happened. Having developed so much sooner than him, and since our parents treated me more harshly than him, I hadn't wanted to talk to him in a while. I didn't hate him for being the boy twin and getting more privilege, but I understood he wasn't much use to me. At home, I was usually causing drama of some sort because of the rules imposed on me, and I think he valued peace. He seemed so innocent, with his smooth skin and big eyes, sitting at the table with the other kids. Our worlds felt so separate then that saying we were twins felt inaccurate. I don't think it would have helped me to have told him what had happened because I didn't even want to think about or understand it. I wouldn't even have known how.

I wouldn't tell my mom about what happened either. I'd just ask her to put me back in another YMCA camp. What happened in the caves was going to sit far back in my mind. I did such a good job burying the memory that I didn't really remember it until I was twenty-one years old, a senior at DePauw University writing about my past when I must have shaken the memory loose. I was alone in a computer lab printing out some articles, and the caves incident seemed to drop directly onto my head, a cave kiss. Emotions I didn't allow myself to feel years ago overcame me. I had to sit. I saw a metal boat on water and kids in it. They seemed far away, their faces peach smudges. It was as if I was watching from hundreds of feet overhead, as if the caves had cracked open below.

—ɯ—

BUCKETHEAD

B.J. HOLLARS

ONCE, A BOY DROWNED AT A summer camp. This was June of 1968. It was early evening, a dinner of fried chicken and green beans already breaking down inside the boys' bellies, and as their counselors shouted numbers to the sky ("ninety-eight . . . ninety-nine . . . one hundred!"), the campers hid, determined not to be found in the all-camp game of hide-and-seek.

More determined than most, ten-year-old Bobby Watson slipped away from his bunkmates and wandered toward the floating docks on the shores of Blackman Lake. He blocked the sun with his hand, allowing his eyes to refocus on the best hiding spot of all. There, glistening at the edge of a dock, was a Kenmore refrigerator. It was powder blue, round-topped, complete with silver handle. Bobby—smitten perhaps by the peculiarity of a refrigerator in such a strange locale—headed toward it.

Bobby knew as well as everyone else that the waterfront was off-limits to campers except during open swim. The head lifeguard—a broad-shouldered, sunburned man—had made this abundantly clear on the first night of camp ("You do, you die"). But it was a game of hide-and-seek, after all, and Bobby, a boy who wanted simply to hide, convinced himself to duck beneath the peeling fence. He jogged toward the fridge, peeking behind him to make sure he hadn't been spotted. He hadn't. No sign of him except for footprints in the sand.

He reached for the shiny handle, pulled, listened for the sound of the door yawning open

Click.

And then, after entering inside, the sound of the door closing:

Click.

The inner shelves had been removed, though it was still a tight squeeze for a boy Bobby's size. Nevertheless, he found that if he tucked himself into the fetal position, it almost felt like a womb. Somewhere in the world beyond the confines of that fridge, the dock wobbled beneath the new weight. Bobby smiled to himself. The boy who wanted simply to hide was quite certain they'd never find him.

Half an hour later, as the game wound down, Bobby's prediction proved true.

Baaaahhhhh-beeeeeee, the counselors' voices droned, followed by the sharper *Bob-be!*

Amidst the shouting, a maintenance man spotted the fridge on the dock and, in an uncharacteristic act, decided not to put off till tomorrow what could easily be done today. Rope in hand, he wandered toward the water, ducking beneath the paint-peeling fence as his work boots clomped toward the dock. He tied one end of a rope around the fridge and the other to the dock post.

The fridge was meant to serve as an anchor to ensure the docks didn't float away, and after the maintenance man double-checked his knots ("This'll hold"), he leaned his stocky frame into the powder-blue box and knocked it into the water.

Nobody knows what Bobby thought as that fridge bobbed twice in the lake. We can imagine, of course. How the water wiggled through the seams like eels. And how it began filling that fridge within seconds, drenching Bobby's shoes, Bobby's socks, Bobby's shorts. Meanwhile, on the other side of that refrigerator door, the maintenance man wiped his hands on his sleeves and headed toward the barn. There was a lawnmower in need of tuning.

Back on land, the counselors continued their search.

Baaaahhhhh-beeeeeee! they cried. *Come out, come out, wherever you are!*

A chorus of prepubescent campers soon joined them.

Hey, Bobby! Game over! Ollie ollie oxen free!

Inside the fridge, the water continued to rise. Past Bobby's orange-and-gray-striped T-shirt, past his slender neck, and finally, as the wide-eyed boy ballooned his cheeks for the last time, past his mouth and nose as well. His hands reached for a handle that was not there, his fingers clawing against the smooth surface. Then, as his cheeks deflated, he just stopped clawing. Just stopped everything. The refrigerator had become a coffin, and in the coming days, as a platoon of sheriff's deputies commandeered fishing boats and skimmed the water, nobody thought to tug on the rope pulled tight to the post of the dock. Nobody thought. Instead, those deputies took solace in the sound of their outboard motors, while Bobby—once a boy—became an anchor.

That night, as the campers slept or tried to, the counselors snuck from their cabins, slipped beneath the paint-peeling fence, and joined the head lifeguard at the waterfront. They were all so terribly young—most not yet twenty—and death, for them, was still an abstraction. As they tugged their damp swimsuits over their hips, the goose bumps served as proof that they were alive.

"All right, let's link up," the head lifeguard called, so the counselors did—locking elbows to form a chain of boys whose high-kneed march plunged their toes deep into the sand. Their toes revealed no bodies that night, but thirty feet away and ten feet below, Bobby Watson's body responded to their ripples.

The days passed like seasons—the seasons like lifetimes—but first, the world stubbornly continued. That week's batch of campers returned home, while the next batch arrived soon after, dragging their trunks along the cabins' plywood floors. In the time between, the maintenance man mowed a lawn, patched a roof, installed a new refrigerator in the mess. When the new campers arrived, the counselors knew better than to talk about Bobby. Though the boys kept inquiring what all those sheriff's deputies were doing bobbing about in the water, the counselors remained mum, except for the one who lightened the mood by making some joke about bank-robbing bass.

The head lifeguard, too, spent the following week staring out at the boats from his place at the edge of the dock. The summer was blazing then, and every half an hour or so he'd reach for a white bucket, fill it with lake water, and send the water sizzling across the scalding docks. He repeated this action—a kind of keening—though one afternoon, as he walked to the boathouse to retrieve the goose poop broom, he returned to the dock to find his bucket missing.

This is the part of the story that gets gruesome, the part that, forty years later, when I am a counselor there myself, we are encouraged not to tell.

According to lore, that bucket didn't just disappear but was taken—by Bobby, whose body had broken free from the fridge, though it was hardly his body any longer. His bones were intact and most of his skin, though the fish had fed on his face.

A week after his disappearance, young Bobby—trapped in some transitory state (not quite dead, certainly not living)—was said to have broken his seaweed-speckled hand across the waterline and retrieved the bucket, slipping it over his fish-eaten face to spare others the view.

All of this, we told our campers by flashlight, *might have been different had Bobby just followed the rules. But he didn't. He just didn't. And that was the end of him.*

—⚬—

Before serving as a camp counselor, I was a camper, and for a week each summer, I'd unfurl my sleeping bag on a hard mattress in the Apache cabin, unpack my sunscreen and calamine lotion, and begin using words like *kindling* and *rucksack* and *bug juice*. Each week, our counselor told us the tale of Buckethead, reminding us of the importance of never wandering into the waterfront unattended ("You do, you die").

Years later, when I became counselor of that cabin, I began leading my own tribe of rucksack-carrying, bug-juice-drinking, kindling-finding boys. And I repeated the Buckethead legend as it had been told to me, adding a few flourishes, of course, including the pencil-scrawled initials "B. W." on one of the bunks to prove that Bobby Watson, too, had been an Apache. A necessary detail, I thought, to connect us with our fabricated past.

I probably took it too far—provided too many details on what it might feel like for water to rise in a confined space. Yet I told myself that my vivid recounting was meant merely to reinforce the cautionary tale; that if I told it well enough—true enough—I might scare these kids back to the safety of the shoreline.

During my second summer as a camper, I, too, was scared for my own good. I'd been scared the previous summer as well, and as I slipped my duffel beneath the familiar bunk once more, my hand grazed a white bucket tilted sideways like a bowling pin. I reached for it, though I stopped when I heard a cane slap the plywood floor behind me.

My eyes followed the cane up to the blind boy carrying it. He said hello ("Hi!"), his name was Dennis ("I'm Dennis!"), and wondered whether he'd found his way into the Apache cabin. It was the first time any of us had ever seen a blind boy, and my bunkmates and I wanted to know how he kept from tripping over all those roots in the path leading up to the cabin.

"Hell, I trip over shit all the time," announced Randall, the kid on the bunk above me. This, I later reasoned, might have been Randall's only glimpse of empathy, though our counselor misread it, told the kid to watch his damn mouth ("Or else").

That night, after a campfire spent fending off mosquitoes, the Apache tribe marched back through the woods to our cabin. Our counselor promised us a scary story if we could get in our sleeping bags without playing too much grab-ass ("Randall, Paul, I'm talking to you!").

We wanted the story, so we did as we were told, peeling off sweat-soaked socks and shirts and curling—like Bobby—into spaces that were nearly too small for us. With the lights off, he told us about Buckethead, about Bobby Watson, about the refrigerator that clicked shut and did not open.

Since I knew the story, I mostly just watched the expressions on the other boys' faces. Across from me, Dennis's eyes emitted terror but not nearly as much as Randall's.

"What a crock of shit," Randall grumbled, wadding up his pillow, though the tremor in his throat was unmistakable.

The week dragged on—days spent shooting bows and threading lanyards and trying to steer our canoes to the safety of the shoreline. We learned songs and then forgot them, built fires and put them out. We dedicated hours to sand volleyball, took turns at tetherball, measured the arc of our piss streams by the cattails.

Dennis couldn't take part in everything, but most of us did what we could to make him feel a part of our tribe. We took turns sitting next to him at dinner, trying hard to anticipate his needs, our eyes focused on the eyes that couldn't focus on us.

A few days in, Randall said something to Dennis—don't ask me what, it was all so long ago. Nevertheless, I remember feeling that his comment had seemed unnecessarily cruel, spiteful even, and though we were just innocent boys back then—still scared by the minnows that nipped our toes—we knew we had to retaliate.

Later that day, while Dennis slapped his cane along the blacktop, four of us sprawled ourselves on the lodge porch plotting against Randall. We knew Buckethead was his weakness, so we figured we'd scare him. We wanted him to feel cruelty too.

As we tried to figure out how, I offhandedly mentioned the bucket beneath my bunk.

"What kind of bucket?" asked Paul.

"The right kind," I whispered.

That night, after campfire, we marched through the woods to the shower house as we'd done every night that week. We were an awkward bunch—some of us less suited for the wilderness than others ("Something bit my butt!")—and our three-minute trek always seemed to stretch on much longer. Somebody (usually me) was always dropping his shower caddy in the leaves or getting his towel stuck in the craggy arms of the branches. That night, I broke a spider web with my face and felt terrible for what I'd done to that poor creature.

Who knows where our counselor was, probably attending to a scraped knee or a poison ivy outbreak. Years later, when I was the counselor, I could confirm that these injuries were endless, that it was impossible for nine-year-old boys not to sprain ankles or stumble into wasp nests. Whatever our counselor's alibi, it meant we were momentarily alone in that shower house, our mud-caked shoes tromping against the moldy tiles while we bit back guilty grins. The overhead lights gave us shadows, while a screened window invited in the summer heat. It was not hard to imagine decades of summers of boys just like us being baptized beneath those showerheads. Or if not there, then in the lake, or the mud, or half-drowned in the smoke around those campfires. I have seen black-and-white photographs from those ancient times, pictures of boys in war paint who—with the exception of Bobby (if there ever was a Bobby)—were lucky enough to grow to become old men.

Yet we thought little of history or our place in it as we kicked our clothes into a pile and positioned ourselves beneath those showerheads. We thought little of the story we would become. Our thoughts remained on Randall as he snapped a towel or two our way ("Take that, suckers!"). We did. We took it. He would get his soon enough.

A light flickered, a bug zapped, and I began reciting my line.

"Guys," I said rather unconvincingly. "I think I saw Buckethead out the window."

Refusing to look for himself, Randall pretended to study the soap in his washcloth.

"Did you?" asked Dennis, reaching for my arm.

"Aw, he didn't see jack shit," Randall said.

"Then look," someone pressed. "Why don't you look?"

Newly emboldened, Randall marched bare-assed toward the screen and peeked out.

"See? Nothing out there but . . ."

We killed the lights as Paul pounded his plastic head against the shower house screen. His moans were louder than ours, more desperate, how I imagined a sheep might sound in the final thrusts of labor. I couldn't see Paul's face behind the bucket, but I thought of Bobby's, what his might've looked like had his tragedy been true.

Randall screamed—it was all we wanted from him—so we flicked on the lights and told Paul to remove his bucket. But what we saw with the lights on was far worse than what Randall had seen with them off:

Dennis—our friend, our charge—curled naked on the mossy tiles.

We'd underestimated the effect of confusion on a blind boy.

"Hey, Dennis, it was no one," I said, hovering over him. "We were trying to teach a lesson." The others gathered around him, touching his shoulder and his forehead to let him know they were there.

Dennis kept shaking, and as we repeatedly asked if he was all right—if he'd pull through—he just kept shaking, not quite a yes or a no.

Who can remember what happened on the walk back to the cabin that night? Randall shut his foul mouth for a change—I remember that much—and a pair of us may have threaded our arms through Dennis's as we led him back through the woods.

That night, for the first time, we went to bed without talking.

"Finally tuckered you out," our counselor said upon his return. "About time."

While the others slept, I became newly afraid of the dark. I'd never needed a night-light before, though I needed one then—the sliver of moon refracting off the lake seemed suddenly insufficient. Still, I took comfort where I could, reminding myself that the bucket was back beneath my bunk, that for the moment it wasn't hiding anyone's flesh-eaten face.

The box fan on the windowsill out-hummed the crickets, but I still knew they were out there, chirping as Buckethead's sea-weeded shoes dragged along the overgrown trails. My imagination conjured him so clearly—a boy more scared than scary grasping in the dark, hoping for something to touch or to touch him.

Across from me, Dennis lay in his bunk, his hands folded across his chest. I couldn't tell if he was awake or not, if he was afraid or not, so I balanced on my elbow to have a look.

"Hey, you still up?" I whispered. He didn't answer.

But his eyes, like mine, were wide.

—⟋w⟍—

QUICK FEET

KIESE LAYMON

A FEW WEEKS INTO THE SUMMER, ONE month before the start of eighth grade, two days after that psychologist's directive to "count to ten in case of emergencies and limit your intake of simple carbohydrates," you dropped me off with Grandmama in Forest, Mississippi. Before speeding off, you wiped away your tears. You said you were sorry. You kissed the roundest parts of my cheeks. You said you were sorry. You claimed Grandmama would make everything okay.

You said you were sorry.

I loved Grandmama, but I didn't really love going to her house any day other than Friday. Every Friday, Grandmama let me watch *The Dukes of Hazzard*, a show you said "operates in a world even more racist than the one we live in, where two white drug dealers, who keep violating probation and making fools of the police, in a Confederate-flag-topped red Dodge Charger called the General Lee, never go to prison."

The Friday night I was sent to stay with Grandmama, I asked her if black folk like us could ever get away from the police like Bo and Luke Duke could.

"No," Grandmama said before I could get the whole question out. "Nope. Not at all. Never. You better never try that mess either, Kie."

The one or two times we saw black characters on *The Dukes of Hazzard*, I remember Grandmama and her boyfriend, Ofa D, getting closer to the screen and cheering for them the same way they cheered if the Georgetown Hoyas were playing, if Jackson State won, or if there was a black contestant on *Wheel of Fortune*.

Like most black women in Forest, Grandmama had a number of side hustles in addition to working the line at the chicken plant. One of her side hustles was selling vegetables from her garden. Another side hustle was selling fried fish, pound cakes, and sweet potato pies every Saturday evening to anyone who would buy them. The most important of Grandmama's side hustles was washing clothes, ironing, cooking, and doing dishes for this white family called the Mumfords.

After church that Sunday, on the way to the Mumfords, I complained to Grandmama that my slacks were so tight I had to unzip them to breathe. Grandmama laughed and laughed and laughed until she didn't. She said she wouldn't be at the Mumfords for long. I always saw the Mumfords' nasty clothes next to Grandmama's washer, and their clean clothes out on the clothesline behind her house.

I hated those clothes.

The Mumfords lived right off Highway 35. I was amazed at how the houses off Highway 35 were the only houses in Forest that looked like the houses on *Leave It to Beaver, Who's the Boss?,* and *Mr. Belvedere.* When I imagined the insides of rich-white-folk houses, I imagined stealing all their food while they were asleep. I wanted to gobble up palmfuls of Crunch 'n Munch and fill up their thirty-two-ounce glasses with name-brand ginger ale and crushed ice tumbling out of their silver refrigerators. I wanted to leave the empty glasses and Crunch 'n Munch crumbs on the counter so the white folk would know I'd been there and they'd have something to clean up when I left.

Grandmama left the key in the ignition and told me she'd be back in about twenty minutes. "Don't say nothing to that badass Mumford boy if he come out here, Kie," she said. "He ain't got a lick of home training. You hear me? Don't get out of this car unless it's an emergency."

I nodded yes and sprawled out across the front seat of the Impala. Damn near as soon as Grandmama went in the house, out came this boy who looked like a nine-year-old Mike D from the Beastie Boys. The Mumford boy was bone white and skinny in a way Grandmama called "po'." Grandmama didn't have much money, and her six-hundred-square-foot shotgun house was clean as Clorox on the inside but raggedy as a roach on the outside. I always wondered why Grandmama never called people with less stuff than us "po'." She called them "folk who ain't got a pot to piss in" or "folk whose money ain't all the way right" or "folk with nan dime to they name," but she never used "poor" or "po'" to talk about anything other than people's bodies.

Without knocking, the po' white boy opened the door of the driver's side of Grandmama's Impala. "You Reno's grandson?" he asked me.

"Who is Reno?"

"You know Reno. The old black lady who clean my house." I'd never seen this po' white boy before, but I'd seen the shiny gray Jams swim trunks, the long two-striped socks, and the gray Luke Skywalker shirt he had on in our dirty clothes basket and hanging on our clothesline. I didn't like how knowing a po' white boy's clothes before knowing a po' white boy made me feel. And I hated how this po' white boy called Grandmama "Reno, the old black lady who clean my house."

I got out of the Impala and kept my hands in my pockets. "So you Reno's grandson?" the boy asked. "You the one from Jackson?"

Before I could say yes, the Mumford boy told me we couldn't come in his house but we could play in the backyard. The phrase "I'm good" was something I always said in Jackson, but I didn't know I had ever meant it as much as I meant it that day.

That's what I felt before I looked at the size of the Mumfords' garage and saw a closet door open in the left corner. I walked toward the room and saw a washer, a dryer, and a scale on the ground.

"What y'all call this room?" I asked him.

"That's our washroom," he said. "Why y'all stay shooting folk in Jackson? Can I ask you that?"

I ignored the po' white boy's question. At Grandmama's house, our washer was in the dining room and we didn't have a dryer, so we hung everything up on the clothesline. "Wait. What's a scale doing in there?"

"My pawpaw like to weigh himself out here."

"That washer, do it work?"

"It work fine," he said. "Good as new."

"And the dryer too?" I looked at the two irons on this shelf hanging above a new ironing board. I didn't know how to say what I wanted to say. I stepped on the scale in the corner. "This scale, it's right?"

"Don't ask me," he said. "I never used it. I told you it's my pawpaw scale."

I walked back to Grandmama's Impala, got in the driver's seat, and locked the doors. I remember gripping the steering wheel with one hand and digging my fingernails into my knee with the other hand. I wondered how fat 218 pounds really was for twelve years old.

Less than a minute after I was in the car, the Mumford boy came back out. Without knocking, he tried to open the Impala's driver's side door again.

"Come on in and play, Jackson," he said again from outside the car.

"Naw. I'm good," I told him and rolled the window down.

"You wanna shoot squirrels in the head with my pellet gun in the backyard?"

"Naw," I told him. "My mama don't let me shoot squirrels in the head. I'm not allowed to shoot guns. I'm good."

"But all y'all do is shoot guns in Jackson."

I sat in Grandmama's Impala with a rot spreading in my belly for a few seconds before Grandmama walked out of the house carrying a basket of dirty clothes. An envelope sat on top of the clothes.

When I told Grandmama what the Mumford boy said to me, she told me to leave these folk alone. "Do you know who you messing with?" she asked me. "These white folk, they liable to have us locked up under the jail, Kie."

I kept looking at Grandmama as we drove home. I was trying to decide if I should ask her why she had to wash, dry, iron, and fold the Mumfords' nasty clothes if the Mumfords had a better washer than ours, a working dryer, a newer iron, and an ironing board. I wanted to ask her if there were better side hustles than washing nasty white-folk clothes on the weekend. But I didn't say anything on the first half of the way home. I just looked at Grandmama's face and saw deeper frown lines around her mouth than I'd ever seen before. I wanted to shrink and slide down those frown lines.

I understood that day why you and Grandmama were so hungry for black wins, regardless of how tiny those wins were. For Grandmama, those wins were always personal. For you, the wins were always political. Both of y'all knew, and showed me, how we didn't even have to win for white folk to punish us. All we had to do was not lose the way they wanted us to.

I kept wishing I would have gone in the Mumfords' house and stolen all their food. Stealing their food felt like the only way to make the rotten feeling in my belly go away.

Before going home, Grandmama took the envelope she'd gotten from the Mumfords, wrote your name and address on it, and put it in the mailbox downtown.

"Grandmama," I said as we turned down Old Morton Road, "do those white folk know your name is Catherine, or do they think your name is Reno?"

"I know my name," Grandmama said, "and I know how much these white folk pay me every week."

"Do you tell the Mumfords the truth when you're in their house?"

"Naw," she said. "I shole don't."

"Then what you be telling them?"

"I be telling them whatever it takes to get they little money and take care of my family."

"But do you ever wanna steal they food?"

"Naw, Kie," she said. "They test me like that all the time. If I ever stole from them folk, we wouldn't have nothing. You hear me? Nothing. I'm telling you what I know now. Do not steal nothing from no white folk. Ever. Or you likely to be off in hell with them folk one day."

In Grandmama's world, most white folk were destined for hell, not because they were white but because they were fake Christians who hadn't really heeded their Bibles. Grandmama really believed only two things could halt white folks' inevitable trek into hell: appropriate doses of Jesus and immediate immersion in Concord Missionary Baptist Church. I didn't understand hell, or the devil, but I understood Concord Missionary Baptist Church. And I hated most of it.

My slacks were too tight in Sunday school, so they were always flooding. My shirt choked my esophagus. My clip-on tie looked like a clip-on tie. No matter the temperature, Grandmama made me wear a polyester vest. My feet grew so fast that my penny loafers never fit. Plus, she stopped me from putting dimes or nickels in my penny loafers because that was something only mannish boys did.

Inside Concord Missionary Baptist Church, I loved the attention I got from the older black women for being a fat black boy: They were the only women on Earth who called my fatness fineness. I felt flirted with, and like most fat black boys, when flirted with, I fell in love. I loved the organ's blended notes, the aftertaste of the grape juice, the fans steadily moving through the humidity, the anticipation of somebody catching the Holy Ghost, the lawd-have-mercy claps after the little big-head boy who couldn't read so well was forced to read a greeting to the congregation.

But as much as I loved parts of church, and as hard as I tried, I couldn't love the holy word coming from the pulpit. The voices carrying the word were slick and sure of themselves in ways I didn't believe. The word at Concord was always carried by the mouths of the reverend, deacons, or other visiting preachers who acted like they knew my grandmama and her friends better than they did.

Older black women in the church made up the majority of the audience. But their voices and words were only heard during songs, in ad-libbed responses to the preacher's word, and during church announcements. While Grandmama and everyone else amen'd and well'd their way through shiny hollow sermons, I just sat there, usually at the end of the pew, sucking my teeth, feeling super hot, super bored, and really resentful because Grandmama and her friends never told the sorry-ass preachers to shut up and sit down somewhere.

My problem with church was I knew what could have been. Every other Wednesday, the older women of the church had something called Home

Mission: They would meet at alternate houses and bring their best food, Bibles, notebooks, and testimonies. There was no instrumental music at Home Mission, but those women, Grandmama's friends, used their lives, their mo(u)rning songs, and their Bibles as primary texts to boast, confess, and critique their way into tearful silence every single time.

I didn't understand hell, partially because I didn't believe any place could be hotter than Mississippi in August. But I understood feeling good. I did not feel good at Concord Missionary Baptist Church. I felt good watching Grandmama and her friends love one another during Home Mission.

—⁂—

When we pulled into our yard, Grandmama told me to grab the basket of nasty clothes and put it next to the washer. I picked the clothes up and instead of stopping at the washer, I walked into the kitchen, placed the dirty-clothes basket on the floor in between the fridge and the oven.

I looked around to see if Grandmama was coming before stepping both of my penny loafers deep into the Mumfords' basket and doing "quick feet" like we did at the beginning of basketball and football practice. "I got your gun right here, white nigga," I said, stomping my feet all up in the white folks' clothes as hard and fast as I could. "Y'all don't even know. I got your gun right here, white nigga."

I was doing quick feet in the Mumfords' clothes for a good thirty seconds when Grandmama came out of nowhere, whupping my legs with a pleather blue belt. The little pleather blue licks didn't stop me. I was still doing quick feet like it was going out of style.

"Kie," Grandmama said, "get out my kitchen acting like a starnated fool."

I stopped and took my whupping. Afterward, I asked Grandmama whether she meant "star-nated" or "stark naked." I told her I'd rather be a "star-nated" fool because I loved stars even though I didn't think "star-nated" was a word. Grandmama and I loved talking about words.

She was better than anyone I'd ever known at bending, breaking, and building words that weren't in the dictionary. I asked her what word I could use to make that Mumford boy feel what we felt.

"Ain't no need to make up words for words that already exist, Kie," she said. "That ain't nothing but the white you saw in that po' child today. And you don't want to feel no kinds of white. I feel sorry for them folk."

I looked at Grandmama and told her I felt like a nigger, and feeling like a nigger made my heart, lungs, kidneys, and brain feel like they were melting and dripping out the ends of my toenails.

"It ain't about making white folk feel what you feel," she said. "It's about not feeling what they want you to feel. Do you hear me? You better know from whence you came and forget about those folk." Grandmama started laughing. "Kie, what you call yourself doing to those folks' clothes?"

"Oh," I said and started doing it again. "At practice, we be calling this quick feet."

"You gave them white-folk clothes them quick feets?"

"Not feets," I said, laughing. "It's already plural, Grandmama. Quick feet."

"Quick feets?" she said again and kept laughing until she almost fell out of her chair. "Quick foots?"

"Grandmama," I started, and sat next to her legs. "I hate white-folk clothes. I'm serious."

"I know you do." Grandmama stopped laughing. "I don't much appreciate them or they clothes either, but cleaning them nasty clothes is how we eat and how I got your mama and them through school. You know I been washing them folks' clothes for years, and I ain't never seen one washcloth?"

"What you mean, Grandmama?"

"I mean what I said. Them folk don't use no washcloths." I waited for a blink, a smirk, a slow roll of her eyes. I got nothing. "And the one time the little po' one who was messing with you asked me how to use a washrag, I told that baby, 'If you bring that washrag from your ass to your face, that's between you and your God.' And this baby just stood there laughing like I'm telling jokes. You know I was serious as a heart attack, Kie."

While I was dying laughing, Grandmama told me she whupped me for acting up in her kitchen, not for messing up them folks' clothes. She said she spent so many hours in white-folk kitchens and just wanted her children to respect her kitchen when she got home.

I asked Grandmama why she whupped me on my legs when I was doing quick feet and not my head or my neck or my back like you would. "Because I don't want to hurt you," she said. "I want you to act like you got good sense, but I don't ever want to hurt you."

Grandmama stood up and told me to follow her out to her garden. We went outside and picked butter beans, purple hull peas, collard greens, green tomatoes, and yellow squash.

"You know why I love my garden, Kie?"

"Because you don't want to have to rely on white folk to eat?"

"Chile, please," Grandmama said, walking back to the porch. "I ain't studdin' nan one of those folk when I'm at my own house. I love knowing directly what the food that be going in us has been through. You know what I mean?"

"I think I do," I told Grandmama as we sat on the porch, hulling peas and talking more about quick feet. My bucket of peas was between my legs when Grandmama stood up and straddled my tub.

"Kie, try hulling like this here," Grandmama said. I looked up at her hands and how they handled the purple hull peas. When she reached for my face, I jumped back. "I ain't trying to hurt you," she said. "What you jumping back for?"

I didn't know what to say.

Grandmama took the bucket from between my legs into the kitchen. I sat there looking at my hands. They wouldn't stop shaking. I felt sweat pooling up between my thighs.

—m—

At supper, Grandmama apologized again for whupping my legs and told me when I wrote my report on the Book of Psalms later that night, I could write the way we talk. Like you, Grandmama made me do written assignments every night. Unlike your assignments, all of Grandmama's assignments had to be about the Bible.

Later that evening, I wrote, "I know you want me to write about the Book of Psalms. If it is okay I just want to tell you about some secrets that be making my head hurt. I be eating too much and staying awake at night and fighting people in Jackson. Mama does not like how my eyes are red. I wake her up in the morning and she be making me use Visine before school. I try but I can't tell her what's wrong. Can I tell you? Can you help me with my words? The words Mama make me use don't work like they supposed to work."

I wrote the words "be kissing me in the morning" "be choking me" "be beating my back" "be hearing her heartbeat" "be wet dreaming about stuff that scare me" "be listening to trains" "be kissing me in the morning" "be kissing him at night" "be hitting hard" "be saying white folk hit the hardest" "be laughing so it won't hurt" "be eating when I'm full" "be kissing me" "be choking me" "be confusing me."

At the end, I wrote, "Grandmama, can you please help me with my words?" I gave Grandmama my notebook when I was done like I had to every Sunday night we spent together. Unlike on other nights, she didn't say anything about what I'd written. When she walked by me, I didn't even hear her breathing.

Later that night, before bed, Grandmama got on her knees, turned the light off, and told me she loved me. She told me tomorrow would be a better day. Grandmama looked at that old raggedy gold and silver contraption she called her phone book before she got in bed with me like she always did. She looked up your name and number, Aunt Sue's name and number, Uncle Jimmy's name and number, and Aunt Linda's name and number.

Before both of us went to sleep, I asked Grandmama if 218 pounds was too fat for twelve years old. "What you weighing yourself for anyway?" she asked me. "Two hundred eighteen pounds is just right, Kie. It's just heavy enough."

"Heavy enough for what?"

"Heavy enough for everything you need to be heavy enough for."

I loved sleeping with Grandmama because that was the only place in the world I slept all the way through the night. But tonight was different. "Can I ask you one more question before we go to bed?"

"Yes, baby," Grandmama said, and faced me for the first time since I gave her the notebook.

"What do you think about counting to ten in case of emergencies?"

"Ain't no emergency God can't help you forget," Grandmama told me. "Evil is real, Kie."

"But what about the emergencies made by folk who say they love you?"

"You forget it all," she said. "Especially that kind of emergency. Or you go stone crazy. My whole life, it seem like something crazy always happens on Sunday nights in the summer."

Grandmama made me pray again that night. I prayed for you to never close the door to your room if your boyfriend was there. I prayed for Layla and Dougie to never feel like they had to go back in Daryl's room. I prayed for Grandmama to have more money so she wouldn't have to stand in that big room ripping the bloody guts out of chickens before standing in that smaller room smelling bleach and white folks' shitty underwear. I prayed nothing would ever happen again in any room in the world that made us feel like we were dying.

When I got off my knees, I watched the back of Grandmama's body heave in and heave out as she fell asleep on the bed. Grandmama was trying, hard as she could, to forget one more Sunday night in the summer. For a second, though, she stopped heaving. I couldn't hear her breathing. When I finally climbed into bed, I placed my left thumb lightly on the small of Grandmama's back. She jerked forward and clenched the covers tighter around her body.

"My bad, Grandmama. I just wanted to make sure you were okay."

"Be still, Kie," Grandmama mumbled with her back to me. "Just be still. Close your eyes. Some things, they ain't meant to be remembered. Be still with the good things we got, like all them quick foots."

"Quick feet," I told her. "It's already plural. I know you know that, Grandmama. Quick feet."

—ɯ—

THE ELVIS ROOM

KATIE MOULTON

MAMA IS DIGGING THROUGH A CABINET, looking for a spare picture frame, when she pulls out a cassette tape in its see-through case. She hands it to me.

"I thought this was lost forever," I say, turning it over.

"You can have it," she says and smiles, then goes on rummaging.

The cassette tape is beige, affixed with a generic label that looks like it's been soaked in tea. Two lines at the top. Next to *Title*, it says "My Way." Next to *Artist*, someone misspelled my last name before correcting it with Sharpie. The tape coiled inside is mostly bright yellow, which means the recording is short. There's a lot of space left on the tape.

On a road trip in 1978, my parents stopped in Memphis on a hundred-degree dead-summer day to pay their respects at Graceland. They were twenty-two and twenty-three, already married a couple years. Elvis Presley's humble mansion wasn't yet open to the public, but there were souvenir shops set up across the street. The strip mall is still there today, billed as the Official Graceland Outlet, much of its parking lot reserved for employees of the new Presley exhibition center/entertainment complex. But in '78, my parents pulled over on suburban Elvis Presley Boulevard and browsed the shoddy postcards and teddy bears, then walked into a storefront called Graceland Recording Studio. My dad stepped into the booth, which was just a small closet lined with cast-off carpet and insulation. Inside, his head of long, wavy brown hair bumping against the ceiling, he put on headphones, aimed his voice at a microphone, and made his own Elvis record.

—ɯ—

In our house, Elvis Presley always got a bigger room than I did. To be fair, my parents had him first. We were the only house on the block with a boombox propped on an empty kitchen chair, *Little-sister-don't-you* jumping against the clink of rinsed dishes. A hushed Saturday made suddenly dramatic by the hit-your-knees *searchin' for you!* of "Kentucky Rain." A tongue-in-cheek *Uhhh thank yuh, thank yuh very much* whenever someone passed the salt. But in our house, Elvis wasn't just in the air.

No, Elvis had an actual room. The King of Rock and Roll is the many-headed icon of a shrine that still fills a large room in the lower level of Mama's house. The walls are a kaleidoscope of Presley's face: calendars, clocks, spoons, Elvis in leather, Elvis in rhinestones, Elvis-on-Wood, long-lashed Velvet Elvises on canvases of every size and crudeness. A glass display case is stocked with porcelain statuettes, karate-chop action figures, *Elvis Is Alive!* VHS tapes, and a cardboard model of Graceland. For decades, these objects have never moved. Nothing even gets dusted.

At the center of the Elvis Room is The Bust. It doesn't really look like Elvis; the vibe is much more Mary-Magdalene-in-drag. His face is textured like chalk and painted in pastels, and there's a sheen to the black matte of his hair. His parted pink lips curl softly upward. He measures two feet tall and two feet across at his widest point, where the shoulders of his white plaster jumpsuit jut off in opposite directions. His eyes—a little askew—are as blue as his silk scarf and tilted towards heaven. Blocking his view like a styrene halo is a powder-blue lampshade with a trim of burnished gold.

The lamp sits at eye-level atop a sound system that was state-of-the-art in the '90s, rising from shelves cluttered with CDs. Gold and platinum records checkerboard the walls: they're sales awards plaques, certified by the Recording Industry Association of America, bestowed on my dad back when he managed a Musicland, one in a long-defunct chain of record stores. His store was the largest in the St. Louis metro area, and so he reported its sales to the Billboard charts. In the '80s, label reps would still fly in to record stores to make sure their artists were displayed prominently, persuading managers with tickets and backstage passes. Tucked in front of a LaserDisc player is a framed photo of the time my dad met Lionel Richie backstage somewhere, sometime before I was born. According to the family account, my dad made a joke, to which Lionel Richie exclaimed, "Dave . . . you knock! me! out!" I don't know what the joke was, but the photo, Richie's expression, is our proof that a moment passed between them.

An only child learns early: a lot happened before we showed up. We get absorbed into a society of two. The intimate culture of my parents took root in summer 1975 when they were given ten-dollar tickets to see Elvis perform in the small arena in their Indiana hometown. They were nineteen, too young for Elvis. He had scored his first hits the year they were born. By '75, Elvis was bloated kitsch, both beloved and reviled. Forty-year-old Elvis did karate moves and vamped with a cape across the stage, and housewives caught the baby-blue scarves he threw into the front row like sweaty sacraments. At the climax of a gospel medley, he looked like he might keel over or implode. America's biggest music star had long been hurtling into his black hole of self-destruction, and everybody knew it. But my dad was curious about *what Elvis meant*. According to Mama, seeing him live in concert "cemented the fascination." He loved his voice. Their friends laughed and asked, *Why would you go see Elvis?* When I ask, Mama says, "We just thought he was beautiful."

—⁄w⁄—

My dad died when he was forty-seven and I was about to turn seventeen. We were very close. He bought me my first records, recommended music from Hendrix to Alanis Morrissette to N.W.A. He left Chaucer and Tom Robbins on my bedside table. We shared subscriptions to *Rolling Stone* and *Spin*, played basketball for hours in the driveway, and saw stupid movies together—*Half Baked*; *Austin Powers*; *Pootie Tang*; *Dude, Where's My Car?*—turning to each other in the dark theater with tears streaming down our cheeks. He was monumental to me: six-foot-four, 240 pounds, salt-and-pepper hair, handsome in a way that made people comment, smart and sharp, but gentle to his core. So gentle that even as a kid I saw how easily he could be hurt, that he needed protection. For longer than any of us could remember, he struggled with alcoholism and depression. By the time I was a teenager, I was angry—even as I understood how he felt, recognized his darkness in myself. I was angry because I could still clearly see the flashes of who he had been and who he could be behind his addictions. One morning, he woke up to his skin yellow and swollen. Less beautiful, suddenly. He asked to go to the hospital. I don't like to remember the artifacts of those last weeks: a stack of dialysis reports, the stuffed bunny Mama tucked into his shirt pocket in the casket, the mostly empty bottles I found hidden in corners and closets until I graduated high school. Those things, we didn't keep.

—⁄w⁄—

The Elvis Room is a collection, sure, but *shrine* is the better word. Meaning, it's not curated but haphazard—strange memorabilia discovered in the wild—and very personal. There's the custom-made neon light, which beams *Elvis* in cursive glass lettering, a violet glow you can see a quarter mile down the road.

There's the photo of my young parents at a Halloween party: my dad svelte in a white jumpsuit, his features obscured by a rubber Elvis mask. Mama's dolled up as Raggedy Ann, her red hair caricatured with a yarn wig, real-life freckles highlighted with marker, clutching my dad at the waist and chest and grinning, even though the mask looks like it's melting his face.

When playing tour guide for first-time visitors to the Elvis Room, I point out one bust in particular. Made of thick white porcelain stuck to an ugly brown base and embossed *ELVIS, 1935–1977*, it looks rough-hewn but was mass-produced. I turn the bust around to where a brass plate reads *McCormick Distilling, Weston, Mo.* I unscrew the corked knob to show where you pour out the liquor.

Fans of Elvis forged him into a weird saint, his purity put into relief by the weakness or excess that killed him. In *Dead Elvis: A Chronicle of a Cultural Obsession*, Greil Marcus describes this moment from a phone-in radio show: "I have a friend who has a shrine to Elvis in his bathroom," the caller says, flummoxed. "When you flush the toilet, these lights light up. He's got Quaalude bottles in front of it."

The phenomenon of Elvis shrines in private homes has been around nearly as long as Elvis himself. But the practice of hoarding Presley ephemera as a form of devotion took on a decidedly more religious bent after his death in 1977. He died at age forty-two of cardiac arrest likely caused by his abuse of pharmaceutical drugs. In *Afterlife as Afterimage: Understanding Posthumous Fame*, historian Erika Doss writes, "Associating material culture abundance with Elvis piety is not only a sign of being a true fan, but of being true to Elvis: fans repeatedly say that by collecting and displaying Elvis memorabilia they are 'taking care' of Elvis, keeping his memory alive and rescuing him from historical oblivion." Many fans took the memory-keeping to the extreme: denying that Elvis died at all.

—∿—

I haven't heard my dad's voice since I was sixteen. As far as I know, this tape is the only recording of him that exists. I've heard that the first thing you forget about someone is not their smell or touch or face—there's a difference between types of sensory memories. Our brains are much better at converting visual memory, called *iconic*, into longer-term storage. We can scan an image and close our eyes and see it still. On demand, I conjure my dad's face, the particular light of an eye glinting between dark lashes and ruddy cheek, an expression that was never exactly captured in a photograph. I'd know his cologne immediately across a crowded mall. My grandmother says sometimes she still feels the pads of his fingers squeezing her shoulders when she needs it.

We can't do that with auditory, or echoic, memory. *Echo-ic*, echo. By defini-
tion, the sound is fading, already and always going away. Of course, we would
recognize a familiar voice if it somehow returned, snuck up behind us. But after
absence—and it's shorter than you'd think—it's almost impossible to call up
another's voice with our own.

When I try to imagine my dad's voice, I can only *describe* it: versatile, rangey,
warm like a woodwind. A voice with an ironic, inviting edge. A voice that
instructed, pleaded, reeled. When things were bad, I learned to listen for gra-
dients of lucidity in the give between words, in a garble at the back of the throat.
From a note of his voice, I could tell how far gone he was, how drunk or high,
how lost in his own memory, how far from being my dad. But now when I try
to *hear* his voice again, I'm clouded by doubt—*was it pitched higher or lower? Is
that laugh his* real *laugh, or was it forced? Am I making it up?*

Perhaps we lose the voice because the "voice" is not technically a body part,
not an entity unto itself. The voice is created when two tiny vocal cords tighten
as air pushes through, and the tongue, lips, and teeth give form to sound. Voice
is a mutation towards a need, a trick of evolution, totally unique to the capacity
of its vehicle.

And Elvis was quite a vehicle—container of a supreme voice. Critic Henry
Pleasants called it "an extraordinary compass." Robert Plant said Elvis "created
a euphoria within himself"—a transfiguration. The voice is rafter-rattling, a
glorious and spasmodic wail. It is also, by turns, a hiccup, a come-on. Elvis was
a baritone *and* a tenor with a range beyond two octaves. The voice was a risk-
taker, a shapeshifter of emotive forms: soul shouting, operatic bombast, tender
lullaby. The voice was a mimic and thief, filtered through the quirks of self. The
voice could deepen or obliterate the meaning of a lyric. That voice—recorded,
referenced, remixed—endures: an echoic memory the world is not allowed to
forget.

In the first home video where I appear, I'm alone. I'm an infant in only a
diaper, with light curls and a pink slash across my lip where stitches are heal-
ing. In the background, you can hear the rolling tempo and gale-force chorus
of Presley's "Burning Love"—*just a-hunk-a-hunk-a—ahhhh!* You can hear my
parents' voices, my name. I stand, wide-legged and shaky on the brick hearth,
then start to rock back and forth.

I've been trying to recall my dad's voice for a long time. I've sat alone, eyes
closed, listening for it. Gone searching for it in vinyl records and far-flung cit-
ies. I've imagined it into other bodies. I've tried molding my own voice into
something approximating his. I know his catalogue of wounds, his flashes of
greatness, his potential. Who else could do it, who was closer?

—⁂—

As soon as Mama hands the tape to me, I want to play it—but I hesitate. Even the highest-quality analog tape wasn't built to last. My dad's tape, recorded in 1978 at the height of the technology's short heyday, looks as decrepit as the beige strip mall where he made it. What if I stuff this artifact into a tape deck and the mechanism swallows it whole? In online forums, users recount attempts to play old cassettes only to hear the sound of the tape cinching and crinkling: "all of a sudden, it's *squeak squeak*, then *jam*! Loop-mash city!"

Sound information on tapes is encoded on magnetic particles, bound within a polyester-urethane adhesive. Exposed to heat and humidity, the tapes become sticky and eventually begin to shed pieces of the binding, a condition called *sticky shed syndrome*. In "Orpheus Unglued," ethnomusicologist Dr. Michael Heller writes, "In the squealing instant of shed, tape ceases to function as memory . . . The archive breaks down at the very instant we wish to hear it." He equates this moment of loss with the moment that mythic Orpheus turned back to look at Eurydice—and in doing so, sealed their separation forever.

The analog-heads in the internet forums recommend the only known way to salvage tape, which even then only makes the tape playable for one week. The remedy? It's literally *baking*: Remove the tape's plastic casing, stick it in the oven, and cook at a low temperature. I imagined watching my relic melt and catch fire, burning away all it held.

Instead, I email the local photo center to inquire whether they digitize vintage audio, and I play it cool, mentioning casually that the recording is "precious." An employee named Mike assures me they can handle this, but he explains that an old tape might get stuck together—a glitch called *crossover*, where data seeps between layers so it sounds like two tracks playing at once. There might be literal fungus growing on the tape. He writes, "Just letting you know that it is worth doing, because it's precious, but it may not sound like when it was originally recorded." He signs off, "We will do what we can. Mike."

My head swims. Should I risk destroying the tape in the attempt to hear his voice again? Or is it better to hold onto the tape and preserve its potential, as something pure but inaccessible? I mean, what happened to Eurydice after Orpheus *almost* led her back into the world of the living? When she died a second time, was there even less of her? I mean, look what they did to Elvis. Look what Elvis did to himself.

—⁂—

I can picture the room where my dad made the tape. I've been there with him and without him, wandered those souvenir shops, spun the mobiles of keychains. I'd been to Graceland before I'd been to kindergarten. We drove through Memphis nearly every year on the way to see family on the Gulf Coast. We rolled south from St. Louis on I-55, following the Mississippi River. Even if we didn't stop, my dad marked our passing through Memphis. As we neared the exit, he reached into the cupholder and put on the sunglasses he kept there. The shades were cheap plastic, flaking silver. Aviator-style lenses, a chunky frame wrapping around the nose and ears. Etched into the arm: a lightning bolt and the letters *TCB*. He'd curl a lip and we laughed. He'd pop Paul Simon's *Graceland* out of the tape deck (what else could you listen to on '90s road trips?) and cue up an Elvis steamroller like "Suspicious Minds." *We're caught in a trap.* He'd turn up the volume real loud. *I can't walk out.* With the chorus strings soaring at our backs, we'd fly over the river, whether shining or sludgy, all three of us boogying in our seats and trying to sing like Elvis, trying to mark this passing—*because I love you too much, baby.* This was our ritual, an ironic fandom so deep it transfigures into devotion.

Once, my parents drove us west on Interstate 70 to Wright City, Missouri, home of the Elvis Is Alive Museum. The theory goes that Elvis faked his death to escape the chains of unprecedented fame and exploitative contracts. Death-deniers are split, however, on whether Elvis began a new "normal" life, worked undercover for the CIA, or rejoined the aliens. The "museum" was founded in 1992 by Bill Beeny, a Baptist minister who had organized segregationist, anti-communist, and pro–Vietnam War actions in the 1960s. I don't remember much of that building, just the claustrophobia of narrow halls crowded with too many images. The bad white light. But I remember one room in particular, perhaps because I have a photograph of it. This was the room with the casket. Inside, laid out on cheap lace, was a wax dummy of Elvis. He was wearing sunglasses like my dad's. This was a replica of a replica, the sham body that Beeny and others believed to occupy Elvis's actual coffin. I left the funeral room almost immediately, but my parents lingered. In the photo Mama snapped, Dad wears a Hawaiian shirt and poses beside the casket. He's looking down into the mannequin's face as though deep in thought, paying his respects. He's playing and not—one palm pressed flat against his own heart.

Elvis's fall was always part of his story. Even as a kid, I viewed him as totally tragic: complicated, manipulated, profoundly sad, capable of greatness, generous—and ultimately unable to overcome. Yet I reacted viscerally against the death cult of Elvis. I disliked its religiosity and the mocking it inspired. "The fascination [with Elvis] was the reality showing through the illusion," writes Dr. Linda Ray Pratt in "Elvis, or the Ironies of a Southern Identity," in *The Elvis Reader*. "The illusion of invincibility and the tragedy of frailty; the illusion of complete control and the reality of inner chaos . . . Elvis had all the freedom the world can offer and could escape nothing."

Yet the ballooning devotion to Elvis after his death mutated the popular image of him—from provocateur and outsider artist, bellwether of changing social mores, to a paranoid puppet, a pitiable figure of ego and excess. The rhinestone jumpsuit, death-on-the-toilet, even his outsized beauty: His image got passed around and replicated like a garish Mona Lisa. Elvis stood in for everything simultaneously wrong and great about America.

The Elvis faithful use their material fandom to "construct his immortality," writes Doss. "The images and objects in these rooms are highly charged and passionately loved, antidotes to Elvis's absence, fetishistic substitutes for Elvis himself." At the Elvis Is Alive Museum, Mama bought VHS tapes of a program called *Elvis: Dead or Alive?* The cover promised *new FBI evidence!* She stored the tapes in the basement and called them "hospitality gifts," offered as a joke prize to anyone who would spend the night on the twin-size trundle bed in the Elvis Room.

—⁓—

The world's audiocassettes are dying of old age. The recordings on magnetic tape are actively degrading, and many will reach the end of their "playable lifetime" without being preserved or digitized. The Cultural Heritage Index estimates that US museums and archives hold forty-six million magnetic tapes, including VHS and cassettes, but due to limited time and equipment, archivists don't know the quality or playability of 40 percent of these. Elvis's voice will never disappear, but what about those voices that were only put down once, like my dad's, and on audio technology that was outdated just a few short years later?

I keep the tape beside my computer as I research. Eventually I find articles on a technology called infrared spectroscopy. It's a method of analysis that can be applied to everything from determining blood alcohol content to the pigments of ancient illuminated manuscripts. A lab at the University of South Carolina published a paper in 2015 on the technology's application to old audiocassettes that the Library of Congress had deemed in danger of degrading. Here was a noninvasive method for determining whether my dad's tape was playable without sticking it into a playback machine or an oven and crossing my fingers. I imagine driving to the lab, watching through thick windowpanes and goggles as the lasers . . . do whatever it is that lasers do. I track down the lead investigator's contact information and conduct hypothetical conversations about what he believed he was preserving. Could his belief bolster my own?

I used to work for university scientists, so I know better than to cold call the head of a major lab. Instead, I internet-stalk every coauthor on the infrared spectroscopy paper. Samantha Skelton, who had been a research assistant early on in the project, answers my message. She has since moved from chemistry to working as a conservator of paintings, honing her skills as a craftsman in what was sometimes called *heritage science*. When she agrees to an interview, I tell her I'm a bit of a "heritage scientist" myself. Luckily she doesn't hang up.

Skelton explains that the study's goal was to develop a cost-effective way to quickly discern "healthy tape" from gummy, degrading tape. If the scientists figured out which materials were in the most danger, then archivists could approach them more efficiently and with less destruction. The lab applied Fourier-transform infrared spectroscopy (FTIR) and developed a statistical analysis to "suss out very small patterns" about the tapes' fitness within an enormous data set. Skelton's duties included figuring out the precise conditions for the best analysis, which meant determining *what kind of crystal through which to shoot a laser*. Many labs use diamond crystal, but Skelton recommended germanium because it provides "a less noisy spectra."

I ask how she got into this work, what she was after. "It's this idea that we as a species have a tangible cultural history that has been gathered and stood the test of time," Skelton says. "But it's also been edited down through intentional destruction or iconoclasm or the elements of time or natural disasters. We have this physical record, and it says so much about us. It's all we have."

—⚮—

I've had a friend since sixth grade who refuses to enter the Elvis Room. She said Elvis was the height of *creepiness* and *corniness*, like a clown, and she was *afraid* of him. Naturally, at sleepovers, our friends and I put on the Elvis mask and chased her or snuck up behind her holding a ceramic Elvis bust, made it peek over her shoulder. We tricked her into entering the Elvis Room, then held the door shut while she yowled and pounded. No one believed her Presley-phobia. To be honest, it insulted me. I believed Elvis was, objectively, important, beautiful, complicated. I rejected the one-dimensional view but also rejected any version of Elvis other than my own, the one built within my family's culture, our foundational mythology.

I rejected the obscene cartoon versions of Elvis and the death cult of Elvis. I hated any kind of mourning that turned people into saints or angels, that flattened whole lives into one cheesy glamour shot settled on a mantelpiece. I resisted when anyone tried to tell me that my dad was—points skyward—*up there, watching over me*. It didn't comfort me to think of him fixed overhead;

I wished that he were still uncontainable. I wished that I didn't get to decide what he was, that it wasn't down to me to form one image from the relics we have left.

———————

There's a difference between absence and loss. There is a way we can pretend that Elvis is just in the next room, that the man is somehow contained in his ephemera and vinyl. But this cassette tape could mean another death for my dad and me. I can remember some of his voice—melodious, but strongest when doing an impression, singing a made-up lullaby. What if I listen to the tape, and what I hear—*that* voice, unknown, unfamiliar—replaces whatever remnants of him I hold in my mind? Would my dad be that and only that from now on? Would he be reduced, and therefore lost again?

Orpheus turned around to look at Eurydice in order to solidify his connection, to be sure that she was still within reach. *Possessable.* We all know that Orpheus should not have looked back. But perhaps more than that, he should have listened harder for Eurydice's footsteps behind him. He should've trusted the sound.

"A dead person is vulnerable in ways a living person is not," Greil Marcus writes in *Dead Elvis.* "When the subject of a book is living, he or she can always make that book into a lie by acting in a new way. A dead person can be summed up and dismissed. And Elvis is especially vulnerable, because for much of America he has always been a freak."

Worse than a freak, a man becomes a symbol. An *icon*: memorable but static. I knew about this. When your dad is an alcoholic, or addicted, or depressed, or dead, or all of the above—that becomes the whole story. But what about a life beyond its destruction? The complication and capacity. What about the charisma, the kaleidoscope, the music? What about the time he met Lionel Richie and made him laugh? What about Graceland?

I realize that whether I listened or not, I've been trying to recapture my dad. I'm still trying to protect him, to ward off the flattening of time, of addiction. It's understandable, but in doing so, I'm trying to possess him, to control the end of the story. That's not how it works between people, not even a dad and a daughter. I can't keep treating the tape like an illuminated manuscript. Maybe every grief deserves infrared spectroscopy, but I can't wait any longer, can't keep the voice protected behind glass. The only way that the voice has even a chance of *living* again—as a separate entity, an expression made by a separate person—is this: *Play the tape.*

———————

I drive to the local photo center. The tiny bell rings above the door, and the middle-aged man behind the counter is not Mike who had emailed me. When I mention *baking* tapes, he widens his eyes and clutches his pearls. He says he can transfer the tape to a CD by Friday. It's Monday.

"Oh," I say, ". . . or as soon as possible?"

"Probably," not-Mike says.

I put my hands on the counter and singsong, "I sure hope it doesn't get ruined!"

He stays thin-lipped, but his eyes are sympathetic. "We will do what we can," he says.

I leave him with the tape, walk into the parking lot. I get in my car and drive away, but I only make it across the street. Wander the aisles of Food Lion. Pick things up and put them down. I can't imagine standing in front of that man or other unsuspecting customers as the tape of "My Way" jams and rips apart in the cassette player. But if the tape is about to be destroyed, I also can't stand to not be there. *We will do what we can.* I hightail it back to the photo center and ask to listen to the tape right then.

"Oh, sure," not-Mike says. He brings out a portable tape player, but he has to dig around for headphones and new batteries. He presses buttons and the gears squeal. This is my low-tech nightmare. This is my expert, my holy heritage scientist? But then not-Mike hands me the player and walks away. Here I am, headphones plugged in, standing alone at a counter in the center of the store.

When I found the tape, I had been disappointed that my dad had chosen to sing "My Way." It's best known as a Frank Sinatra song, though I've always preferred Elvis's version. Sinatra seems to sneer, denying any regret about his choices all the way to the end.

Elvis sobs.

I wonder how my dad would sing it: would he be over-the-top and vulnerable like Elvis? How much pain would I hear, and whose, and could I take it?

I press play. The cassette wheel turns, and there he is.

My dad rumbles, "Uh, *thank you*, thank you very much."

The first Elvis impersonator, after all, was Elvis himself. I can already tell: My dad is holding back laughter. He's using the lounge-act voice I recognize: deeper and self-serious, yet playful. He's doing late-era Elvis, Elvis in Vegas. The strings of the backing track swell. And he sings. Even though he's playing, he really sings. He starts low, ponderous, then shoots for those delicate notes—and actually hits a few. He fakes a vibrato, and it hits me the same as the real thing. He stays in character, pausing between lyrics to make jokes as though he's striding across some casino stage, blinking into the bright lights: "*I did it myyy waaay*—buck naked in the recording booth! Ha-ha!" He pretends to shake hands with Sammy Davis Jr., and he tells the Jordanaires to cut loose. He tells the crowd they're wonderful. As he reaches the big finish, he cries, "Now everybody, let's sing the last part together," before breaking into that final verse, the one that really means something—

For what is a man? What has he got?

If not himself, then he has naught

Here's the truth: We, the faithful, know that Elvis is dead. But what does *dead* have to do with us? What does it have to do with love? We were there. We've got the tapes.

My dad is singing into the microphone nestled between my ears, and it's so beautiful and burning I can hardly listen. He sounds exactly like I remember: multifaceted, flashing, ironic but profoundly tender.

But, of course, he doesn't sound exactly like I remember. He couldn't. He made the tape years before I even existed. Before he was my dad, when he was a young man on a long trip with a red-haired girl. He was pretending to be Elvis. He's not one thing or another. His voice is closer than it's been in fifteen years, and yet he's less accessible again, the way the living are. I can't predict what this voice will do next.

It's true that in each remembering, each replay, something is lost again. I look around the quiet store, boxed-up technologies set on pedestals. Our icons die, our dads die. They didn't slip out the back of the building or disappear into a black Cadillac. They can't be recalled if you learn the right notes or if you pray to their images or if you want it enough. We can only play it through.

On the tape, his voice is nothing like Elvis: that belting, lunging with an operatic need, near tears. Because my dad is laughing. By the end, he cracks up completely. He laughs like he can't believe it—how great this is, how *silly* and how great. He steps back from the mic and goes right on chuckling to himself. That's how the song plays out. That's how the recording ends. The gears keep respooling the yellow tape. For a few more beats, I listen to it whir.

—ɯ—

USELESS BEAUTY

SCOTT RUSSELL SANDERS

IN A NICHE ABOVE OUR HEARTH, alongside books and rocks and birds' nests, my wife and I keep the shell of a chambered nautilus. My mother bought it for us at a flea market more than thirty years ago, thinking we might welcome a reminder of the ocean here in landlocked Indiana. Like the shell of a lowly snail, and like our galaxy, it has a spiral shape. When the nautilus was in residence, it would have floated with the knobby core of the spiral uppermost and the curving tail pointed down. As large as a saucer and thinner than fine porcelain, our shell has been sliced down the middle in such a way as to produce two symmetrical halves, which we display side by side, one half showing the exterior and the other showing the interior. On the outside, wavy stripes the color of butterscotch radiate from the center of the spiral, contrasting with an ivory background, which is faintly grooved, as if from brushstrokes in glossy paint. The lustrous interior reveals a sequence of chambers resembling crescent moons, thirty in all, which the nautilus fashioned as it grew, beginning with a cranny too small to see without a magnifying glass and increasing, step by step, to the size of a child's grin. It is a marvelous feat of construction—as if a baby fashioned its own cradle, and then, having outgrown that first home, went on to make a crib, a bedroom, a hut, a cottage, a mansion, on and on, all life long.

Over the years, visitors have often admired the shell. Many ask if they might look at it more closely, and I am always happy to reach the two pieces down from their niche and lay them in curious hands. The visitors run their fingers over the tigerish stripes on the exterior, tilt the half shell to catch the sheen of its pearly interior, examine the spiraling chambers. They marvel at how a deep-sea animal could produce such elegant patterns and captivating colors. Some visitors go further and ask a question that the nautilus shell has long posed for me—not *how* this beauty is produced, but *why*. Why such beauty in a seashell? For that matter, why such beauty in a sunset, in blossom or birdsong or butterfly wing, or anywhere at all?

Allow this innocent question into your mind, and it will be followed by a host of others that philosophers have pondered for ages: What is beauty? Is it an intrinsic feature of the world, like the mass of an apple, or is it an artifact of human perception, like the apple's red color? If beauty is an aspect of reality, independent of our perceptions, how does it arise—purely by the operation of physical laws, or by design? If by physical laws, how do they happen to generate a quality so pleasing to us? And if by design, then who or what is the designer? Whatever its nature and whatever its source, why does beauty appeal to us so deeply? Why do we crave it, savor it, and seek it out, and why do we strive to create beauty with our hands and minds and voices?

Despite having devoted thousands of pages to these questions, philosophers disagree about the answers—as they tend to do about all the perennial puzzles, such as how we know what we know, how we should act, what the universe is made of, and why there is a universe at all. As an amateur, I will leave the great enigma of beauty to the experts and merely reflect on one small piece of the puzzle, which I stumbled across while reading about the chambered nautilus.

According to scientists, the pattern on the outside of the shell, which we find so lovely, provides camouflage from predators and prey. The wavy butterscotch stripes, thick and dark on the portion of the shell that floats on top, gradually fade as the spiral opens, leaving the bottom portion clear. Seen from above, the stripes obscure the outlines of the shell and blend into the darkness of the deeps; seen from below, the unmarked ivory blends with light from the surface. That we find these markings gorgeous is a happy accident. What seems beautiful to us is beneficial to the nautilus, a legacy of evolution, helping its kind survive for some five hundred million years.

But what about the shell's interior—that mother-of-pearl luster, that exquisite series of crescent-shaped chambers—all invisible to predators? This beauty gave no benefit to the nautilus; indeed, it sealed its doom, for the only predator that knew of this hidden splendor was the two-legged kind that fished the shell from the sea and sliced it in half and introduced it to the marketplace of beautiful objects. Although of no use to the nautilus, this interior beauty has kept the fragile half shells intact as they passed through innumerable hands, including my wife's and mine and those of our curious visitors.

—ᴍ—

Among the things in nature we find beautiful, many, like the outer pattern on a nautilus shell, are the result of natural selection, adaptations that improve the chances of survival for an organism or a species. Think of the peacock's tail, attractive to mates. Think of the monarch butterfly's cautionary orange and gold, or the Day-Glo colors on rain-forest frogs, warning of the poisons they carry. Think of the zebra's stripes, confusing to predators, or the scent of roses, alluring to pollinators. Consider the chameleon's shifting colors, the buck's imposing antlers, the song of the canyon wren, the beaks of humming-birds exactly fitted to sources of nectar, the white crowns of clover seductive to bees, the courtship dance of sandhill cranes or the daredevil flights of woodcocks, the flicker of fireflies, the cries of spring peepers, the fiddling of crickets—all can be explained as resulting from natural selection. You could discover as many examples as there are living species, for if you carefully observe anything alive, you will find something biologically useful that is also beautiful.

In addition to that useful beauty, however, you will discover something more, an extravagance of design, an opulence of materials—like the pearly interior of the nautilus shell—that serves no evident purpose, other than to make the natural world inexhaustibly interesting. If you study flowers, for instance, you will find quite a few that seem fancier than they need to be. Look at fuchsia, with its blossom of purple pantaloons overtopped by a pink tiara. Look at bleeding heart, with its plump valentine blossoms dangling from the stem like charms on a bracelet. Look at iris, with its streaked petals flung out in all directions, like the blurred arms of a whirling dervish. Or look at wild columbine, which might be a scarlet moon lander, with five spurs thrust skyward like spiky antennae, five pointed sepals spread out like wings, a white interior for a firing chamber, and yellow threads of stamens shooting downward like the tracery of rockets. If color, odor, and beckoning shape are the key signals to pollinators, why all the flair and filigree?

The same lovely extravagance shows up everywhere you look or listen in the living world, from the dazzling patterns of microscopic diatoms to the sea-filling arias of humpback whales. The wings of butterflies known as painted ladies resemble the stained glass on Tiffany lampshades, a fanciful collage of swirls and curlicues and eye-shaped spots. There are beetles covered in polka dots, beetles as shiny and colorful as new cars in a showroom, beetles bearing scrawls on their backs as jazzy as urban graffiti. There are fish gaudier than clowns, salamanders flashier than neon signs, medusas like alien spacecraft, birds as flamboyant as Victorian Easter hats. Look anywhere you like—at mon-keys or mushrooms, cacti or dragonflies, fritillaries or ferns, leafhoppers or leaves—and you will discover designs more various than any vocabulary we might use to describe them.

Even if this seeming excess of beauty could be accounted for as biologically useful, what of the glories in the nonliving world? What of sunsets and sunrises? What of the northern lights? What of the moon, our fellow traveler, with its captivating phases? What of the stars, those faithful Muses? What of the sea, with its troughs and swells, its rhythmic drumming on the shore, its vast expanses for the eye to roam? What of canyons and crevasses, waterfalls and glaciers, the play of current in rivers, the restless ballet of clouds?

There's useless beauty everywhere, even among seemingly stolid rocks. Here in the limestone country of southern Indiana, for example, our creek beds are littered with brownish lumps of mineral sediment called geodes. Ranging from the size of peas to the size of basketballs, they are dull on the outside, with little to catch the eye, but if you find one that has been cracked open, or if you split it yourself with a hammer, inside you will find translucent crystals of quartz, or bands of purple amethyst, orange agate, pale-blue chalcedony, or sultry-red jasper, colors and forms as resplendent as anything a jeweler could offer.

Our remote ancestors paid heed to such earthly and heavenly glories, painted them on the walls of caves, wove them into religions and rugs, etched them into stories and stones. In the past few centuries, however, our ingenious technology has revealed beauties from realms our early ancestors knew nothing of. Telescopes, microscopes, cameras mounted in satellites or in deep-sea submersibles, receivers capable of reading the whole spectrum of light and sound, and a slew of other devices have greatly extended the range of our senses. If you graduated from childhood without having looked through a microscope at the menagerie of beasts in a drop of pond water, or through a telescope at craters on the moon, you were deprived.

More powerful instruments reveal even more astonishing designs. The compound eye of an ordinary housefly, viewed through a scanning electron microscope, might be mistaken for the head of a sunflower or a geodesic dome; at higher magnification, the facets of that eye look like hexagonal pastries crowded onto a baking sheet. Undersea rovers have photographed luminous creatures more exotic and majestic than anything conjured up by the makers of science fiction films. The Hubble Space Telescope has brought us mesmerizing close-ups of our sister planets and of our own precious globe; peering into distances that stagger the imagination, it has also brought us images of quasars, supernovae, black holes, and other spectacular phenomena that were unknown even to astronomers a century ago. Moreover, thanks to computers, databanks, and the World Wide Web, you can summon up such revelations in your home, school, or library, or through a gadget that will fit into your palm. You can listen to whale song, watch meteor showers, trace the motions of amoebas, study a lattice of carbon atoms, or glimpse exploding stars. If you have access to this technology, you can behold riches that were hidden from every previous generation.

—ɷ—

Wherever we look, from the dirt under our feet to the edge of the expanding cosmos, and on every scale from atoms to galaxies, the universe appears to be saturated with beauty. What are we to make of this?

If you believe that so much stunning design can only be the work of a cosmic Designer, then the Designer must be inordinately fond of beauty (as the British biologist J. B. S. Haldane is said to have remarked about God's regard for beetles). It would seem to follow, for anyone who holds such a belief, that this beauty is sacred to the Designer and is therefore deserving of our care. We can't protect the glittering stars or flaming sunset or cycling moon, but we can protect the streams that salmon need for spawning, the high plains where sage grouse dance, the ancient forests required by spotted owls, the Arctic calving grounds of caribou. We can defend the last groves of redwoods from loggers, the creeks and mountaintops of Appalachia from miners, the ocean floor from trawlers, the atmosphere from polluters.

On the other hand, if you believe these ubiquitous beauties can be accounted for entirely by the operation of material processes, you may nonetheless treasure them. Indeed, you may treasure them all the more, as gifts we have no reason to expect from an indifferent universe. You may feel an obligation to protect whatever falls within your reach, not because it is divinely created, not because you can eat it or wear it or display it above your hearth but because you love the beautiful thing itself a creature, a species, a place. Even if you happen not to marvel at salmon or wolves, even if you've never seen an unplowed prairie or unlogged forest, you might still favor the protection of these and other natural beauties out of a respect for the people who do know and love them.

Or you might take yet a third view of these matters, a view that will long since have occurred to the philosophers in my imagined audience. You might argue that what I call *beauty* is not a feature of the universe at all, sacred or secular, but only a quality of experience, a certain inner weather, like sorrow or joy. Even on this view, if *beauty* is merely a label for a feeling, that inner state is so enthralling, so invigorating, so nourishing, you might wish to protect whatever source outside of consciousness gives rise to it, for your own sake and for the sake of others who could enjoy the same experience. If it thrills you to hear owls call from a deep wood, you want the woods and owls to survive, and you want your own children or children yet unborn to have a chance of feeling the same thrill.

Whatever our philosophical or scientific or religious views, a close attention to beauty in the natural world ought to inspire in us an ethic of ecological care. It ought to make us live lightly. It ought to make us ardent supporters of laws aimed at protecting air, water, soil, endangered species, and wilderness. Ought to—but frequently doesn't. Those who regard *beauty* as only the name of a pleasurable feeling might find all the stimulation they desire in movies or music or mathematics, without recourse to nature. Those who regard the universe as a machine that has been grinding away for billions of years, without purpose or direction, might regard natural beauty as having no intrinsic value, but only as a commodity to be used up or discarded to suit our appetites. Those who believe in a beauty-loving Creator often claim, based on a literal reading of the Bible, that the universe is only a few thousand years old, and that everything in it, on Earth and beyond, was created for humans to exploit.

Our collective behavior suggests that the dominant view, at least in America, is that nothing in nature has value except insofar as it is useful to humans—and useful today, not in some future generation. What good is a wilderness if we can't drill it for oil or mine it for minerals? What good is an ancient forest if it doesn't yield board feet of lumber? Why protect wild salmon if we can grow fish in concrete vats laced with chemicals? Why worry about any nonhuman creature if it stands in the way of our plans?

This is not a minority view. These utilitarian sentiments resound from legislatures, boardrooms, and editorial pages; they permeate economics textbooks and the buy-it-now babble of advertisements; they guide shoppers looking for the cheapest deal.

Measured by its consequences, the utilitarian ethic has proven to be disastrous. A child born in America today enters a world chock-full of human comforts and contrivances, but sorely depleted of natural wealth—topsoil lost, rivers dammed, air and water poisoned, wetlands drained, roadsides and oceans littered with trash, resources squandered, species extinguished. We are trading forested mountaintops for cut-rate electricity. We are swapping the sound of meadowlarks and the sight of prairie coneflowers for casinos and parking lots. We are sacrificing rainforests for hamburgers, coral reefs for island cruises, glaciers for SUVs. With every upward tick of the GDP, the richness and resilience of the greater-than-human world declines.

Of course, that same child born in America today may never know what
has been lost. She may take the diminished world as the way things *must* be, if
we are to enjoy what Madison Avenue and Wall Street call progress and pros-
perity. With each passing year, Americans on average spend more and more
of their time inside human constructions—buildings and vehicles; symbolic
zones made out of numbers, musical notes, or, like this essay, out of words; and
inside the trance of TV, video games, and the burgeoning empire of cyberspace.
Cut off from direct contact with natural beauty, people make do with crude
substitutes—plastic flowers, air freshener, Muzak; with artistic imitations—
films, photographs, and recordings; or with tokens—flowers in vases, flowing
water in fountains, nautilus shells above the hearth. If those counterfeits and
borrowings are all we know of nature, then natural beauty is in jeopardy, for
we will not protect what we do not know.

—⁓—

A final look at the interior of our nautilus shell suggests a possible way out of
this impasse, a way of reconciling the world we've made with the greater world
that made us. By compressing nitrogen into those inner chambers, the nautilus
can regulate its buoyancy, ranging in its seemingly fragile hull from the shallows of tropical seas to depths of two thousand feet, nearly ten times as deep as
a scuba diver could safely go. More intriguing, the pattern of crescent-shaped
chambers illustrates a mathematical rule, first described by Descartes, called
a logarithmic spiral. The formula can be written out in a string of symbols
shorter than the title of this essay. The same pattern appears widely in nature
in the bands of hurricane winds, the spiral arms of galaxies, the array of seeds
in sunflowers, the heads of certain broccolis, a hawk's curving approach to its
prey, even in some wave-scoured beaches.

This congruence between nature and numbers does not lead me to conclude,
with Pythagoras, that the universe is mathematics writ large, but rather the
opposite—that mathematics is the universe writ small. Indeed, this conso-
nance between the patterns we make and the patterns we find in nature rein-
forces my sense that not only mathematics but also music, poetry, painting,
photography, storytelling, dance—all forms of art and symbolic language—
are manifestations, through human beings, of the cosmic penchant for creating
beauty. The universe out of which we have evolved is inscribed in our intel-
ligence and imagination. This does not make us gods, nor does it justify our
dominion over Earth, but it does confirm that we belong here, in spite of what
otherworldly religions claim. The creative genius of nature runs right through
us, as it runs through the chambered nautilus.

I will let the philosophers define what beauty is. But I think I understand some of what beauty *does*. It calls us out of ourselves. It feeds our senses. It provides standards for art and science, for language and literature. It inspires affection and gratitude. How then should we live, in a world overflowing with such bounty? Rejoice in it, care for it, and strive to add our own mite of beauty, with whatever power and talent we possess.

PART 2

POETRY

ORCHIDS ARE SPROUTING FROM THE FLOORBOARDS

KAVEH AKBAR

Orchids are sprouting from the floorboards.
Orchids are gushing out from the faucets.
The cat mews orchids from his mouth.
His whiskers are also orchids.
The grass is sprouting orchids.
It is becoming mostly orchids.
The trees are filled with orchids.
The tire swing is twirling with orchids.
The sunlight on the wet cement is a white orchid.
The car's tires leave a trail of orchids.
A bouquet of orchids lifts from its tailpipe.
Teenagers are texting each other pictures
of orchids on their phones, which are also orchids.
Old men in orchid penny loafers
furiously trade orchids.
Mothers fill bottles with warm orchids
to feed their infants, who are orchids themselves.
Their coos are a kind of orchid.
The clouds are all orchids.
They are raining orchids.
The walls are all orchids,
the teapot is an orchid,
the blank easel is an orchid,
and this cold is an orchid. Oh,
Lydia, we miss you terribly.

LOOKING FOR MUSHROOMS

DASON ANDERSON

Not looking for mushrooms
because at night it's been too cold
to sleep without you.
Because we can't just walk
into the woods like we used to,
out the back door, past the big oak
tree with the tarnished trunk,
over the rusted barbed wire
fence, and following
the dry creek bed to the secret
cave where it opens from the hillside,
spilling cold breath, spilling
water now, in spring, water
that doesn't make it far, pooling in
abandoned tires, sinking into bedrock,
getting lost in dams of last year's fallen
leaves. Where on the hill,
above the cave, there were mushrooms.

Not looking for mushrooms
because cool April has turned downtown
into a veritable Shire, where booze abounds
and fresh herbs mingle with music
in the park, and velvet flowers sway
like butt cheeks in a breeze of East Coast
mental pollution. It ain't so bad,
finding salvation in a pint of OJ

and champagne. Wondering if
my hair looks OK, not wondering
if I'll find any dimpled morels
over this next beech-crested hill.

Not looking for mushrooms
because I didn't think I'd find any
anyway. Felt good waking in a spill
of sunlight and promises, felt good
foregoing the hunt and sleeping in.
Abandon greasy diner, abandon
sylvan sanctuary—who needs
an escape anyway. Find joy
everywhere you are. Know that
last time you took a shortcut
to mushrooms, you fell crying
in grey leaves, in a creek bend,
in a bed of fresh pepper root,
blood root, yellow root, squirrel corn,
trout lily, etc., in remorse, regret,
in not finding food, well-being,
forgiveness, in not finding mushrooms
where you've found them before.
In finding someone else's tears
crystallized behind sunglasses
as you fret over what to do with yourself,
what to waste your money on,
in replacing money with more booze.
Hoping you wouldn't have found anything
today anyway, so nothing's wasted.
So better luck next time.

THE CREATOR TAKES THE STAND

NOAH BALDINO

I see I see but that's not
the worst part I can't
help anybody They have ideas
of heaven I didn't give them
I just wanted them to have
fingernails and blades
of grass Do you know how impossible
to replace a single blade of grass with
its own particular folds and edges I didn't mean to
make these perishables before
I invented foresight See
in the beginning there were
limitations Humanity was just
a knot in my throat Now even
the courtroom sketches
accuse me
I am mudslide murdered infant smashed
glass sparrow I have wreaked
no small havoc
I'll plead guilty
if it saves just one socket
from a knuckle or returns every
long-dead parent Objection Objection
My guilt changes nothing I forgot to create
accountability

This world keeps happening
without me It tends
to its own evolutions and cries
in a voice like a dog whistle I didn't
invent the dog whistle
or the leash only
the ear I'm so sorry for the ear I meant
to do no harm I won't fit
in a jail cell I invented
escape but also forgiveness Do you
remember forgiveness
What about the mango or the juice
that drips off the lip to sweeten
the ground See I'm good
Everyone's a good person
aren't they Aren't they

ATMOSPHERE IN OUR BULLSHIT LITTLE TOWN

BRYCE BERKOWITZ

Most days, we skateboarded
like the sky was spilling out of our pockets—
our crusty teenaged hearts stuck in a cyclone
of a going nowhere town, of our wheels
knocking the sidewalk gaps to Wendy's,
to high school, to the futures we'd walk away from.
We named ourselves,
tagged hoppers and auto racks,
but we never shot up the crooks
of our arms with hornets or pink dahlias.
On Saturday night, we waited for Bryan
to quit Long John Silver's
by pinching crispies or crunchies
or whatever the fuck those fried-gold bits were
into our mouths; those questionable
unknowns we'd never fork
into our now thirty-five-year-old bodies
out of fear of descending
into a pile of broken candles.
There's so much life you'll never escape.
When I ask my father,
What was I like back then?
I feel myself disappear.

RED-WINGED BLACKBIRD

JOE BETZ

On corn tassels, dew. On our jeans, dew.
From his lips, a boy wipes sweat thick
as pickling salt. Today no one is resting,
not even the sun high and burning like
a cross in misanthropic minds. On the radio,
love. On our minds, love. In the field
we're slipping wet hands in corn until we
walk slow as clouds plumping west to the
farmer asleep in his truck, rocks and lunch
boxes behind our burnt backs, red as apples
now cooling to peel. No one is resting.
Our plan to bang these rocks, whip these
boxes for wild music, we slink. We are
children; mustard weed on pant legs. And in
fifteen feet, we will later say we knew
an engine's backfire did not ring but popped
to nothing, and in fifteen feet, we will
later say the sound was not the tractor's
basket clipping another well. We are children.
We smell him first. And in the early afternoon,
if you watch, a red-winged blackbird will
sit on a phone line for you silent
as waving hands, a plane in the sky.

PRETEND

CALLISTA BUCHEN

For a while, my daughter worried about a catastrophic hole in the ground wherever we were going. *Mom, what if the library is just a giant hole? What if the cereal aisle is a big hole?* She imagined canyons replacing each familiar landmark. At every intersection, every turn, I promised her there would be no hole. She'd plead: *But what will we do? You'll see,* I would say, *everything will be fine.* When she stopped asking, I grieved her lost worry like the death of an imaginary friend; but since she's first stacked the blocks in the living room, she's understood that what we build we can crash. *Anything can go boom,* she says now to her little brother, who wants the tower higher, higher still. *Mom will hold it,* she tells him. She pauses and adds, *for now.*

DEER WHISPERER

STEVE CASTRO

Sitka deer are excellent swimmers, so you have to be careful.
I wouldn't be surprised if they swam across the Ohio River
in order to do something criminal. I almost got killed by a deer once.
I also had an individual with a deer head shoot an arrow right over my head.
In my backyard, I once fed an apple to a deer in need,
and he came back the next day with his entire mob. They held me hostage
until I gave them all of my fruit and vegetables. They didn't even leave me
a single papaya. I once started a letter with the words *Deer Susan*,
and I was so embarrassed when Susan showed me the error.
It is said that wolves are the deer's worst enemies, but deer are their own
     worst enemy.
Once a week, I visit my local deer cemetery, and I see deer eating grass,
picnicking with their families, lamenting over their loved ones,
and some even gossiping as to why I might be there.

HELLO, MY PARENTS DON'T SPEAK ENGLISH WELL, HOW CAN I HELP YOU?

SU CHO

Are you the head of the household?
Because I am
Calling about the census—
Dear, I need to speak with an adult
Even if they don't speak English well.
For every call like this, my mother
Gestures wildly as if we
Haven't done this a million times.
I'm sorry, I say back to the voice.
Just do it, just once, and I shrug, listen to my mom saying she's sorry,
Korean, yes. She stumbles over the practiced phrase, please
Listen to my daughter
My English
No good.
Once I called her stupid for
Packing my field trip lunch with
Quick sesame rice balls even though that's what I
Requested. This isn't true. I called her
Stupid after she hit me for low grades in English class.
The truth is, I hated my friends
Upset over the sesame smell sprawled over
Verdant lawns of the IMAX theatre. A field trip, perfect
Weather. The expensive sticky rice, stones in my stomach.
X-rays of what I eat at home scattered for my school to see.
Yet twenty years later, I am on the phone in a different time
Zone, speaking for my mother, how we just want some accountability.

ODE TO THE TONGUE

NANDI COMER

Click. Twist. Flutter. Once again
you stick a tepid towel sound in my mouth.
We are in a café, in a hotel, in a store
trying to order coffee or cookies, and there you go.

The long *u* of you in my lap. I am a fractured
figurine. Language is made of spackled sounds
flitting past my eyes. We play naming games,
guess each mouth-shaped word made soft in their lips.

What you call imitation is a clanging arrest, a sour
misuse of the throat. I trip over syllables. I feel
sweat trickle between my breasts, let these
faraway words lie like fuzz on my teeth. Tongue,

have you noticed how troubled you have become?
I cannot maneuver conversation without you slipping
out of place. You twist around like a trapped bull.
I have tried to force you out of your silent ending.

We are native to people who can't stop speaking
foreign languages. There is no space for timidness,
tongue. Loop into a long word like *lung*. Lay
the lengthy trills on the backside of *paladar*.

At some tables, tongue and language
are the same. Don't bother translating decorum.
Each country sets, with its own formal address
and common clatter, a shock on the mouth.

In this mouth, let's send a curled *g* galloping
across some desert with the *r*'s rolling ribbon heart.

FEAST GREEN AND STAINED

PAUL CUNNINGHAM

I am wasted on thought-so's and photo-ops

so-so's and S-O-S cries and the lit flare

I burn I intuit I follow your light

look at the way you go into the tall grass

into it   you light

        you moth

look at your shirtless body behind the tall grass

look at me on my knees

a poem is a lot like a grass stain

I want to do what a grass stain does

—*w*—

THIS AFTERNOON, KIRKWOOD AVENUE BREATHES

MITCHELL L. H. DOUGLAS

Behind the counter at the corner bookstore,
              a woman sings Tori Amos—well.
Nose stud and outlined lips,
she arranges new porno mags
                  like the order matters.

I browse *Poets & Writers*,
                  search for salvation,
then retreat to the used bookstore
two doors down where two men
             salivate for authors I don't know.

His mouth tired of praise,
one man hoists a box of hardcovers,
quips, "I need another book
like I need a hole in my head."
                We all could use that kind of space
I think, as I pick Natasha Trethewey
from a pile of paperbacks,
             pretend not to eavesdrop.

LITTLE EAGLE CREEK IN SEASONS

M. A. DUBBS

I
Brown ice seals the creek,
a plump chickadee curls its
toes around bare branch

II
Pink redbud petals
frame creek bank, a muskrat bathes
on a stone island

III
At dusk, cicadas
hum in the tulip trees while
fireflies dance along

IV
Crisp fire-tinged leaves
layer muddy bank, blanket
the smallmouth below

OUR RELATIONSHIP AS EMBRACE B/W ICARUS & LIGHT

SAMANTHA FAIN

the sun sees Icarus & tries to shift orbit
but he already flies so close
(too close) & the sun sees beeswax ((coming closer))
wings & feathers & briefly wants to hold him
& imagines the touch [   ] like popping off
a fanta lid: all orange fizz / a good explosive /
the sun tastes it / on his orb & delights & shines warmer
& so Icarus   slips
melts into the water leaving
the sun trembling /
weeping with no one to listen:
[   ],
[   ],
[   ].

SELF-PORTRAIT AS HAMMER

MAGGIE GRABER

The grip is everything.
Then the swing-back
and journey down,
song of steel
forged in a forge.
Let me do the work.
The marriage
between the body
and the tool,
the way I bend gravity
in your hand.
Before I could build
anything, I had to learn
what God gave me:
a bag full of nails,
the stone
my body becomes
in thought.
Look at the nail
planted like a stem—
what we can build
and take apart.
To make a bird,
you need two birds.
To make a hammer, you need

another hammer, fire,
and a handle long
as a neck. Otherwise,
you got no song.

QUIET AFTER RAIN IN INDIANA

JOE HEITHAUS

Drips, distant hum of a combine,
train rumble, fly buzz, and the inside
sighs and coos of thought, a line

that won't meet the horizon's wide
passage to the clouds. Children
nap in this hour, a lid

slips off a coffee can, a spoon
scoops up a heap, and one person holds
another against the afternoon

chill that came with fields
of puddles silvering pink when the sun
appears again and the quiet folds

into the after-clatter in the run
of a creek mixed with the caws of the crows.

JUNK FOOD

ALLISON JOSEPH

One day I nearly cracked my skull wide open,
feet flying out from under as I fell
down a series of slate stone steps
iced over by Indiana winter
because I had to have a bag of Oreos.
I didn't care that ice was everywhere,
that my breath hung, a frozen vapor.
I wanted to lick that creamy white middle,
let its sugar dissolve all over my tongue
and teeth, to crunch those round
black cookies, savoring them with a glass
of milk colder than the air outside.
Fool for sweetness, I would have
run out naked had there been free bags
tossed in the snow, bounty from a jackknifed
Nabisco truck. No substitute would do,
no supermarket brand or nearest competitor—
I wanted no other crumbs on my lips, fingers,
table. So when I roused myself,
dazed from the fall, the cold,
my head a heavy weight that bumped
all three steps on the way down,
I still craved a taste sweeter
than anything upstairs in the house,
a certainty even winter couldn't kill.

BESAYDOO

YALIE KAMARA

While sipping coffee in my mother's Toyota, we hear the birdcall of two teen-
 age boys
in the parking lot: *Aiight,* one says, *Besaydoo,* the other returns, as they
 reach
for each other. Their cupped handshake pops like the first, fat, firecrackers of
 summer,

their fingers shimmy as if they're solving a Rubik's cube just beyond our sight.
 Moments
later, their Schwinns head in opposite directions. My mother turns to me,
 revealing the
milky, John-Waters-mustache-thin foam on her upper lip, *Wetin dem bin say?*

Besaydoo? Nar English? she asks, tickled by this tangle of new language.
 Alright.
Be safe dude, I pull apart each syllable like string cheese for her. *Oh yah, dem
 nar real padi,*
she smiles, surprisingly broken by the tenderness expressed by what half my
 family might call

thugs. *Besaydoo. Besaydoo. Besaydoo,* we chirp in the car, then nightly into our
 phones
after I leave California. *Besaydoo,* she says as she softly muffles the rattling of
 my bones
in newfound sobriety. *Besaydoo,* I say years later, her response made raspy by
 an oxygen

treatment at the ER. *Besaydoo*, we whisper to each other across the country.
Like

some word from deep in a somewhere too newborn-pure for the outdoors,
but we

saw those two boys do it, in broad daylight, under a decadent, ruinous,
sun.

THE INDIANAPOLIS 500

CHRISTOPHER KEMPF

"Mike Conway injures left leg in airborne crash"

—The Indianapolis Star, *May 30, 2010*

This too we stole from the gods. Robbed
fire and driveshaft and strapped
both to the back of a man more bird now than human. How,
in Ovid, the gods look on
with indifference at Icarus slipping from the sky.
That vaulted waterlock.
Listen. For miles the whine
of Hondas drowns even this place's cicadas. The stadium
thrums, hums its love song
of steel and heat and the hundred thousand
pink-faced race fans who flock—all feather—to the dead,
fuel-injected center of the state. It's something
Roman almost. Like aqueduct. Like dome. Roman—
our wanting just this exact catastrophe to happen. Our wanting
to watch. A man enters myth
only so many ways this century. Proficiency
at killing things is one. Another
is up-cycling your six-cylinder in the middle
of turn four where the fans
know already it will end
in mangled carbon fiber and flame. In the weightless
cicada shell of your car
spinning across the sky like a discus. Which,

like columns and democracy and their intricate system
of sewers, the ancients gave us. How Phaëton,
doubting his sun-god father, robbed him
of his chariot and carried the sun from one
pedestal of the heavens to another, blood-colored
hair roiling in his wake. What hubris,
the gods cried out, seeing his strung musculature—
the curved breast, the burnished
hips and thighs. This also
from Ovid. Who wanted
to explain the way we learn violence
is by trying to fly and falling. Who watched the sky
draw back like an affronted lover above the floodgates, a place
we can't imagine anymore,
in the starved architecture we built this century
to watch our sons come crashing back. The ones
who got up and walked.

PORTRAIT OF BOY IN GREYHOUND BUS WINDOW

PATRICK KINDIG

We are halfway between Indianapolis and Ann Arbor
when I see his fingers make a decision. Beneath

the blackened television screen, beneath the cover of
an electric blue hoodie, beneath the bus's bone-shaking

music and its sacral echoes, his zipper opens
like an eyelid. Outside, the world is an indecipherable map

of penises—silos and pylons, the soft curve
of a pine tree rising from uneven ground. Inside

there is just the one. The air conditioner drowns
out all sound, and now the only sign of it is

the gentle rocking of his lap, imperceptible
to anyone not looking for such things, the sheer and simple

audacity of this act for him like a colossal pair
of lips. He looks through the rain-wet window

at his own reflection, one corner of his mouth curling
upward like an animal intent on the task

of population. This is misleading: he is here not for business
but pleasure. He finishes in his palm, still

secret beneath the blue hoodie, still silent, and
he handprints the seat beside him sticky. His face shimmers

in the window, soft brown on a field of grey and green,
and he smiles at himself. What contentment! What

intimacy! The white of his teeth flashes a promise
to the glass: You are all I will ever love.

PORTABLE CITY

KAREN KOVACIK

after Yin Xiuzhen

My city fits in a suitcase,
all steeples and spires,
White River zipped up for the night.
When I open my city, I hear the slow jazz
of a dozen waiting rooms.

Inside, there's high humidity.
My staid navy swimsuit
dreams of chlorine.
Tiny war memorials spin
through the air like chess pieces.

You never know what
will fly out of my suitcase.
It has its own airport,
planes, and terrorists.
It bulges like a B-movie bomb.

In Paris, my city smelled
like French fries and Big Macs.
In Beijing, it swelled
to panda size. In Venice,
the gondolier refused it.

Sometimes I open the case in public
like an aunt on a park bench,

folding up the lawns in cute little squares,
slipping the strip malls and parking lots
into side pockets.

My city can never be too neat.
You won't find much graffiti in my suitcase.
But you'll see racecars lapping each other
and peace pipes unsmoked
for a hundred years.

More than once, I schemed
to ditch my city,
to forget it in the trunk of a cab
or watch it orbit for half an hour
on some airport's black belt.

Instead I cling to its leash.
Heel, I yell. Stand! Stay!
At home, I hoist my city
onto the bed to see
what earthquakes have wrought.

Hooray! The city still stands,
though its one-way streets heave
this way and that. My hands
tunnel through underwear
like the subway cars my city never had.

At night, when sewer grates weigh down
my lids like tin coins, I plumb the hollows
where only bone resides. Bone
that speaks Miami or Delaware.
Bone among beech pillars in the rain.

MATURATION THEORY

KIEN LAM

You grow older
with each spider
you eat
in your sleep.
The silk gathers
in your mouth
until you dream
you can't breathe,
your limbs
caught in a wet
web, your tongue
a wet spider,
a red carpet laid
from the throat,
the voice box,
the one still
in need of air,
still muted, caught
on the Earth's
tongue, the Earth
playing with its food
because it never learned
how to swallow,
how to hide
its toys

from mortality.
This is what it means
for your skin to crawl.
This is how you were
born. You slipped
into the Earth's
mouth. The mouth
took a breath.
The breath took
you in. It is a cage
you cannot escape.
You don't want to be
swallowed. You are
not a spider,
but the mouth is wet.
The tongue is loose.
You try to leave a leg
for the Earth to find
when it wakes up.

THE MERCHANT SEAMAN'S WIFE

JACQUELINE JONES LAMON

These days, I'm spending time and pocketing
the change. In the afternoons, the sun hits strong,
reminds me of my need for warmth, my life
absent of caress. These long, silent, luscious days.
On schedule, I walk to the docks, sit with my back

unsupported, imagine the hour of his return. I wonder
if I will want him—his hands sure to be stiffened,
and calloused, snagging against what I've strived
to keep taut, his vision of me a conjured oasis,

his legs unaccustomed to the dance we once learned
to do on land. This time, it's been eight months
of single plates and coffee cups, smoothing my side
of our bed—not the first time, not the last. The hard
part is reentry—this coming and going, like tide.

Imported spices. Foreign cars. Our Indonesian clothes.

GOOD FRIDAY

REBECCA LEHMANN

The stench of dung encased the countryside
with threats of the pastoral. Was it with pride

the trilling robins dropped their spring-pale eggs
into their slap-dash nests? Their twiggy legs

performed brute magic—holding them above
the ploughed-up ruts of finally thawed mud.

You stood beside the truck. I'd had a headache for three days. I called to you. The dead

flies on the windowsill didn't answer. In
some other bleached-out towns we would've been

the heroes of this story, circling
pathetic homestead barns left crumbling,

waiting for the Fire Marshal's match
to touch the gasoline-soaked wood, to catch

and burn a hundred fifty years of disappointment. But here the squirrels chase and kiss

their brothers. The grass droops, damp with sinful dew.
I knew you in the morning sun, and you

knew all the ways to scare the kittens from
the haymow—their too big heads and pupils like some

crazed god's wet dream, their stubby tails a shake
of fur and bone. There is no way to take

apart this landscape. Often loneliness
became our ally, pushing us to dress

the facts in flowery language. No one felt
the fear, the runaway heartbeat of the calf

we butchered that Good Friday—the snot that glazed
its huffing, widened nostrils—the panic-blazed

wide planets of its eyes that searched and took
us in—its one last bellow. No response. No look

of empathy. The barn was not the land.
It stood apart. I went to hold your hand.

It held the knife. We couldn't touch. The spring
air was an accusation. Let me bring

you, shaking, to the half-plowed final field
next to the cow pond. We can lie, unreal

below the wandering caul-gray clouds—pretend
we're kids again—the summer no dead end,

the irises reaching up not harbingers
of a too-ripe season's manic, fertile whir.

THE POET ENCOUNTERS
A MOOSE IN WINTER

JOHN LEO

look at this ol' boy his shoulders
are endless his antlers great gravy scoops my
stars are themselves the fenceposts
that order this particular land but this moose
is borderless his shoulders bleed into the starfield
his blood is starry his bellow a hagiography
of all Canadian saints my rifle retreats
into the folds of this buckram apology
I have never met a god I could not name but
this old boy bedevils taxonomy his name
is MANIFEST my name is Johnny his hooves
berate the earth for its indignity I raise
my wimpy chin my spit my tongue my stars
if I had a truer name I would speak it now

MUSEUM

KEITH LEONARD

I walked the three floors
of the local antique store
and imagined white plaques
adorning each room
—but unlike museums,
I could touch the displays
and could take a seat
at a beautiful walnut table—
I could wonder about the moment
its palm-stained patina
went from simply dirty
to expensively antique—that
singular moment the thing
became slightly more
than a thing by simply
continuing to be
the very same thing—all its cracks
thick as the edge of a quarter—
all its smoothed over corners—
all its dark knots flourishing—
and I thought I could live
for awhile in this very
same body—and did, somehow,
and was loved, somehow,
into a third body, which totters
across the living room,

and whose knees I kiss
when he stumbles,
and the difference between
just now and *not*
is an aperture's quick snap—
is breath-delicate—
it must have been Luck
—I see it—that saddled me,
the blind horse rising
and falling as the carnival
blared from the brass pipes,
as the carousel twirled
its crown of lights,
and one by one the bulbs
went dark—and so it is,
this life—this goddamn
lucky life—the organ
sounding off the melody,
the platform winding down,
and the horses still bounding.

NIGHT SWIM AT SHADOW LAKE

ANNI LIU

I can barely swim but I don't tell them that.
At the beach, the guys joke about leeches
longer than my hand. They strip

and hoot with pleasure as they leap off
the slick rock. I keep my underwear on,
feel my way in, the rocks first becoming dirt,

then a soft sucking silt. Without my glasses,
the lake surface gleams, oiled with stars.
Someone told me once to imagine the water

holding me up to the air, buoyant,
but all I do is sink. The lake's long fingers
plug my ears, grip me like a hand closing.

Panicked, I plash back to the shallow muck
and wait. In the car back to the farm,
I sit with a towel stuffed between my legs.

No one tells any jokes. In the tensed
silence, I realize they'd meant for me
to take off all my clothes. I roll down

my window, let in the night and its shrill
insect trills, its sharp slaps of wind. My entire life,
I have been afraid of the wrong things.

UMBRA

NANCY CHEN LONG

Swarms of newcomers invade the park.
As the light fades into an odd blue
hue, the boy stares upward, in his hand
a fortune cookie. The scope of the sky
doesn't matter when the noon-day
moon invites you to escape.
A gaggle of befuddled geese escape
to a moss-covered pond. Scooters park
along a picket fence, bringing in more day-
trippers impatient for an eclipse. The blue
sunlight edges toward gray, but the sky
is still bright. The father fidgets, his hands
arguing with a camera. The boy hands
his father the fortune. *No one escapes
alive.* He pockets the fortune as he eyes the sky.
In an old pickup truck, the mother arrives. *Park
the picnic basket there*, the father points to a blue
tarp weighted with limestone. *Every daydream is a ready answer*, she thinks, her day
overrun with dreams. Her right hand
holds a blank book, while her left holds blue
orchids. A turquoise-tinted humming bird escapes
detection, zipping toward her. The park
floods with tourists the way the sky
floods with birds. *Soon there will be no sky
to see*, a passerby whispers to the boy. Today

is the boy's birthday and the ballpark
is where he'd rather be, trying his hand
at magic. Once, the boy narrowly escaped
disappearing into a crowd. Once, out of the blue,
the sun was swallowed by the moon. *A blue
moon is not an abomination and the sky
is not the limit*, says the mother to the sun. *Escape
is in the mind*, says the father to himself. The day
inches along, people hand-in-hand,
singing, in love with astronomy. Park
rangers pass out glasses in the parking lot. Blue
petals spill from the mother's hand. The father escapes
into a daydream. Their son stares at the prophetic sky.

BERRIES

ALESSANDRA LYNCH

Berries breed and brood and darken
in scarlet dusk. Their viscera
visible. Their contortions
evident. A smear on the pave.
A tiny massacre.
Seed-eyes dull with sun won't meet yours.
You who had stepped over them
Proclaiming *it's the order of things*.

TELEVISION, A PATIENT TEACHER

ORLANDO RICARDO MENES

Never a nag, mean word, our color Quasar in the sunroom
where Mr. Rogers purled droplets of praise, and I could forget
the clang of Miss Dorns burro bell when I said *shadow*
like *chado*, stretched the *O*s of wood and good into a *U*.
Mama's gleaming bathroom, a language lab, where I stood
before the gold mirror to chew in Cronkite monotones,
pop like bazooka gum those plosive *P*s, *B*s that pummeled
Batman's foes. After a hot bath, I'd practice the tidal schwas
of Captain Kangaroo, my vaporous face breaking up,
drips and streaks on cold glass, the mouth swollen, rubbery,
a cephalopod in eddies. Within three years, I could pass
for a Hoosier or a Buckeye, Mamá proud I'd mastered a tongue
that to her sounded like a sick dog. *El castellano* retreated
into memory, dreams, the once proud hidalgo humbled
to chatter. No quitter, it began to lurk, mind's liminal wilds,
borderlands between the conscious and unconscious,
a *guerrillero*, a trickster, resisting English, his usurper.
As in a game of musical chairs, El Padre Nuestro lost
his throne to the Lord's Prayer, but any requests, my talk
with God, in sovereign *castizo*. To break writer's block,
think like a child, I freewrite *en español*, squelching any intrusions
by Lord English. After an argument with my wife,
those words I regret are hard nasals, caustic fricatives,
but *cariñito* cloys like guayaba paste on a sticky afternoon.
Colleagues call me *cubano*, rounding out vowels like smoke,
which pleases me enough to wear *guayabera*, pestle cumin
with garlic, fix saints to the dash, let rice boil over the pot.

SELF-PORTRAIT, WEARING BEAR SKULL AS MASK

MICHAEL MLEKODAY

The world looks like fangs.
You look like fangs to the world.
Everything is quieter
so you shout, slang and other language
coming out warbled and hungry
as a barbed arrow.
The world does not care what you eat
so long as it is not them,
but motherfuck, they all look ripe
from the inside of a mouth.
The mouth is a cave and you are the fire
within, or you are the cave painting,
the ghost of something slain by something larger,
or the mouth is the scope of a rifle
and you are a boy away from home.
You are a boy in the shape of an animal
and in the dark everything feels like the woods.
The sweat, the fresh smack of spring
brings blood to your face,
but you are still just skull and imagined claw
to the world, just the dumb perfect body
of death. You stopped speaking long ago.
You haven't eaten yet today,
and the world looks bright as winter.

FIRST MILK

DANNI QUINTOS

After all that birth, the legs you've used your whole life
are now wobbly & the lake where your son used to swim

trickles from between them. The spaces between your fingers
feel sticky. The first thing the baby does is search for the warmth

of you, his face a small suction cup for the mounds you've been
building. Those first golden drops, thick as honey, spill from you

& the nurse rushes to catch them with a plastic spoon. God forbid
they soak your hospital gown or run down your rib cage. Once, you were

a girl with two breasts like the smallest constellation, an incomplete ellipsis.
Today, they find new purpose. Today they are nourishment & comfort,

food, water, some kind of magic. They work so hard after years
of thinking themselves merely decorative.

STILL ANIMALS

SAM ROSS

In the chicken coop, Jill and I found a headless one.
We cleaned up, and she told me it's what skunks do—

snap a neck in their jaws, twist the head off.
They guzzle the yellow fluid from the eggs. They leave

the carcass untouched but lap up the blood
as if it was honey. How could I pretend it wasn't a thrill

to hear this in the morning? It came back to me after
I received your letter, the one cataloging shapes

our bodies make together at night. I imagined
red threads tied to each of a bird's talons, then to us

arranged in the position you called your favorite:
my mouth at your neck, barely, and you feigning sleep.

MAP

BRUCE SNIDER

There ought to be a fire somewhere in Indiana,
not this night across the fields in Indiana.

And God said let there be light, and there was light.
And God said let there be corn, and there was Indiana.

I kiss my love, taking his hand near the deer stand.
Honey is fragrant on the table, and there is thunder in Indiana.

And what of Amy Blaine, who drowned when she was twelve?
Nights, I feel her in the cold rain of Indiana.

For the rest of my life, I'll feel the wet hair plastered to her face.
I'll feel darkness and the magpie's feathers in Indiana.

But I'm not interested in grief, just the sound of the yellowthroat,
just the warblers in the thickets of Muncie, Indiana.

I don't need a communion wafer.
I need the autumn mist of Indiana.

Arcola, Goshen, Nappanee. Remember a place where the river bank
passes through you, where the Amish girls spread their skirts in Indiana.

Remember a place where spring breaks the yellow news of the pawpaw tree,
where a pan of grease hisses against a flame called Indiana.

Lord, the boys touch other boys, eating fried dough
and glazed apples, lips sticky with syrup and heat in Indiana.

Bach winter, sleet turns the cornfield into a cemetery.
It's epitaph reads: Indiana.

My father's pulse slows between systole and diastole,
between the frozen creek beds and the grain silos of Indiana.

And you will ask: Where are the lilacs?
And I will answer: Under the snows of Indiana.

Soon, spring buds will thrust their sex organs into the mouths of bees.
Their story is the story of Indiana.

If there are a hundred ways to recall the dogwood in bloom,
this is the one where your parents make love on a battered sofa in Indiana.

Stamen and pistol, pollen in the air, the field of poppies knows lust
spells its name: I-N-D-I-A-N-A.

What's death, after all, if not the Wabash wearing down river stones,
if not the muskrat flicking its damp tail in Indiana?

Are those angels' trumpets? Is that God calling
Bruce? Have I reached the end of the world? Or Indiana?

BARE NECESSITIES

LANA SPENDL

I walk into her office to give her papers
and she comes to mine to return them.

My walls are bare. Just a table, a chair.
Coffee pot in corner, next to a lamp
a coworker gave.

I block the embarrassed space with my body
and talk and talk. Her office was warm,
in reds, filled with things, and her home
with her partner must be the same.
Full of trinkets she lifts and examines
and places on shelves. She can walk out
the door and not wonder if they'll stay.

And I think of the war in Bosnia
that made me lose home and friends,
and I think of that Bosnian writer I just read
who in the war feared losing his books.
All it would take is an attack in the night
to jolt you awake and you could only carry
two plastic bags of books as you run
down building stairs.

But which books to take?

MOTHER'S COAT

MAURA STANTON

Take it, my sister says, *it just fits you.*
She hardly wore it for she went nowhere,
just to the doctor. So it's almost new.
I lift it off the hanger—full of air—

and slip my arms into the long black sleeves
and zip the zipper tight up to my chin.
I like the way the narrow waist achieves
real elegance, making me tall and slim.

Oh, she thought she looked pretty in it too,
my sister says, plucking a fine light hair
off the collar. She holds it up to view.
We know it's her hair. It floats off somewhere,

and I shrug deeper into the downy space
of the coat that held her in its light embrace.

RED STATE

JACOB SUNDERLIN

Appetite for Destruction was recorded here
in a pile of burning leaves. My cousin prayed it,

the hand grenade from the comment stream.
Now he hoards shotguns out in the shed.

For "Christ." I get it. Liking the imaginary
to be god-hurled. Walking out the piers of yourself

in a gas-can helmet, garden hose to breathe,
a bootleg pearl diver watching the bioluminescent

whatever-they-are of rage
hum up from the squid muck in your mind.

Diving in. On Teen Mom, all the beer
has blurry labels. It's been hard to hear

through all the stomas. There is a Coleman lantern
& a blanket & a boombox by the river

where I am saying this to you:
at work, why is it that men talk this *our-grandmothers—*

slept-with-brass-knuckles-so-immense—
they-could-never-lift-them-&-so-we-shook-them-with-alarm—

in-the-stillness-&-named-our-first-band-The-Vendettas—
bullshit. It has never been easy for me

to tell who is lying. I once heard you say
the ghosts of steel & iron ore ships

are never coming home. You weren't lying?

TRAIN PEOPLE

GIN FAITH THOMAS

Don't you think the front of the Moon and River Café in Schenectady grins out at the cracked streets because life's just that damn funny and the evening breeze smells like the rust kicked up by passing trains? Knock knock, who's there, my feet hurt. Did you see the deodorant and dental floss lined up next to the gluten-free muffins? How much for a ham sandwich? "We get a lot of train people in here," the owner told us. We're train people now. Can you ever forgive me for my pinky-hitching falseness? Look, the hippies have come rolling in to play Beatles songs with their rattling guitars and drink night coffee, their voices are full of tambourines. Do you remember how the houses near the river are stacked on top of their bricks like cats stuck on fence posts? And what about that river chuckling past, all debris and fishlessness—what a gas. Knock knock, who's there, coffee, coffee who? Pinned to the walls are articles and ads, signs and sayings, probably somewhere here there's a good joke. We were kids once. Isn't that hilarious? Now we're train people, and we try not to skip too much through the dark to the hotel. A block away, a woman is yelling at a man full-throated in the street. They're probably dating. They'll probably go home and laugh until they curl in on themselves like pill bugs. You're the closest I'll ever come to having a sister so maybe you'll get this one: Knock knock, who's there, I don't know, I don't know who? Yes, yes. That exactly.

THE FENS AT MOUNDS STATE PARK

CHUCK WAGNER

"Listen," this shallow rivulet says
as it washes over stones, smoothing
everything that is rough or jagged
that would complain or cry out, "and I
will whisper a story in sibilance
and rounded vowels that will slow
the racing pulse and arrest the hurried
heartbeat, that will suspend the jogger
and the hiker in a moment of stasis
spun from the footsteps of all who have
crossed this fen, fed upon its sedges
or settled into its slough and sediment
through the slow centuries, a story
of ancient mineral-rich artisan springs
that will entice you to your knees
to partake of my flowing silver body
in the crude cup of your hands."

FIRST FLIGHT

SHARI WAGNER

Richmond, Indiana, 1884

It quivered in the roll and turn
as Orville banked a curve,
spun from his hubs
downhill to the river.

And a dream caught
in Will's spokes, too, as he pedaled
to the rear, reading the cursive
of turkey buzzards, how they'd

coast with wings extended,
feather-tips twisted to balance on air.
Something tugged them both
away from their mother,

wasted balsa wood thin, delicate
as the kite frames
she helped them build.
Their pockets packed

with pennies and love notes,
the ballast of loss,
they raced what snapped
at their heels—tomorrow's move

to Ohio. Under cirrus clouds,
dirt roads flew beneath them,
spokes twirled like a whirligig's
blades, like a flyer's spruce propellers

to lift them to the sky.

INCIDENT WITH NATURE, LATE

MARCUS WICKER

Clean, the gust, prying
me open for the first time
this week—as I—
not exactly wind-
like in the running
thirty & already hunched
over after three stoic
blocks & one big sloppy
knock into the neighbor's
knotty fence decide it
as good a place as any
to stop, pant
& smell the roses—
except there are no
roses, proverbial
or otherwise, except
a nondescript shrub
quivering
with what I hereby dub
the "piney-ness
of an Indiana March"
& oh my God
it feathering my nose
hairs stirring in me
a place where finally
I decide to quit

dicking around
& dig my face in it
low bent, hands cupped
over kneecaps
my eyes adjusting
always for some throbbing:
this sweet bumblebee rushing
through an interstate
of arteries & wishbone
forks in the bush's gut
for a derelict cherry
bloom wearing blush
that hummingbird
in hot pursuit, humming
little drone holy
shit I swivel too late
& she hammers
her needled beak
through my ear drills
hard the run of bone
behind my lobe
& sticks—
All my life, I've been
biblically acquainted
with the donkey-face sting
of avertable night:
usually some small game
slight, some gnat-sized fowl
wedging itself in
where there had always been
light, but just then, momentarily
less—so predictably me
I wave it in, let it pitch a tent
in my living room, bore
heavy-duty stakes through
the Pergo floor, let it crack
walnuts with my violet
mini-stapler, split dishes
with the weight
of peat moss-bricked
lasagna, this lazy ache

I let him knock around inside
my record crates, floss
his beak with the grooves
of my favorite 45
until all I am is a busted song
of nerve tentacles swimming
beneath the pink umbrella
of a redbud tree or all
I am is a singing
saw through a bell
of flesh—the point
being not the ear
but maybe the thorn
is god, little-winged
& hovering here, quietly
in me, when I sit real still
to feel my nature opening
its mouth to speak.

WORLD OF DESIRE

BRANDON YOUNG

We live in a house one block from railroad tracks.
We learn to stack our desires like pennies there
with our fingertips, place them on the track—returning
to them flattened by a force we have taught ourselves to
ignore. Our desire is a humid heat. It clings to the skin
as we soak up more than we will ever release.
The train shakes the floors of our house as it speeds up,
desire is the vibration of skin & metal passing by.
I am ten—the boy I love bikes across
the tracks, bare arms washed by sun. It's late summer,
his father also works in the auto factory, which means
he & I are ordinary, which means we desire in more ways
than one. It's late summer & the flowers have stopped
blooming. The boy & I take turns drinking from the hose
between rounds of our never-ending summer games—
his love for me is metallic, reflective, & wishing
for the freeze of the hose water or colder times.
The question I ask is—how can I ever keep
the boy or all the pennies melted together
by the train, the sun-scorched day. What force.
That coming Christmas, I open my stocking to find
an orange, an apple, a handful of walnuts—
I make a world of desire as I eat them all. I shove
my fingertip into the orange. Begin to peel away

with my thumb the encasing I then form into a globe
of what it once contained. My desire is a sticky
hollow—my desire speeds up on course to somewhere.
& right there on my skin, I begin to feel where I'm going.

PART 3

FICTION

YOU PERFECT, BROKEN THING

C. L. CLARK

WHEN I LEAVE THE KILL FLOOR, my legs are wasted. I shuffle to the women's locker room. I can't stand anymore, but I know if I sit, I'll never get back up. At least, not for another hour.

I prop myself up on my open locker. My hands are shaking too. My fingertips are blue, my skin receding from chawed-down fingernails.

"You don't look good." Shell, one of my training partners, spooks me from behind. Her blonde hair is half brown with sweat. "You can't afford to train this hard, Coach. You won't have anything left *for* the race."

I don't meet her eyes. I can't. She's right. But she's also wrong. I know my body. I'm so far gone I *have* to win the cure. If I don't at least place, I probably won't survive Race Day, even if I stop training for the next two weeks. Placing in the top three means two shots of the good stuff. One for me, one for Honey.

I straighten up, push my sopping curls off my forehead, and smile. "I just need to eat," and curl up in a corner to die. Plenty of time for that later though.

"Here." Shell hands me my water bottle, refilled. I must have forgotten it on the kill floor. I dump in my usual posttraining powders: the medrazine to steady the shakes, peradone for the pain I can already feel radiating from my quadriceps and up my spine to throb in my temples. And, of course, a standard berry-flavored recovery mix to wash it all down and make me forget I'm training for the last chance to save my sorry life.

"Where's everyone else?"

"Rowboat is stretching. You should too. You can't nag me about yoga and then skip out."

I wince. But I can't stay. I'm half a minute away from fainting or vomiting, and it's all I can do to keep one Shell in focus. "Gotta get home. Honey's waiting, and I have to plan Little's workout for tomorrow."

Shell smiles. I swear, you've never seen so much love and pain in one look. "Go easy on her."

"Since when do I go easy?"

Shell snorts. "Start tonight. I'm gonna tell Honey to dump your ass on the couch and sit on you. Rest. We'll clean up the floor."

And that doesn't sound half bad, honestly. I make it a plan. Her skin is clammy with sweat when we hug.

Even though we call it the kill floor, no one's died there. Not yet. Every day we train, though, we pull the disease a little closer to us. We, me and Shell and the others, take a calculated risk to train for the race. Training accelerates the disease, but it makes us stronger, faster, when we have to hit the dirt and drag ourselves to the finish line.

This is not my first race.

—◊◊◊—

The night doesn't go as planned.

Honey takes one look at me and says she'll make dinner.

I use the railing like a cane, all my strength bent to keeping my feet for one, two, three, four. Five, six, seven, eight, nine. Ten, eleven, twelve. Thirteen. Fourteen stairs. My hips scream at the end, without the railing to support my weight. My desk, on the other side of the office, is impossibly far from the doorframe where I gather my strength.

It can't be more than five steps away.

I don't make it.

The carpet is thin and cheap and rough against my cheek, but clean. We only rent, but it's a nice place. It smells like Honey vacuumed it while I was gone.

"Honey?" I call.

It takes a long time for the lightning pain in my ankles, knees, hips to dissipate to a dull throb. When it finally does, it only takes a ginger test, pushing myself up, to send it flaring back. Bright and illuminating. With my eyes closed, I see constellations of my future—the hero, the lover, the companions, the enemies to slay.

Her footsteps on the stairs, then, "Ah, shit, babe." She wedges under my armpit and helps me drag myself to—she angles me away from the bedroom. "Nuh-uh. You smell."

I sit on the closed toilet while she runs hot water and dumps in Epsom salt. I crawl into the tub and sink down to my neck, eyes closed, legs crossed to keep them in that glorious heat. Honey sighs, and I raise one eyelid.

"Hm."

"Hm. You know what 'hm.' Is it worth it?"

"It will be when we can be happy and alive together. You can dance again."

"Or you race yourself into the ground, and I'm heartbroken and alive alone. If you stop, you can level out. It won't be a long life, but we'd stress less."

I close my eye. The minutes draw on, and then she leaves. I can almost hear her shaking her head.

—⟋⟍—

I pick up Little when she gets out of school and take her to the kill floor. Before I get the fans turned on, she's monkeying across the wall.

"Hey, punk! Get down here!" If she falls and breaks her neck, Shell'll break mine, and Honey will let her.

I think of my own fall on the carpet at home; my body is still sore from the impact. The drugs helped me sleep though, and I feel better. All the same, I'm happy to take the day off.

Little will be eight in December. As she scrambles down at my orders, I watch the play of her small muscles, so young they don't even look like muscles, just smooth skin. That doesn't stop her from flexing a junior bicep when she lands in front of me.

I secure her into her harness and make sure our carabiners are locked tight. "Ready, punk?"

"Aye, aye, captain!" She salutes me.

And then she's racing up the wall, thinking through puzzles and struggling to reach holds she has no business reaching for, and I am most definitely not crying.

—⟋⟍—

We train without incident—without *major* incident—for the next week. But Race Day creeps toward us. We all manifest anxiety in different ways. Shell hasn't been eating. She bonks through sets she used to crush. Rowboat eats even more, hoping another protein shake or spoonful of peanut butter will grow new myofibrils out of nowhere. I know what my problem is. We all do. But I ignore it.

Six days out, we're at the kill floor again. We just finished our wind sprints. I beat everyone, and the air I pull into my lungs feels purer than anything I've breathed in weeks. It might be my preworkout, kicking me into overdrive. It might be fear of my own inadequacies being my downfall.

I hunt for my climbing harness, and everyone snaps out of the postset stupor.

"Coach." Rowboat's hands are on his knees as he huffs for breath. "Shut that shit down. You just ran . . . a mile's worth of sprints."

I didn't need him to tell me that. I calculated our needs the night before, our weak spots. I accounted for his lack of stamina, for Shell's lack of speed. My pain. Our weakness will come with us to the race. The wall will be there too, and I need to be able to take it.

I slap the gray wall with the flat of my palm. "Just one time, quick. Promise." I let Shell double-check the harness. We won't have harnesses on Race Day, but that doesn't mean I want to tempt fate sooner than I have to.

Shell glances back anxiously at Rowboat, up the wall, and back to me. "You want me to belay?"

Rowboat growls and snatches the biggest harness we have. "I got it. But if you hurt your dumbass, Coach, I swear to shit—" he grumbles as he shimmies and buckles himself in.

I shake the lactic acid out of my legs and swing my arms across my chest. It makes me wonder what it would be like to stretch wings out and soar across open sky. I imagine it feels like sprinting, nothing in my way but the air on my face.

The colorful rubber is rough under my fingers. I think of Little and try to imitate her gibbon's grace. Each contraction of my lats pulls me higher, and my biceps thrill at their strength. My legs forget their fatigue, and I'm—

I'm a goddamn orchestra.

Until I'm not, and numbness webs across my back, a note out of tune. Maybe it started in my fingers and I didn't notice, and now it's too late.

"Row—!" My scream starts but doesn't finish. My legs are gone, and I catch a face full of bright pink handhold before I bounce away again.

Below me, Shell is shrieking. I crash again, arms useless to push me away. They shout below, only blurs as Shell scurries and Rowboat lowers me.

"I'm okay," I slur, lying on mat-covered ground.

"I'm calling an ambulance—"

"No!"

They stop at my outburst.

"I can't afford it. And if they lock me down there, I won't get to race."

No one tells me I shouldn't race anyway, not in this condition.

I'm dying. We all are; it's the only condition. Degeneration from the inside out, one broken-down cell at a time. I'm just a lot farther along than anyone expected.

No one can voice it.

Now the rest of the kill floor knows it too.

— ⁓ —

The day before the race, Honey and I host the crew's traditional last supper.

Shell comes with Little and a bottle of fancy sparkling water since no one drinks, not even Honey, who doesn't even have her race performance to worry about; Rowboat shows up with an armful of board games; we eat pasta with chicken and fancy Kalamata olives, heavy on the pasta, except for Little, who pushes all of her olives to the edge of her plate so I can steal them, and I return the favor when she wants to steal bites of my chocolate cake; it's this same cake that Rowboat sneaks a third piece of—half of a third piece, since I manage to snag a hunk of it and run away with my mouth full to hide behind Honey, who's strategizing with Shell over their half of the co-op game; but Honey gives me that "not my circus, not my monkeys" look, so I hide behind Little instead, and Rowboat tackles her with tickles until she yells, "I'll pee on you, I'll pee on you!" and laughs even harder; of course, I do too, and chunks of chocolate cake land on Rowboat's cheek; and then we're all laughing, and the game's forgotten, and the race is forgotten, and the pain's forgotten too.

Finally, they leave Honey and me alone.

The house should feel too quiet, like the blood's been let out of it, but it doesn't. It feels like burrowing down to your ears in a blanket your grandma made you.

I don't want to tempt the ache in my body, but I don't want to die tomorrow without remembering the good things my body does. So we're two bodies, in flexion, extension, the slow eccentric stretch and the isometric clenching hold, over and over, until we can release.

When I fall asleep, I dream of falling off the wall.

— ⁓ —

The next day, Shell, Rowboat, and I march to the starting line like pallbearers. Some of my other gym rats are there too, young enough that this race is just a trial for them, to help them strategize future runs. There are so many of us for one city. Eligible entrants between eighteen and forty, no criminal records, no outstanding government debts, etc., etc., etc.

Honey kisses me one more time, while Shell squeezes Little until the little girl complains—then Shell squeezes some more. Honey takes Little to get popcorn and wait.

I breathe. I check my shoes. Breathe. Squeeze Shell's and Rowboat's hands on either side of me. Breathe. Release them.

The starting horn blows.

—⁓—

I surge forward, hoping to get just far enough out of the press to pace myself I'm hit pushed scratched the blood tickles I'm shoved and tripping and sliding in my tennis shoes across muck that smells like cow shit smeared on someone else's calf unlucky they've fallen and probably won't get up for a while and I didn't stop to help them up there just wasn't time to do anything but dodge an elbow cracks into my jaw I'm still standing I think I'm pulling clear and sliding again one foot two foot feet three across more mud and into the first obstacle a foxhole so close close close forward someone on my ass but really just my feet and elbow by elbow I drag myself forward and fuck but how did I forget how dark it would be get a fucking move on he says to my feet fuck yourself I yell go die he yells you first I yell and then the sun is out again and I push myself up don't let that shithole pass you don't let him and I keep ahead two steps his arm flies for me as he passes I dodge left mark him with his yellow laces gray shoes perfectly bifurcated calf muscles I hope he tears with a matching yellow watch telling him everything how fast how long how far where on earth where in the race pace split pace how many goddamn heartbeats he's wasting—

I know none of that. Only what my heart is whispering to my throat, the hurried message, "Isn't this fun, my love? You perfect thing?"

My throat growls back, a laugh—yes. Yes.

I don't register the obstacles until I reach the wall. I have to crane my neck to see the top. Four stories easy. Maybe more. A wall built to keep people out. Shoes slick with mud. Hands dry thanks to the terry cloth wristbands. Black. I swipe my hands on them one more time and go.

There is no feeling in the world like knowing the only thing in the world between you and a plummeting death is your own strength.

There is no feeling in the world like knowing that and knowing your strength cannot be trusted.

The thought freezes me, two and a half stories up, hand cramped like a dead spider, and all I can think of is how badly I don't want to die in cow shit. Better a hospital bed. My couch, next to Honey. Crushed under a bar on the kill floor.

Someone passes me. "Let's move it, champ. You got this." He wears ratty shorts but almost-new shoes. Good luck charm and a sensible breaking-in period. He doesn't reach out with his hands. He doesn't need to.

"Closer to the top than the bottom," someone else grunts. She's got a shaved blonde head and a black headband—already looks like a skull.

They go. Uncurling my fear-clamped body, reaching up, it is amazing. It is awful. I hear them whoop, I don't know who, and then we are going, all of us are going.

When I finally drag myself over the top and rappel down the other side, my angels are gone. I don't pass her until the monkey bars from hell, wet, slick, and wobbling. I pass him at the net crawl, where he fights to unsnarl his almost-new shoe from a loop.

—⋙—

I catch up to Shell, and together we slide unbelievably into the top four. Number one gases out, slows to a broken jog as he sees us coming. Too fast out of the gate. Not my business. Not his Coach. His wide eyes roll with horse-fear as he watches us take his chance. My chance. Our chance. If we take second and third, that's four shots, four cures.

The other one jerks and shudders at the live wires. Too wet or too much zing or a weak heart. Short hair on end. The shock burns, grabs me and holds me still for one, two seconds, and then it's me and Shell and the mud pits and a straight shot to the finish line on the other side.

Only she's not beside me as I wade through the sucking expanse of water like chocolate milk. No yelp, the earth didn't bubble after it swallowed her—she's just gone.

"Shell?" I yell. I swish my hands in the water, reaching for a waterlogged ponytail, a bra strap, anything.

Someone else—yellow-laced bastard with perfect calves—crashes through. He spares me half a glance before stalking through, the mud sucking at his thighs. And then another comer, blonde skull woman. This time, she doesn't look back.

Still no Shell. I don't know why I'm still here. It's a matter of life and death. If she's stuck under this muck, no air for—how long? I calculate the wasted seconds of my lead.

She isn't in the mud. She can't be. And I don't have it in me to go back.

Another runner comes for my pit. I roar at them, guarding my territory.

What good is this body if I can help no one else? *What good is this work?*

One leg is an iron barbell, the other one is numb. Me and Wannabe-Third-Place come out of the mud at almost the same time. Almost.

They beat me out of the water.

My gooey fingers catch their singlet by both arm loops, and I pull, pull, pull. We slip under the muck, together.

Everything goes mud and sputter and cough as we wrestle in the pit, but it's not me putting out less and less fight with every gasp of shitty water. It's not me who goes still.

I drag my sorry carcass out of the sludge without looking to see if they crawl out. I walk.

Family members shout for their loved ones to run faster, to overtake me. Did Honey just watch me kill someone? Does she care if I did?

Who else will I kill, just by winning?

Shell. Rowboat and maybe every other kill floor buddy I have.

But I can sleep the night through. Honey and I can make love anytime, and nothing will hurt. We won't taste the breakdown of our bodies in our sweat.

I stagger across the finish line and drop to my knees.

Third place.

—◆—

Mud drips off my body or clings in sticky clumps, like a smeared diaper. I smell like one too, if cows wore diapers.

On my hands and knees, I finally look up. Rowboat has Shell draped around his shoulders as they cross the finish line. They don't bother to run. There are no more prizes.

And there's Little, grinning as she bear-crawls toward me. Like this is all a game the grown-ups play, a game that she'll get to play too. She writhes like a spider above the ground, small fingers splurging mud, miniature shoulder muscles flexing on her slight frame. She'll be a compact athlete, like her mother. Sometimes the light ones with endurance are the winners. Sometimes they aren't.

The victors' tent is full of nurses, all sterile, sharp needles, and sharper smiles. They usher my family in behind me, Honey's arm on my sweaty, muddy back as I limp.

They guide me into a chair, and a nurse tries to clear a patch of skin on my flaking-dirt arm. I can't feel her scrape at me, but I jerk away anyhow.

"Her first." I point to Honey.

The nurses share a glance, shrug, and give Honey the shot instead, a swipe of alcohol and a jab before she can protest.

The shakes start up in my torso. I put my usual powders in my water before the race, but—it was a long race. Maybe I'll pass out before I can make the decision, and they'll shoot me up regardless. *No.*

"Hey, Little. Auntie's big girl. You're not afraid of needles, are you? Take Auntie's shot for her?" I pull her up onto my lap.

Honey's neck stiffens with fury, and she's working on spitting something out at me, at the nurses, at Shell—but I shake my head.

"Let her have this," I say, though I don't think anyone else hears.

Honey won't forgive me, but at least she can find someone else after I die. Someone who listens better.

Little bites her lip when the needle goes in. I pull her closer and press my nose into her soft curly puffs.

—⁓—

I open my eyes when someone clears their throat. My family is watching Yellow-Lace Calf-Bastard, standing awkwardly in front of us with one of the nurses from his side of the tent.

He looks healthier than anyone has a right to be, but that's no surprise, not with gear like he has. Still, his brown eyes sit in haunted pits, and I wonder what his training has been like.

"My—I signed up—this was for my mom." He points to his nurse, who holds a capped needle. He blinks hard at the ground. "She didn't make it."

I stare hard at Shell. She hesitates for just a tick, but she can't hold up under my Coach glare. It's the same look I give her when she tries to push through an injury. Ironic.

I hear Rowboat's heavy sigh as Shell gets her shot, and I don't know if it's jealousy or relief, but I feel it too. Little'll grow up. She'll live and love her body without any of this pain, and her mom'll be there for her.

And Honey will live long enough to love and dance again.

Next year, me and Rowboat'll try again. Us and all the people I left behind in the mud today.

If we survive long enough.

But even if we don't, even if I die tonight, on that couch, in Honey's arms, it's worth it. I stroke Little's hair with a trembling hand and kiss her head one more time.

Another throat clears, barely a scrape in the air. The nurse holds her lab coat open, and two more needle plungers peek out of an inner pocket. Her gaze flicks sharply between me and Rowboat.

The nurse puts a finger to her lips. "We do what we can."

INSULTS FOR UGLY GIRLS

TIA CLARK

WE'RE IN NESSA'S BEDROOM, AND I'm showing them the video of the girl who takes out her tampon and puts it in her mouth to suck on the blood. It has over three million views on Worldstar, and it's gotta have at least that on a bunch of other sites too. When we get to the part where she reaches down to grab the string, Tiffany gets up and moves to the bed. I click pause.

"That's revolting," Tiffany says, backing up onto one of Nessa's pink pillows. "She looks like Babe. The pig."

Tiffany's voice sounds like she sucked on a helium balloon and like her voice box is in her nose. She moved to Elmsford from Yonkers over the summer, and where she's from, the girls are prettier and the boys are realer and she went on dates with the realest ones every weekend, allegedly. It's nothing like Elmsford, she claims, this bullshit little village that doesn't even have enough kids in the school for a football team.

Nessa thinks Tiffany's snot is gold. "You're such a bitch!" She laughs her big laugh while she hits the desk and stomps on the floor. "Babe, though? Rude!"

Tiffany doesn't smile; she twists her face up like she can smell something through the computer screen. "This is the grossest thing I've ever seen. Easily." The way Nessa laughs, Tiffany's gotta wonder what we ever did without her.

She looks down at her phone. "Wait, wait, Jamaal responded," she says. She's been texting back and forth with him about a house party later. Boys of all grades have been trying to get at Tiffany. She's rich-girl pretty, her nose turned up. And she's fresh meat. It's a small school.

"He says it's on Evarts," she says to Nessa because Nessa's the only one of us that she really wants to talk to. Nessa is pretty too, with absent parents. She also just went with Tiffany to get her nose pierced, and she fidgets with the stud all day long, even though she shouldn't touch it without Bactine. Lynn, who stands by the computer with me, turns to watch their conversation. She doesn't say much when Tiffany's around either.

I wish I was alone. I want to keep watching the video. I want to see the blood.

"Wait, he said he doesn't know who you guys are and to send a picture of all of us," she says.

Nessa complains that her hair is out of control. It's not, but it's in a ponytail, and she hates her ears. Lynn says she can't because she's not wearing makeup, and without makeup, Lynn looks tragically sleepy and unimportant. I don't say anything, but I do have pimples on my chin, bags under my eyes, and hair coming in on my lip. Next to Nessa and Tiffany, Lynn and I will look like a before picture. I would rather be the cameraman.

Tiffany suggests we take a picture of our asses and send him that. She has the biggest one of all. She looks like a video girl, even though she's fifteen. Her stomach is flat and smooth and her belly button is pierced. She told us she's a C cup, and against her stomach, her boobs look perky and perfect. I haven't seen her dance, but she's pretty enough to just bend over or sit on a rapper's lap or play around in a sudsy bathtub. My thin is *skinny* when I'm next to her, like a wood plank. Like a child.

Nessa agrees to the butt picture, and Lynn follows Nessa, and I don't want to be left out. So we take off our shirts. Tiffany's bra is hot pink with lace on the trim. Nessa's is plain black with thin straps. Lynn's is white with blue polka dots. I am beige, wide straps, embarrassed. I avoid Tiffany's face, surely smirking.

—⚹—

We stand in front of the webcam with our arms around each other's waists. Tiffany says to arch our backs; that's how you make your butt look bigger. She says to arch it like you're getting it from behind, something we know nothing about. My arm is cut off in the picture. Tiffany says it's perfect. Hits send.

—⚹—

My older brother Mook is the only one home when I get there since my mom works nights at the halfway house. Mook got suspended from school in the first week, and he's finishing out the second week of his sentence. If one of his friends gets suspended, the others try to get it at the same time so they can go to White Plains or the city or get girls to cut school and come over to the apartment. The teachers are onto it, but what else are they gonna do? Better to keep the bad kids out of the class. Mook is the only one this round, so he's spent most of the days in the position I find him, laid back on the loveseat, watching a cartoon I don't recognize. There are a few fun-size Snickers wrappers by him on the floor. It smells like weed.

I sit on the chair next to the loveseat.

"What you watching?" I ask.

"Some bullshit. Just background noise."

Mook's tank top is pulled up and he scratches his stomach. There's a curly trail of hair below his belly button crawling down to the waistband of his grey sweats. He twirls the hairs between his fingers. He's cut. He walks the house without a shirt sometimes, and he can get his pecs to bounce one by one. I look away and up to his bloodshot eyes.

"You know they're gonna drug test you again."

"Clean piss is a dime a dozen," he says. "Everybody pees. Matter fact, that's why God gave me a good, clean little sister." He jabs the air by my shoulder but doesn't touch me.

"How do you know I'm clean? You haven't been to school in a week. You don't know what I've been doing." You don't know a senior has a picture of my ass.

"Aight, Mother Theresa," he says. When we were young, he used to light things on fire, and I'd cry for him to stop. He'd steal from our mom's wallet, and I'd threaten to tell. I didn't want to take sips of the B&J in the fridge, or smoke our mom's Virginia Slim remains in the ashtray. He didn't claim me in the halls at school. He hated my softness. But at least Mother Theresa made the world a better place, and somewhere deep down, he knows it.

People don't believe it when I say we're siblings. He's got a grown man's muscles. He's a fighter. Girls like him. Including Lynn, who won't admit it directly but always asks about him and tries to play it off like she's interested in me, just making conversation. When he's not around, I smell his things. I watch the girls he watches and try to learn their walks. I want to understand.

Of course he can have my good clean piss, though. I have no use for it myself.

—⁂—

In my bedroom, I go back to the video on Worldstar. She's cut off from the waist down, but she cringes at the camera while her right hand does the dirty work. She pulls out her bloody tampon and dangles it by the string. She's smiling and laughing through it all. It could be fake, maybe cranberry juice, but the dark red clumps around the edges are convincing enough. She puts it in her mouth and holds it in there, sucking like it's a straw.

The Worldstar homepage is otherwise filled with rapper interviews, music videos, fights. I watch one with two girls in a locker room. One chews gum and the other runs her mouth: you're a pussy, ugly, that's why your mother sucks dick for cheeseburgers. Her friends yell at her to swing. They egg her on, call her a punk, tell her "don't start shit you can't finish" and "if you don't swing, I'mma hit her for you." She finally flails her arm toward the gum chewer after two minutes and twenty-three seconds, but her opponent comes at her full force with both arms, punching like a man. She gets the shit talker on the ground, kicks her once, and walks out of the locker room. The shit talker's friends are quiet. The video cuts off.

I get up to make sure my bedroom door is locked. I sit back down and click on the "Honeys" tab.

There's a section for video models, the girls you see dancing with rappers. They're makeup gorgeous, slim, and thick. Sin Monroe does a move where she gets upside down on a pole and spreads her legs into a split in the air and glides down, slowly. I don't understand the physics. When she looks at the camera, I try to see my face. I've put on the same songs and tried to copy her simpler routines, using the heat pipe in the corner of my room as a pole. All I get is frustration and a pool of blood in my head.

There's an interview up of her after one of her strip club nights, showing all the cash she collected in a duffel bag—ones, twenties, hundreds. The cameraman asks her what she would say to any fans, any girls who look up to her. "You can be anything you wanna be." She stops messing with the money. "It's not bad to be sexy," she says. "If you got it, you got it." They ask her if her ass is real. She turns around and grabs it from the bottom and says "All natural, baby." She smiles at the camera, and her teeth are perfect.

There's also a section for regular girls who do their own makeup and film themselves with their camera phones. I try to do what they do. I strip down to my panties when I'm alone and practice rolling my hips on my bed. In the mirror, it looks nothing like sex, feels nothing like I imagine sex feels. Feels like I'm a kid, humping the air, straddling a ghost.

Sex drips off Tiffany's smooth legs and arms, all exposed. She told us about her first time and how it hurt, but how it changed the way she saw the world. Sex is no big deal once you do it a couple times. But it *is* big power. Girls who don't know this get walked all over and disrespected. If you do it right, if you own it, the sex and the attitude, no one will get one over on you. After a few times, it's like breathing.

I go to Tiffany's Instagram and see the kissy faces she blows at the camera, the pictures where she's spread out on her stomach on her zebra print bedspread. I go to my mirror and try again to make the faces. I can't pout without looking sad.

—⁂—

We meet back up at Nessa's before the party on Evarts. She's curling Tiffany's hair so that it cascades over her chest. They both have on shorts that barely cover the basics. Lynn and I wear skinny jeans and sandals, outfits we've worn to school. I suspect Lynn wants to go home and change too.

"Nessa, do you have any clothes they can wear?" Tiffany says after we've been there for a quiet while.

"I'll just go back home and change," I say, before Nessa has to say that I'm too skinny to fit into any of her clothes.

"No, no," she says. "I have dresses." She puts down the curling iron and goes into her closet. "My mom got me this but it's too small," she says. She thumbs through her crowded closet and tosses me a dark green dress on a hanger. The front comes down to a point, for cleavage, and the rest of it is a tight stretch material. She throws another one to Lynn.

Lynn starts to change in the room, in front of everyone, so I do too.

"Mook's prolly gonna be there," Nessa says, back to Tiffany's curls. "That'll be weird."

"I don't know," I say. "He seems pretty lazy since he's been suspended. I haven't seen him get off the couch."

"What'd he get suspended for?" Tiffany says. I'm shocked that she's addressing me.

"I don't know the details. Probably something drug or fight related."

"What kind of drugs?" Tiffany asks.

"Just weed, I think."

"Oh," Tiffany says. "That's not a drug." She looks at me in the mirror and smiles. I have the dress on and it fits, hugging my skin like a second skin. "Much better."

—⁂—

We're the youngest people at the party.

"Let's find Jamaal," Tiffany says, and links her arm in Nessa's. They walk, and Lynn and I follow.

I recognize people who probably don't know I'm big Mook's little sister. Then, I see him.

I don't turn and run or cover up my chest, but I want to. I imagine him grabbing me by the arm and throwing me out or taking my hand and walking me home. I'm five again, and he's telling me to smoke the butts.

Mooks squints, then he opens his eyes wide. "What the fuck? Is that my *sister*?" He leaves the girls he's talking to. "Mother Theresa, what the *fuck* are you doing out of the goddamn church?" I haven't seen him smile so big at me in public. He puts his arm around me. "Little sister crashes the big kid party."

Mook turns me mute. Nessa, Lynn, and Tiffany watch on. He looks at Nessa and Lynn like he always has, but he looks at Tiffany like he looks at women. "Who's your friend?" He nods at her.

"I'm Tiffany," she says. "I can speak for myself."

Mook fake stumbles back and raises his eyebrows. "Well excuse the fuck out of me."

"And who are you?"

"I'm Mook," he says. He swipes his lips with his tongue. And it hits me. Tiffany will have sex with my brother. It might not be today, and maybe not tomorrow, but it's inevitable. He holds out his hand to shake. She gives hers curled with her palm face down like a princess, like she wants him to kiss it. He doesn't. He grabs her fingers and shakes them up and down, "How you know my sister?"

"It's a *very* small school," she says. "I heard you're suspended from it?"

"Damn, sis, you tryna ruin my reputation?" I shrug or I smile or something, I'm not sure, but it doesn't break the rhythm. He looks right back in Tiffany's eyes. "What you drinking?" he asks her.

She holds up her empty hands. "Nothing yet."

"I got you," he says. He heads to the kitchen.

Nessa giggles. "What about Jamaal?" Lynn whispers.

"We're not *married*."

They talk some more, and I look around at the party. Everyone is drinking and laughing and flirting. I wish I was somewhere else. Tiffany will have sex with my brother. Plenty of people have sex with my brother. But I never have to watch the foreplay. It never makes me want to vomit.

Mook comes back with four red cups and three friends. He passes the drinks out and watches me take a big gulp. His big smile.

"This your entourage?" Tiffany says.

Mook points at her with his thumb. "Yo, where did you find this one?" he asks me.

"Yonkers?" I say. Everyone, even Tiffany, laughs.

—◦◦◦—

Paul says I'm so sexy, and he has me by the hand. He kissed me outside and touched me around my belly button and told me in my ear that he wants me, his

breath warm with weed smoke and it tickled me, and now we're upstairs looking for a bedroom. I've had two and a half drinks, the only ones I've ever had.

Paul is a friend of Mook's and I know him and he's big like Mook but he's a
little quiet and he smiles much less and he doesn't have a nickname for me. I
don't know where Lynn is and I don't know where Nessa is and I don't know
where Tiffany is and I'm not sure where I am besides upstairs looking for a
bedroom.

"You're so cute," he says leaning into me. "What are you doing here?" He
turns a knob and opens a door where we see Tiffany bent over a desk and Mook
behind her with one hand on her lower back. He has the bottom of his white
T-shirt in his mouth, so his abs are strong and exposed as he pulls out of her
slow and goes in fast. He has his iPhone in his other hand, holding it over her
arched back. I walk away from the door to the other side, but Paul is standing
there watching. I hear Tiffany yell "shut the fuckin' door!" and Paul slams it
shut. I feel the drinks and everything I've ever eaten swirl around my stomach.
The walls spin me. I've never felt so dizzy. I put my hand on my head, on my
stomach, over my mouth.

"Damn you aight?" Paul says from the doorway. "I bet you ain't wanna see
that."

"I don't feel good," I say. "I feel sick."

"Damn," he says, "you gotta 'url?"

"I don't know," I say. I lean against the wall. "Do you think he saw me?"

"Nah," he said. "He wasn't even lookin' over here. He's busy."

"Don't tell him I saw that," I say. "Please don't tell him I saw that."

"Yeah yeah, no problem." He comes closer to me. He rubs my back. He
kisses my neck. "You wanna smoke?" he says. "I can smoke you out. It's good
for your stomach."

I don't ask what it's like or how long it stays in your system. Instead, I say
okay.

—⁓—

I walk into the kitchen about an hour later, and Mook is there talking to the
girls from earlier. I interrupt.

"You can't have my piss anymore," I say. "I just smoked a blunt with your
friend. My piss isn't clean anymore."

"Dime a dozen, little sis." He pats me on the head like a good puppy. I'm
dizzy. I want to punch him. I want to cry. I want to sit down. "You look high as
shit," he says. I take a deep breath through my nose.

—⁓—

Lynn is on the living room couch, worse off than me.

"I've been looking all over for you," she slurs. "I hate Tiffany."

"Me too."

"Is she with Mook?"

"I don't know," I say. "Who cares?"

"You're right. I hate Nessa too. I hate everybody at this party. Except for you," she says. Her eyelids keep lowering. "You're my best friend," she whispers. "I'mma fuck Tiffany up," she says. "You watch."

She tells me we should be best friends without them. She kisses me on the cheek.

—⚏—

Lynn finally tells me in plain language that she likes my brother. I consider telling her what I saw, but when I think of the words, my mouth waters, sick. I don't feel high or better. Tiffany and Jamaal come into the kitchen. Lynn yells "Slut!" as soon as she sees her.

"Excuse me?" Tiffany says. She gives her drink to Jamaal and steps toward us.

"You heard me," Lynn says. She stands up from the couch and loses her balance for a second. I stand up too. As Lynn inches closer, I inch a little closer behind her.

"Well, at least I'm not ugly like you two bitches. At least I *get* dudes."

"Yeah, *dudes*. Plural," I say.

Jamaal comes between us. "Ladies, take it easy. What's this about?"

"Tiffany's a slut, and I'mma beat her ass," Lynn says.

"Whoa, wow, chill!" Jamaal says.

"I can handle myself," Tiffany says. Jamaal holds up his hands and backs away.

I look around at all of the eyes in the room. People are tuned in. Some are smiling, others are wide-eyed, waiting for the show. Nessa appears in the doorway, and she's one of a few people holding up their cell phones, pointing them at us. I hear someone yell "Worldstar!"

"I dare you to put your hands on me," Tiffany says. "Swing and you're dead. You ugly cunt. You ugly piece of shit."

Lynn wobbles on her feet. Tiffany stands tough.

—⚏—

If our fight goes viral, they'll root for Tiffany. They'll compliment me on how I grab her by the hair and get her on the ground. But I'll be called a bully. They'll ask why no one stopped us when she was on the ground. They'll say it's two on one, that we should've stopped when she had her hands over her face. They'll say we're jealous. They'll say it's always the ugly girls who wanna start fights. They'll say people will do anything to get on the internet these days. Some girls will be disgusted by our ruthlessness and turn their eyes away. Others will watch the whole thing just to see the blood.

CASH 4 GOLD

LAURA DZUBAY

WHEN I WAS AROUND THIRTEEN, MY mother's ex-boyfriend picked me up from school and drove me not to my neighborhood but out to the main highway that carried on north toward Fernandina. We left the dregs of the city and sailed onward up the ratty road, palm trees fluttering along its frayed edges and thrumming with the promise of rain. It took me about twenty minutes to realize that I was being kidnapped.

My mom's ex-boyfriend's name was Con or Conny, short for Lincoln. He hated it when people called him Link. Back when they were dating, which lasted about four years, he used to take me for fun little excursions around town and frame it like it was just the two of us, on an adventure: Conny and Callie taking over the world. Splashing in the shallows at the public beach, slamming go-karts together at Adventure Landing. Lincoln was either a freelancer who was too creatively minded to be held down by a single job or a lowlife drifter, depending on my mother's mood. When my mom had broken up with him about a year earlier, he'd been working at a Smoothie King.

He didn't say a word after we pulled out of the school parking lot, after the initial *Hi Callie—it's me, your old pal Conny. I'm picking you up today.* I'd been puzzled but happy to see him, hadn't asked questions. For several minutes after pulling onto the highway we sat in silence, and I wondered, bumping up and down in the rickety passenger seat of his pickup, what was the proper thing to say after you realize you've been kidnapped. I felt that bringing it up directly would be dangerous because it might tick him off to be accused of something so obviously tasteless. Nobody wants to be a kidnapper. But at that point, every minute another mile between us and town, to politely ask, *Is this just a*

different way of getting home than normal? would have been dumb and probably
pointless.

Shuttling above the Riverside Arts Market on an overpass, I decided
Smoothie King would be a good access point. It was conversational, innocu-
ous. I asked him, "Are you still working at Smoothie King?"

Lincoln blinked a few times and looked over at me as though just then
remembering I was there. "Ah, no," he said regretfully. "Layoffs. That shit, you
know, it fluctuates so much with the seasons."

"Sure," I said, as if I could relate personally.

Lincoln wore an extra-large, stained Carhartt jacket that was big even for
him, and which I knew without having to lean over would smell like Lincoln
himself: musty, warm, cigarettes stamped over time into something not gross
but familiar. It was the same smell of his truck, in which I now found myself,
doors locked.

I looked at the digital numbers indicating the time just below the dashboard:
4:17. Twenty minutes from school, in the wrong direction; thirty-five minutes
from home.

Lincoln saw me looking and misunderstood. "Oh, sorry," he said. "You
wanna listen to the radio? We can listen to the radio."

I looked at him. His nails had gone grimy, clutching the ends of his jacket
sleeves atop the shredded-up steering wheel. His cheeks were reddish, and his
eyes were shiny with a distraught film. I wasn't about to say no.

My lips formed again around the word *Sure* but no sound came out. Lincoln
turned up the volume and found a station anyway, "You're Gonna Make Me
Lonesome When You Go" by Bob Dylan.

—⚒—

I didn't own a cell phone. My mother was one of those traditionalist parents.
Not in every way—like she'd debate me about stuff we saw on the news, and
when we did go out on our rare, special shopping days, she'd take me to any
store I wanted, no questions asked. Aeropostale, Hot Topic, these were distinct
realms to a lot of the other kids at school and therefore, I knew, to their parents
as well, but it was all the same to her. What mattered was that I, a young teenaged girl, vulnerable every day to the pressures and hatreds of a wide and evil
world, felt free to express myself.

Expressing myself through texts was a different story. My mother loved
name-dropping the seventies, that golden era back when the beaches had been
less crowded and people still listened to The Beatles all the time, and she was a
firm believer that my generation would be better off if we all spent a lot less time

hooked up to our devices. What a trite phrase. I had to wait until I was ten to even get an email account—each year, each month, was excruciatingly long—and a phone was out of the question until high school. I was always looped into group plans at the last minute, always grinning awkwardly at the end of some in-joke. My mother saw this as character-building, that I would never need to rely on technology to communicate with other people. That was always the word: not talking, *communicating.* I remembered making a joke about it once, wryly. The new "not like other girls"—"not like other millennials."

My friends at school were Sam, Evana, Jessica. They didn't mind that I couldn't text them—it wasn't their problem—and they all liked my mom. From their softball-field and subdivision vantages, they thought she was adventurous. *Amy,* they'd plea, *tell us about that time before Callie was born when you drove to Atlanta and blacked out. Tell us about when you hitchhiked to California.* Sometimes, us all having had sleepovers together since elementary, they even called her Aunt Amy, a jokey habit that somewhat annoyed but also oddly pleased me. What they really meant by all of this was *Tell us about your men.* Because that's what my mom's stories were: Her ex-boyfriends figured in each of them, sometimes as active players, sometimes as shadows. There was Duane, a mysterious pre-Callie figure, who'd done drugs with my mother, but she'd never tell me which ones. Kevin, who was always trying to take us on road trips to Texas to see his family. Emmett, the army man—to this day the reason we lived in Jacksonville, near the Mayport base, even though he'd been gone since I was about four.

My mother's lapses of singledom were always the briefest windows. Two or three weeks, if that. She never would have admitted it, but she needed a partner around. Somebody to complain to, to lean her head into on the couch, somebody to pick up the groceries or the mail or that week's Blockbuster. My friends never asked for stories about these moments, and my mom never offered them, but they did make up the majority of what those relationships really were. Little errands and kindnesses, all little things, like signals of compassion flashing at one another intermittently from faraway vessels.

Lincoln had always been hard to pin down. Not a drug addict, not an army man. I'd liked him more than the others even though he was a bit anxious, a bit unpredictable. I'd stumble out at six in the morning to grab some breakfast before the bus came, and he'd already be there, although unemployed, sitting cross-legged on the couch and flipping through some old book or a ten-year-old newspaper, or playing a board game by himself. He was strange but benign, which was how I thought of people at school sometimes too.

Forty minutes from school, nearly an hour from home, I decided to broach the subject. "Conny?" I said.

"Mhm."

"Where are we going?"

Again the light came back into his eyes, like he'd been floating through space and just now placed himself back in the car. "Oh! Sorry, I guess I didn't tell you," he said. He laughed nervously. "We're going to go and make some money not too far from here."

"Make some money how?"

A chill had frozen throughout me. But Lincoln reached down into the little compartment under the armrest between us, rummaged around amidst the crumpled bills and McDonald's wrappers, then came up with a Ziploc bag. Inside were a few small lumps of rock, about the size of chicken nuggets. There were even a few sparkly little rock crumbs in the crease and pinched corners of the bag.

"I don't get it," I said.

"It's gold, Callie! This here is some *real genuine gold*. I found it when I was poking around my backyard the other day. Isn't that something?"

He handed me the baggie, and I turned it over in my hands, peering through the plastic. The last time we'd been to see Lincoln had been maybe eight months earlier—so a few months after he and my mom had broken up, but back when they were still flirting with the idea of getting back together. Back then at least, he'd been living in one of those squat ranch-style houses you see off the edge of a highway. One level, a crumbly concrete stoop, and a squashed, tangled yard. We'd driven out there, and I'd waited in the car with the windows open for a humid half an hour, and then the front door swung open and my mom stormed out, Lincoln hollering in the doorway like a wronged kid. I wondered if he was still living there and if that backyard was the one where he'd found the gold.

"Are you sure gold is what it is?"

"Yeah. I scratched it a little; it glints really bright if you just rub the dirt off. You can try if you want."

I didn't want to open the bag. Although I'd asked it, the importance of my own question wasn't quite with me. Even if the answer were yes and it was gold, I'd still been kidnapped, hadn't I?

"So we're going—"

"My buddy knows this guy in Yulee, one of those Cash-4-Gold guys. He says he's really the real deal. I've met him a couple times but never, you know, in this context. But Jimmy, my friend, says I might have a real miracle on my hands and I shouldn't waste it at some pawn shop that wouldn't even know what it's worth."

"Oh." I tried to think if I'd met a Jimmy but couldn't remember if I had. There was a James Foley at school on the swimming team who Sam and Evana and Jessica—and I by extension—were all in love with. "So," I said to Lincoln, and I meant to be like, *Does my mom know where I am*, but the sudden irrational urge to be polite wrangled me into saying instead, "What were you doing in the backyard?"

"Oh, you know. Just poking around," he said vaguely. Then he cleared his throat roughly and sniffed, wiping his nose self-consciously with the huge sleeve of his jacket. "A funny thing happened, actually. Well, not funny, I guess. My dad sort of died. Which is fine," he added in a rush, as if I were about to fall all over him with my sympathies, "we weren't all that close. I hadn't seen him in years. But I was remembering he gave me this really nice silver-rimmed compass once when I was a kid, and then one day, I guess I was about fifteen, I got so mad at him for some stupid thing that I went out to the backyard in the middle of the night and buried it. So I was seeing if I could find that compass, really."

"You really still live in the same house now as you did when you were fifteen?"

"No," he said and laughed. "No, I guess I wasn't thinking all that much at the time. You know how I can get sometimes."

He reached over and squeezed me on the shoulder, grinning slightly as if I were really still his pseudo-daughter. *Were you thinking all that much at the time you picked me up from school*, I wanted to ask, *'cause I get the feeling no.*

"But hey," he said, "we got some gold out of it!"

He seemed triumphant. I nodded graciously and put the Ziploc bag back down among the fast food wrappers.

Trees smeared by the window. The clouds had darkened, and the woods had taken on their way of looking like night in the middle of the day, swaying and ruffling. In Florida, at least the area where I live, everything looks like a place where someone might get murdered, and everything also looks beautiful.

"How's your mom?" asked Lincoln.

"She's good. She's got a boyfriend," I said, which was a lie. "His name is Alex, and he's this big surfer guy." Then I added, I don't know why, "My mom is the most popular of all my friends."

Lincoln gave me a strange sidelong look.

"Well, good," he said. "I'm glad she's doing well."

"She's so happy."

My voice didn't sound angry, but I said it out of anger. I was angry at Lincoln for picking me up without asking my mom, for not thinking about anything ever, for putting me in the position where I had to hate him. I wanted to like him again: Conny and Callie. I hated him for taking that option away. *She's so incredibly happy.*

I tried to remain indifferent about it, but I did feel bad about Lincoln's dad dying. Lincoln really had been one of my favorites of my mom's off-and-on guys, which was why the stupidity of this car ride, this illegal reunion, got to me. I would've been fine if she had married him. He'd had a sit-down talk with me one afternoon about my own dad, totally impromptu during one of our Bruster's trips. I'd been racing the summer heat to the end of a birthday cake ice cream cone, and I don't remember how but Lincoln and I had gotten to talking about my dad, who'd run out on my mom before I was born. He could be any-where in the world, including underground, for all I knew. It was true Lincoln could be spacy sometimes, and sometimes he and my mom would yell at each other until their voices scratched, but he was really all there in that conversation like he could tell it meant something to me. He said he knew it sucked, growing up in such an awful place and feeling like you had something missing but that a lot of different things can be parents if you want them to be. This ice cream cone can teach you about life. This bright red bench can be there for you. He was trying to make me laugh, and it worked.

So yeah, I felt bad about his dad even though they hadn't been close, even though I'd been led astray into Lincoln's pickup. I wondered if it was too early for me to have Stockholm syndrome.

The truck slowed down, and we turned onto a gravel drive that made its metal body bump and rock. The place looked like somebody's house—only meager curtains of trees between here and the other nearby buildings—but there was a windbeaten sign near the front door that read, *CASH 4 GOLD!!!* The sign was orangey-yellow with black letters, standing up on wires like an election ad.

Lincoln looked at me. "You want to stay in the car or anything? I'll under-stand if you don't want to meet my friend, Bobby."

"No. I'll come."

He looked happy about that. We both got out and slammed our doors and walked up the drive, Lincoln holding the baggie full of gold. Before we reached the house, he said, "I'm really glad you came. I would've just gone by myself, but at the last second it occurred to me that you might think this was really cool. You've always been such a cool kid. I was holding this gold and I was just like, Callie would think this was so neat. I should show her this."

He seemed so genuine, so excited. That's me, I thought. Driven off by my mom's ex I haven't seen in months, who isn't really all there some of the time, and I'm like, *This is so neat.*

A big guy in a T-shirt opened the door and stared at us. He had a scruffy chin and wore extra-large faded blue jeans.

"Bobby!" said Lincoln. "Hey, how's it going?" He held up the Ziploc bag like a trophy. "I brought the gold!"

Bobby squinted, even though it was five in the evening and dark out. The trees rustled and whispered at my and Lincoln's backs, warm and blurry gray.

"I thought you were kidding," he said.

"No, man, look. Here it is."

Bobby barely glanced at the lumps in the bag. "Man, I don't think that's . . ."

"It *is*," Lincoln insisted. "C'mon, just look at it. Just really quick, we came all the way here."

Bobby looked from Lincoln to me. He didn't ask who I was, if I was Lincoln's daughter. He just sighed.

Inside, Bobby humored us at a big wooden counter plastered with flyers. The little room contained two or three aisles of pawn junk and precious metal accoutrements: silver necklaces and watches, a bunch of identical white coffee mugs, some embroidery. Bobby handled Lincoln's findings carefully and poked them with little metal instruments, like what dentists use to scratch at your teeth, and examined them through a big magnifying glass.

Lincoln and I waited for the *wow* moment. The, *Oh my God, you've done it—you've really done it!*

Instead, Bobby leaned back with a big stretch and put down the magnifying glass. "It's not gold."

Lincoln didn't get it right away. "Is it *anything*?" he asked anxiously.

Bobby shook his head, glaring. "It's not anything. Anyone with two working eyes can see it's not anything. Now, can you buy something or get out?"

Lincoln looked at me sadly, like he wanted me to tell him what to do. Like that was my job. "Callie? You want anything?"

"No."

"I could get you one of those necklaces."

"I don't want those."

"All right." He sighed. I had pictured him exploding like he did that last time with my mom, screaming and jabbing his finger into the air. Instead, he clapped Bobby on his broad shoulder. "Sorry to waste your time, man."

The first drops of rain were falling when we went back outside, leaving dark spots on my T-shirt. Trees crowded in over the driveway. Lincoln and I got back in the truck and turned onto the main road, heading back the way we'd come.

"Sorry to waste your time, too, Callie," he told me, shaking his head. His voice sounded strangled. "I really just thought you'd think that was really cool."

"Can I have that?" I asked. He was still clutching the Ziploc bag, white-knuckled, over the steering wheel.

He looked startled. "You want it?"

"I guess."

"It's not gold apparently."

"Whatever."

He handed it to me. I didn't even look at it, just held it in my lap.

"Lincoln," I said gravely. It was time. "Does my mom know you picked me up today?"

Lincoln blinked. He kept watching the road but a glaze had come over his eyes as if the question confused him. Then a crease appeared in his forehead, and his face moved in on itself a little, crumpling like a napkin. "Man. I just wanted to show you the gold I found. That's all—"

"So she doesn't know?"

"I just wasn't thinking. I wasn't thinking." As though struck with a new thought, he turned to glance at me. "Shit, I hope I didn't scare you, Callie. I would never've meant to—"

"You didn't," I assured him. "You're fine."

"Your mother was right. I really just never think. I'll take you back to her right now, Callie," he promised me. "Straight away."

I nodded. I could tell he felt bad. My anger and indignation were ebbing away now, into pity, which felt somehow even worse. I pressed my cheek to the window and watched the sky going by over the marshes and the distant dark trees, the rain rippling through the tall grass. I wondered where Lincoln would go after he dropped me off. Back to Smoothie King or some other strip-mall job, back to his empty house with the dug-up yard—what *was* it, I wondered, if it wasn't gold?

Before we got all the way home, before we'd even gotten back into the city, sirens came on in the distance behind us. The lights blurred together in the rain pelting the back windshield, blue and bright red.

Lincoln and I looked at each other. He was already pulling over. This wasn't going to be one of those stories where we ignored the authority and rigidity of the world as if they could never touch us and just drove off into the sunset together, and Lincoln could be my new dad or whatever and we'd both have at least one real friend in the world.

"I didn't mean to scare you," Lincoln said again.

"You're fine."

"I just thought we'd have some fun together like we used to."

"I know."

It was five-fifteen. How far from home was that? I didn't know, didn't care.

I folded the Ziploc bag and slipped it into my pocket while Lincoln parked on the shoulder and shut off the engine. Knowing I'd vouch for him and it wouldn't matter, and I'd get home and there'd be a certain amount of screaming that night and maybe crying and hugging and then I would go to sleep and wake up the next day. Knowing this was the type of story where I'd never see Lincoln again. I leaned back into the seat that smelled like his jacket and watched the thunderous rain slamming the grass and the windshield, suddenly very patient, knowing the story was already over and that I would be OK no matter what.

—ᴍ—

TOM'S STORY

KELCEY PARKER ERVICK

THE FIRST SENTENCE OF THE STORY establishes the fact that the main character is Tom and that he's having a bad day. No mention is made of Gina in the first sentence. The next sentence provides dialogue in which Tom tells someone—the reader does not know whom yet—to fuck off. "Fuck off," it says he says. At this point, it is revealed the person addressed is Gina, that she is Tom's girlfriend, and that she has begun to cry.

A suggestion of conflict having been economically established, a brief description of the setting follows, locating Tom and Gina on a couch in Tom's apartment. Clues are provided to suggest that they have spent a great deal of time on this particular black leather couch, with its large tear on one side, and in this particular apartment, especially at this particular time of the evening when sunlight drains from the room as if there were some sort of leak. It may even be implied that the tension between the couple is either nothing new or has been mounting for some time. While the reader forms a still image of the scene of Tom—slouched, sprawled, and unshaven, staring at the muted TV— and of Gina—looking at Tom and maintaining a protective self-embrace—the narrative introduces Rusty, who has conveniently arrived on the scene. Rusty is described as a mostly-cocker-spaniel mutt with a good sense of timing. The latter information is not intended ironically—for at the literal level of the story Tom is pleased by the dog's arrival and leans forward to tug on its ears—but succeeds in its potential to be understood as such.

By this point, it is clear the narrator is not omniscient but is limited to Tom's perspective, and the account of the situation will be obviously biased and probably distorted by Tom's emotional state. That the narrator will not claim to be Tom (through the use of "I") but only to speak for him, the clever reader will recognize as dissembling, for how can someone who knows the perspective of only one person be anyone other than said person? Less experienced readers, however, will conflate character, narrator, and author, and believe "Tom" is just a substitute for the author himself, even if the story is written by a woman. In which case, they will think she must be a lesbian, a *tom*boy, and that "Gina" is a deliberately shortened form of a word they prefer not to say aloud. (These are not the worst type of readers. At least they are trying.)

Rusty's timely entry upon the scene has allowed for a shift in perspective—in Tom's perspective, that is, as his attention moves from Gina (who has recently gotten an unflattering haircut and who he wishes would stop staring at him with that needy look on her mug) to his apartment and to the dog. The narrative begins to reveal, through thoughts prompted by specific objects within his view (Rusty's food bowl, the beat-up mountain bike, a pile of video games and cords, a table cluttered with used dishes and unopened mail), the failures and frustrations of Tom's thirty-two years. Tom continues to pet Rusty—admitting to himself (according to the narrator, who claims not to be Tom) to being calmed by the repetitive movement and the soft fur but unnerved by Gina's relentless stare—as he surveys the stuff of his quotidian existence with a feeling more of sad regret than the anger suggested in the opening lines. That his current feeling is regret rather than the suggested anger is not a flaw in the narrative's beginning, a red herring, a false clue; it is a true (the limitations of "truth" notwithstanding) reflection of a change, if only temporary, in Tom's mood.

It is revealed, in a long stream-of-consciousness-like narrative paragraph, that what has made this the day, as Tom has decided, to fully and finally break things off with Gina (besides it being a necessary action for the narrative drive of the story) is that earlier in the day he drove by the cross on the side of the highway—the one that he's never been able to turn away from, the one that means he has been spared, the one, in short, that has his name on it—and realized that it has been ten years: Ten years since the Thomas-who-was-not-him died. Ten years since Tom, our protagonist, first drove by the bright white cross and saw his own name intersecting the numbers of the current year. Ten years (this phrase is repeated in this way, for effect) since he promised himself that Thomas (may he rest in peace) would not die in vain but that he (the dead Thomas) would live on as an Inspiring Spirit (here Tom smiles at the term he employed at the time, Inspiring Spirit), as a motivational force for Tom, who would be graduating from college that long-ago June, and who had little more planned than the smoking of vast quantities of pot. Tom had made, the story says, a pact with himself (he even devised a ritual involving candles and the wee-est bit of blood) to do something great enough that he would be able to tell the world about the other Thomas, who had died prematurely (though Tom was not sure by how much for he did not know anything about Thomas except that he was dead and tragically—obviously a car accident), and who had remained with him (Tom) as an Inspiring Spirit. But instead of fulfilling his personal pact, it is explained, all those years ago Tom met Gina and subsequently did nothing.

In a new paragraph, more information is provided about the ten-year period and how specifically Tom managed to ruin it, along with details that allow the reader to question whether Tom had in fact blown it completely or whether (as is often the case) the character is simply not appreciating what is right in front of him: Gina, who is still, Tom can tell out of the corner of his eye as the present situation resumes, staring at Tom and hugging her shins. Just then a scene not in the story but on the television distracts Tom. It is a commercial with several dozen employees of a local company standing and smiling and waving at him in overbright sunlight in front of their workplace, their long shadows stretching behind them like phantoms.

"Do you see that?" It says that he says.

It then says he looks at Gina (who really needs to keep her hair longer), then back to the TV. Creeped out by the smiles, the shadows, the flapping hands that might cause the entire group to fly away or cause a windstorm, Tom, it says, temporarily softens to the familiarity of Gina and all their years together and considers apologizing for the earlier fuck off comment.

It becomes clear that Tom does not apologize, for there follows another paragraph of Tom's thoughts, which appear to be unmediated by the third-person narrator. Tom thinks (without it saying that he thinks) of what he will do if he never gets to tell anyone about Thomas, about the Inspiring Spirit who led him to such greatness. Then he thinks—with no little sense of fury or amazement—that perhaps everything is Thomas's fault after all. If he (Thomas) had been a more *Inspiring* Spirit, Tom might not be stuck where he was. He (Tom) might be something, something worth proclaiming, if Thomas had really stuck with him. Then Tom makes eye contact with Rusty, and it occurs to him that things did start to improve all those years ago when he found Rusty, or was found, as these things go. Life, Tom decides, definitely got better then, shortly after he'd made the pact. He recalls, for example, that he started drinking less. Perhaps, Tom concludes, Thomas did come to him after all: in the form of Rusty. The narrator offers no commentary on whether this is a logical train that has perhaps veered off track. On the contrary, even remarkably, Rusty begins to lick Tom's hand at that very moment, lending credence to Tom's new theory as well as to his belief in Rusty's uncanny sense of timing—both of which now seem related.

The narrator returns to tell the reader that Tom feels reinspired, that he is prepared to make changes, to make up for lost time. (Nothing specific is mentioned in this regard.)

The reader (who has anyway checked the length before committing to the piece, and who even now spies the field of white space beyond the dense woods of words) senses the story is approaching, if not a resolution, an end. The reader is not necessarily optimistic, not about Tom or the story.

Tom stares at and pets Rusty until the reader, who has remembered Gina's presence even if Tom seems to have forgotten, wonders why Tom doesn't tell Gina everything. She seems like a good listener. The reader may even sense the potential dramatic power in an ending that shows Tom embracing Gina as his greatest success (even his only one) and symbolically making *her* the dreamed-of audience for his tale of Thomas.

Instead, Tom looks over at Gina, and she is described as trying to smile. Tom, it is said, finds both her gesture, which does little more than reveal a piece of spinach in her teeth, and her haircut, which needs no further comment, pathetic. A carefully crafted sentence informs the reader that Tom's reaction to Gina's smile and haircut is a simple displacement of the fact that he cannot love and respect a person who loves and respects a person such as himself. He should, Tom concludes, find a woman who will find him intolerable until he makes something of himself.

A further implication is made that Gina would never understand the business about Thomas and about Tom's failures—but that the reader would, that this is why the story is being told at all.

But a clever reader, though flattered, will observe in this, the conclusion of the story, that the perspective has shifted to a restrained omniscience, which describes Rusty turning away from Tom for a quick nibble on his own crotch, and Gina, who is no longer crying, who seems in fact quite done with crying, rising from the couch and casting a shadow from the kitchen light over Tom's face, her own head surrounded by a hazy glow. It seems that while Tom, the narrator, and the reader have been caught up in Tom's story, Gina has been on the terrifying and exhilarating edge of turning a new leaf, of starting a new chapter (book-based metaphors intended) in her own life. She has a great new haircut, for instance, one she's wanted for years. (Here she touches the edge of her hair where it strikes her neck; she loves the feel of the fresh cut against her soft skin.) This is it, she thinks, it's really over. She feels tall and powerful standing above Tom. Though she's not moving at all, she feels inside like one of the people in the commercial that was just on, smiling and gesticulating ecstatically with full arms, waving farewell. Tom, she thinks, can curse if he needs to; she knows that deep down he doesn't mean it. Sometimes he speaks harshly without thinking or speaks carelessly when he's thinking about weird things (which he is obviously doing again) and doesn't know what he's saying. "Goodbye, Tom," she is thinking sadly and with respect for their ten years together, but she is also thinking, "And good riddance." She does not say any of this, however, and the story is back in Tom's perspective so the reader remains unaware of anything other than her expression of—*Could it be pity?* The very possibility makes Tom curse again.

In the end, the reader is left to decide whether to accept the final image in which, though no doors have been opened or sound made, Gina simply disappears from the scene, from the story, and from Tom's life—leaving Tom on the couch alone and still, somehow, in her shadow. Or whether to reject such a physical impossibility as a meaningless trick of narrative.

PENNY AND THE RAKSHASI

SHREYA FADIA

POOR PENNY PRAKASH HAD BEEN UNHAPPY with her life for a long time. She lived with her brown parents and brown brother in a brown house two hours from Atlanta. The baby of her family, with no looks or brains or talent of any sort to speak of, and the only Indian in her entire school until Sonam and Roshni Shukla came to town and took even *that* from her, she always considered herself sorely mistreated. But one fateful day, when she was in her thirteenth summer, Penny's luck changed, and she made a deal she couldn't resist with the monster who lived under her bed.

———

It was all because the Shuklas—stupid Sonam and Roshni and their parents—moved down the street from the Prakashes. Penny's mother, Urmila, was so thrilled they were no longer the only Indians around that she just *had* to go inviting the Shuklas over for chaa. As if they hadn't been perfectly content on their own for all those years before. What, were they going to invite just any old Indian over for tea, share their Parle-G biscuits with every Tarun, Dhruv, and Hari that passed through town? Her father had to trek all the way to the Indian store outside Atlanta to buy those tiny little packets, and here her mother was just emptying whole sleeves of them into the fancy Corningware like it was nothing, like the biscuits were only off-brand Saltines from the corner grocery. But would anyone see reason? Did anyone ask Penny's opinion? No, of course not.

"We've never been able to have anyone over like this," Urmila said, shortly before the hour of the Shuklas' expected visit. "Maybe we'll make a weekly custom of it. Wouldn't that be nice?"

Penny, her mother, and Penny's older brother were all in the kitchen—Vivek at the kitchen table ostensibly studying for the GMAT but in reality probably writing a poem, Penny at the sink washing dishes, and Urmila busy at the table near Vivek, setting out far too many snacks—bowls of chana jor garam, that gross chevdo made with Corn Flakes, chakli, shakarpara, and, of course, the aforementioned Parle-G biscuits, the last of these fanned out like a tiny deck of weird, edible cards.

"Don't you think that's enough food?" Penny asked as she watched Urmila open yet another dabbo and scoop gathiya into a bowl. "How much do you think they're planning to eat?"

Urmila, completely ignoring Penny, continued, "I hear the older daughter is really talented at science. Watch, she'll turn out to be a doctor, with a medical degree from one of those high-ves, Yale or Princeton or Harvard. Or at least from Brown."

She threw a significant look Vivek's way, but he was focused on the books spread out before him and did not appear to notice his mother's glance. Twenty-one and almost a college senior, Vivek would be graduating soon, which apparently meant that he was on the market for a future wife. Penny didn't think Vivek had been apprised of that development yet or that he would be particularly interested in looking—especially, though not only, because he had a boyfriend back in Durham, a fact their parents still didn't know. Technically, Penny wasn't supposed to know about Jamal either, but she happened to have found out because, well, she'd been snooping, as any dutiful and self-respecting younger sister should.

"It's *ivy*, gosh, Mother. And Roshni doesn't have to be a doctor just because she's Indian, you know; maybe she doesn't want to be a doctor. Maybe she wants to teach or, I don't know, go to art school or learn a trade."

"Poonam, stop wasting water. Turn the faucet down."

"For the love of Christ, Mother, would you please stop calling me Poonam? I go by *Penny* now. I've told you a million times. Pennn. Kneee," Penny said, but she did as she was told, even though that meant the water slowed to barely a trickle.

"I'll call you Pen Knee when you start calling me Mummy. Mumm. *Meeee*. Mother is for others," Urmila said, with an annoyingly pleased expression at her own groan-worthy joke. "And what's this Christ-brist business; we're Hindu. Why should you care for this Christ. Say for the love of Shiva or Ganesh if you say anything."

"Whatever—it's just an expression."

Penny did not add that *she* was no Hindu; she was an atheist, thank you very much. But that particular revelation could wait until after Vivek had introduced

Jamal to their parents, whenever that happened. She wasn't stupid. She knew how to time things just right.

"Whatever nothing. Whatever yourself," Urmila said. "How rude you're becoming. I bet Sonam doesn't speak to her mother like that. You could learn from her you know. Taru tells me Sonam and Roshni both speak shuddha Gujarati. Hundred percent perfect. Meantime, you don't even know the difference between tun and tame."

"I wish the Shuklas would go back to where they came from," Penny mumbled, squeezing the sponge so hard that some dirty, soapy water squirted her in the eye.

For a moment, it was like all the air had been sucked out of the room; the change was almost palpable. Penny looked up from the dishes to find her mother and Vivek, who apparently *had* been paying attention to their conversation, both staring at her with the same indignant expression. She resisted the urge to wipe away the foamy streak of soapsuds slithering from her eye down to her cheek, inching perilously close to her mouth.

"Dude, Poonam! That's racist," Vivek said. Of course he would choose to interject only if he could get in a barb at Penny. How like him. His only contribution to the conversation until that point had been a grunt or two, which could have meant anything from *what an interesting point you've made* to *could you both like keep it down—I'm working here* or, more likely, signifying his utter lack of interest in anything not directly concerning him. But Vivek could always be depended on to be totally worthless. "I can't believe my own sister would say something so vile."

"I didn't mean that they should go back to India—they're from Edison," Penny protested. "I meant I wish they would go back to *New Jer*—oh, never mind. Why do I even bother?"

"Arre, can you believe this girl?" Urmila said, turning to Vivek. "What's gotten into her?"

"American teenagers, man. I think you should send her away to India so she can get back to her roots. That would teach her what's what," said Vivek, shaking his head. He had lived with their grandparents in Ahmedabad for three years to attend high school there, and he had been insufferably smug about his so-called Indianness ever since.

Penny knew her brother and mother would go on complaining about her forever, regardless of whether she was in the room. So, muttering under her breath (and saying some things she was glad her mother couldn't hear), she turned off the tap and stormed away, not caring that half the dishes were still unwashed, not caring that her hands were still soapy and dripping all over the floor, not caring that she was probably proving Vivek's point through her admittedly bratty actions. As she made her escape, she took special care to bring each foot down as hard as she could to ensure maximum loudness. The effect was diminished somewhat by her socked feet and the carpeting, but still, it was the intent that mattered, so Penny committed to stomping all the way up the stairs.

In her room, she dried her hands on the towel she'd draped over her desk chair after her shower and then belly-flopped onto her bed, groaning loudly into her pillow. When she had gotten as much frustration out of her system as she could in this way, she sat up.

"Blegh," she said aloud, spitting out a bit of lint and a stray down feather and brushing her tongue with a shirt sleeve, though that only made matters worse.

"It's generally not advisable to eat your bedding or your own clothing. Goodness, I thought by this age you'd have learned better," an unfamiliar voice said from somewhere near the foot of Penny's bed.

Penny sprang back and nearly toppled onto the floor, flailing briefly and knocking the lamp off her nightstand but managing to grab the headboard with her other hand just in time to regain her balance.

"What the—" she said, more frightened than she had ever been in her life. It felt like her heart was thudding inside her *mouth*. "Who's there?"

"Relax. I won't hurt you. I'm harmless," the same voice said, stifling a yawn. Although the speaker was still not visible to Penny, she had the distinct impression that they were stretching as they spoke, luxuriating like a cat rousing from slumber. "If I wanted to eat you, I would have done so absolutely ages ago. I've had plenty of opportunities—I've been living here under your bed for a long, long while now. Biding my time for a moment just like this one."

Penny *should* have screamed until someone came running. She *should* have tried to dart out of her room to the safety of her family's company downstairs. She *should* have thrown something at whoever or whatever it was that was speaking to her, a book or her alarm clock from the bedside table, anything at all.

But she did none of those things.

Instead, moving slowly, cautiously, she crawled forward toward the foot of her bed. "Who are you?" she asked, almost whispering the words.

"You can call me Rakhi," the voice said. "I was a woman once, and it was my name then. I will answer to it."

"What are you now?" Penny said, creeping forward still.

"So many questions for so little in return?"

"What do you mean you've been waiting for this moment?" Penny said, now just inches from the edge of the mattress, hardly daring to breathe, the gray comforter beneath her clutched tight in both hands.

"Go on," Rakhi said, her voice caressing, languorous, strangely alluring. "Come closer; there now. Why don't you get a nice, long look at me."

Penny couldn't help herself. It was like she'd lost all volition and her body was being propelled forward by some unseen force. But no, that wasn't the full story; surely there was some part of her, somewhere deep down, that wanted to see, that wanted to know.

And then she did see, and then she did know.

—w—

It was an easy choice. Actually, it hadn't been a choice at all. It was a foregone conclusion that when the monster who had taken up residence under her bed offered Penny Prakash the deal of a lifetime, she would accept, and gladly.

"I can have anything in the world that I want? Really and truly? This isn't a trick?"

"Have I steered you wrong yet?"

"Well, I did only just meet you," Penny said. She was trying *very* hard not to look at Rakhi directly or to sit too close to the edge of the bed or to breathe in the monster's—the rakshasi's—pungent, ferrous stench, but she was only partially succeeding at just one of these things. And she had a bad feeling about this, sort of nagging at her, almost but not quite like an itch, prickling the back of her neck. Persistent. Uncomfortable. "I don't think you've steered me any-where yet."

"Right you are, my dear Penniless one. I suppose you'll just have to trust me then, have a little blind faith," Rakhi said, pulling her dark, shadowy shape up from the floor so that her face—or the skull that passed for a face—was in line with Penny's. "Do we have a deal? Just one small favor, a tiny thing, really nothing at all, a mere pittance, in exchange for the one thing you want most in the world."

Penny felt a cold, fluttering touch on her chin, like a wisp of fabric brushing against it. The rakshasi's hand was turning Penny's face so that Penny had no choice but to look right into those gleaming, red eyes. That empty pit of a mouth was so close to Penny's own that she could feel the rakshasi's breath, breathed it in so that Rakhi's breath was her own breath, and she nearly choked on the metallic, loamy taste of it.

"We have a deal."

—w—

Poor Penny Patterson had been unhappy for most of her life. She lived with her white parents and white brother in a white house two hours from Atlanta. She had pale, sallow skin, lank hair the color of mouse fur, and dull, gray eyes. The baby of her family, with no looks or brains or talent of any sort to speak of, she always considered herself sorely mistreated. But still, she knew she had a perfectly ordinary, all-American life—or at least she *would* have had one, if a lying fuck of a monster hadn't taken up residence inside of her.

—⚉—

The sun glinted on the hood of Penny's car, the light gathering in a pool, blinding her. She lowered her sun visor and considered but then thought better of honking again. It was, after all, still early in the morning, and people were probably only now waking up, settling down for breakfast or to take a shit. No use getting the neighbors all in a tizzy.

Absently, she rubbed the tattoo on her left forearm through the wool of her sweater, her fingers on their own accord following the shape inked there, that tiny, perfect replica of the rakshasi's face that she had carried with her for the past five years, etched onto her skin in blood red ever since the monster had climbed in through Penny's mouth, squeezed itself into her, become part of her. The memory of that afternoon was inscribed on Penny's body forever, no matter how hard she scrubbed, no matter how sharp the blade she used and how deep she dug; it was seemingly seared through all the layers of skin, even on the subcutaneous fat, probably on the bone itself, though Penny had given up before she got that far.

Something thumped loudly against the driver's side window, and Penny, startled, jumped in her seat and slammed her knee into the steering wheel. On impulse, she reached for the pepper spray she kept in the cup holder, her knee throbbing and the world a blur until she wiped the tears from her eyes with her free hand. She let go of the pepper spray when she saw Zachary's grinning face peering in at her through the window.

"What the fuck, Zachary. I've told you not to do that," she said once he had come around to the other side of the car and slipped into the passenger seat. "I nearly had a heart attack."

"You're fine, babe," he said, leaning in for a kiss, but Penny pulled away from him. He shrugged and ran his fingers through his hair so that it fell like a blonde curtain over his left eye. "I was only messing with you."

"I don't like it when people sneak up on me."

"You're *fine*," Zachary repeated. "God, someone's a real monster today. But that's okay. I know how to help." He looked slyly at Penny, his blue eyes narrowing, and then, lowering his voice, trying to sound sexy but just sounding like the dick that he was, said, "Nothing a good fucking can't take care of." As he spoke, Zachary slid his hand up Penny's thigh, up to the belt loops of her jeans, tried to reach below her sweater. "No one's home right now, you know—the 'rents are both already at work."

Penny wasn't having any of it. Exasperated, she lifted Zachary's hand off her stomach and pushed his arm away from her, back to his side of her car.

"Don't fucking touch me. I'm not in the mood," she said, through gritted teeth. "And I'm on my period anyway."

"That explains a lot."

"Oh, right, hormones, blood, real funny," Penny said, as she started the car and pulled out of the Reynolds' driveway. "You're so hilariously funny."

"Jesus, Penny. Lighten up."

Penny tensed but didn't respond. Zachary shifted in his seat so that he was turned almost completely toward the passenger side window. Good. Let him sulk. She didn't want to talk to him anyway.

Can we eat him?

The question sounded from some hidden place deep inside Penny's mind, the same skulking, languid voice as always, and then came a growling from the pit of her stomach and the gnaw of hunger.

Stop it. We're not eating anyone. You know I'm vegetarian. I don't eat meat, and I most definitely do not eat people.

But I'm sooo veerry hungry. It's been decades since I've had a proper meal. And you didn't tell me you were vegetarian.

You didn't tell me you were going to climb into me and inhabit me forever.

I gave you exactly what you wanted, didn't I?

I didn't ask to have a fucking parasite inside of me.

Penny felt a sudden cramp of pain somewhere in the region of her uterus, but the rakshasi didn't otherwise respond. Rakhi was sulking too now. Good. Maybe Penny would, for once, have some peace and quiet.

The rest of the drive to school was uneventful, except that Penny's cramps got even worse. By the time she parked in her usual spot beneath the shade of the huge, gnarled oak tree, the pain was so bad that Penny was nearly doubled over and couldn't get out of the car. Zachary, however, left without looking at her or even thanking her for the ride. She was so dumping his ass. Well, as soon as she could move again.

And then we'll eat him?

Penny jerked her left sleeve up and pinched the skull tattoo on her arm, hard. *You know that doesn't do anything to me. You're only hurting yourself.*

Penny tried her best to ignore Rakhi's purring voice. She leaned the seat back all the way and curled up in it, hugging her knees to her chest. She closed her eyes tight as a paroxysm of pain spasmed through her abdomen. Her stomach growled again with hunger, and she felt a sort of smug satisfaction—Rakhi was obviously pleased with the effect she was having on Penny. For the second time that morning, Penny's eyes began to water. The tears at least, unlike everything else she was feeling, were her own.

Penny had grown used to the pain, to the monster's prodding and poking whenever she didn't get her way; she was used to Rakhi's angry fits, more like tantrums really than anything else. But Penny still couldn't get used to sharing the rakshasi's every emotion, to feeling satisfaction and hunger and anger and boredom and sadness and arousal that were not her own.

She squeezed her knees hard, trying to brace herself as another spasm of pain coursed through her, this time jolting down her back, twisting her stomach, clenching her whole body in its fist. Rakhi was angrier than she had been in a long time and making sure that Penny knew it.

All of this was, Penny knew, the price she had paid for the thing she had wanted most in the world, to trade a life and an identity that was not her own for any other. She had gotten what she wanted, hadn't she? And all she could do now was live with it.

—⁂—

Poor Penny Prasad should have finally been happy with her life. She lived with her brown husband and brownish daughter in a blue house an hour from Atlanta. She had a deep orange tan, hair box-dyed the color of ravens, and brown contacts she popped out before bed. As for the rakshasi who lived inside her, Penny had learned that some Lithium with a chaser of Vicodin could keep Rakhi more or less subdued. And if there were times Penny had dreams of sinking her teeth into human flesh—well, they were usually gone by morning. Yes, Penny had a life that she was mostly okay with. Or at least she *thought* she had one—until one day, in her fortieth summer, she stood and listened at a door.

—⁂—

Penny saw a shadow at the door of her office, looming and monstrous through the frosted glass. She sighed, closed her laptop, and leaned back in her chair. She waited. The shadow shifted a little, and Penny heard the wood beyond the door creak under the weight of a foot, but then the shadow was still again.

Penny crossed her arms. She knew what this was about, and she'd had just about enough. She'd been in the middle of writing a tense scene: Rama was finally going to rescue his beloved Sita and confront the demon Ravana, had gotten as far as picking up the sword that would end Ravana's pathetic demon life, make Ravana pay for the misery and torture and mayhem, that evil ten-headed fuck—

Penny felt a gurgling in the pit of her stomach. She closed her eyes, breathed in deep, opened her eyes, tried to sweep the anger away. It was no use getting worked up, she told herself. Rama and Ravana weren't going anywhere, and she could finish the scene later, no big deal, everything was dandy. Just A-OK. She was fine. She unclenched her fists—she hadn't even realized she'd been making fists, hadn't noticed her fingernails digging into her palms, pressing crescent moons into them. It was fine. Penny settled her gaze on her rain-streaked office window and the blur of trees and grass and cloud visible through it. She was *not* upset. Penny reached for the stress ball she kept on her desk. She'd taken it from a bin in her therapist's office, the blue and green model Earth stamped with *Breathe* and beneath it, the number for a suicide prevention hotline. She was *not* upset. She squeezed the Earth tight in her hand.

But it was too late. Penny felt something shifting within her, like water beginning to churn. She winced—it had been so long since she'd lost her grip—and braced herself.

She heard a yawn, and something pushed against her ribs from within. Penny's stomach lurched, and then she heard that familiar voice, perhaps a little less familiar now but as abhorrent and unwelcome as ever.

Who reads this garbage anyway? If you ask me, she's doing you a favor by interrupting you.

I didn't ask you, though, did I?

It's not even accurate. Everyone thinks Sita was kidnapped, but I was there, and she knew exactly what she was doing when she left that self-righteous ass of a husband.

Penny considered this for a moment but then shook her head, as if to physically cast the voice out, though years of trying to do just that had taught her that there was no getting rid of Rakhi. She squeezed the stress ball again, but it was useless now. She set it back on her desk.

It's not like I like being in here, the voice said. *But you know*—and at this, Penny felt a strange sensation, a silken caress that wound its way through her—*we could make another deal. You could be free of me. I'd only need one small favor, a little thing, a pittance, in return.*

Do you really think that's going to work on me again?

Well—frankly, yes.

"I know you're there," Penny said, speaking loudly, in a feeble attempt to drown out Rakhi's voice. "You might as well come in."

A moment later, the door to Penny's office opened, first an inch, then another, and then all the way. Penny's thirteen-year-old daughter, Kavi, stepped part of the way inside, looking sheepish but with a hint of a smile and something like hope in her expression.

"I don't remember telling you that you could leave your room," Penny said.

"It's been hours. Haven't I suffered enough? I'm really sorry," Kavi said. She paused, as if weighing her words carefully. "And I wanted to ask you something," she said.

Penny raised her eyebrows but didn't otherwise respond.

Emboldened by Penny's silence, Kavi took another step into the room, drew in a breath, and continued, "Have you given any more thought to my going to India to visit Mitali over Christmas break? I know I shouldn't have been on my computer, and I'm sorry, but I was just researching flights, and there's a great deal on a round trip on the eighteenth. I've worked it all out. I can just take a cab and then MARTA right to the airport. You and Dad wouldn't have to do a thing. I can even book the tickets myself if you give me your credit card."

Penny narrowed her eyes at Kavi, who was watching her expectantly. "I already said no, and that's final."

Kavi looked as though Penny had slapped her—clearly, she'd thought things would go differently. "But *Mom*," she said, elongating each word, stretching the *Mom* into two syllables. "That's *so* unfair."

Rakhi snorted, but Penny ignored her. "You're not going to India all on your own. You're only thirteen years old. You can go when you're older."

"But I won't be alone. Mitali lives with her older sister, who's twenty-two, and Mitali said they could meet me at the airport in Delhi and everything."

"This isn't a discussion, Kavita," Penny said. "Honestly, I don't understand this sudden desire to go to India. Last month, you refused to go to the temple, and now you want to go all the way to India? What's going on?"

"You wouldn't understand," Kavi mumbled.

"Well, then, help me understand."

Blegh, the voice in Penny's head said.

Penny felt her stomach contract. She swallowed and closed her eyes again, and waited for her body to settle. But there was no shutting Rakhi up now.

If she were my daughter, I'd—

You'd eat her, yes, I know. You really don't have much in the way of imagination, do you?

Says the brown girl who wanted to be white. If I had a penny for every time I heard that one . . .

You'd what, buy yourself a nickel?

That makes no sense.

You make no sense.

"Are you even listening to me?"

Startled, Penny looked up at her daughter. For a moment, Kavi appeared blurred and unfocused, almost like she was two Kavis—a second Kavi superimposed clumsily over the original. But Penny blinked and her vision cleared again, and then it was just the one Kavi, scowling at Penny from across the room.

"Of course—of course I was listening," Penny said.

Liar, Rakhi said.

"I *was* listening."

A liar and an awful mother, and ugly too. You're a real winner, you know that?

Cut it out, Penny thought. And then, aloud, she said, "What is it you don't think I'll understand?"

"I'm so sick of being like this. In the middle. Maybe I just want to be Indian," Kavi said. "But forget it. Just forget I said anything; you wouldn't understand. How could *you* possibly know what it's like?"

"What's that supposed to mean? I know a lot more about it than—" Penny started to say, but then she let the thought dangle, unfinished.

Kavi's scowl had turned into a look of utter disgust. "You're unbelievable," she said. "As if the fake tan wasn't bad enough. You're a joke. You're an embarrassment."

"That's it," Penny said. "You just bought yourself another week of being grounded. Go to your room."

At that, Kavi groaned so loudly that it was almost a scream, and she swept out of the room, slamming the door behind her so hard that Penny worried the glass would fall out of the frame. The door slam was followed by a long series of thumps—Kavi was stomping all the way to her room—and then another, more muffled slam, presumably of Kavi's bedroom door. Then the house lay still.

Penny let out a heavy sigh. She rested her head in her hands, suddenly exhausted, almost like she'd just run some great distance. She felt, too, the throb of an incipient migraine.

She's right you know. You can pretend all you want. But you're stuck like this forever, aren't you? Rakhi said. She sounded positively gleeful.

Penny knew she had screwed up. She was just out of practice with dealing with Rakhi—she'd grown lax over the years, could almost pretend Rakhi didn't exist, wasn't part of her still. But of course it couldn't be so easy. And what was she going to do with Kavi? Kavi, who had once been so sweet, now, seemingly overnight, had become a veritable caricature of an adolescent. Why couldn't anything ever be simple?

I know how to make things simpler. An arm, a hand, a foot. You don't even need to cook her. I like them raw and bloody.

"Stop it," Penny said aloud to her empty office. "I've told you, I'm not eating my daughter."

—⚹—

Kavi didn't leave her room again for the rest of the day, not even to come to dinner—although that wasn't surprising considering that Penny, feeling resentful, had made khichdi, a meal Kavi abhorred. Once, in another life that she scarcely thought of now, back when she'd been Poonam, Penny had hated khichdi too, had always refused to eat it. But now, to the surprise of her Gujarati husband and in-laws, she cooked it herself, ladled kadhi over bowlfuls of it, eating with a gusto even they could not muster.

But that day, Penny didn't have much of an appetite. She was exhausted. She'd finally—*finally*—gotten Rakhi to leave her alone. It had taken a hearty dose of Nyquil to do it, but because she couldn't explain to her husband why, in the middle of July, with no cold or cough to speak of, she'd taken the medicine, she fought to stay awake through dinner.

"Why don't I take her up a sandwich," Amit said as they cleared the plates after dinner. He looked anxiously up at the ceiling, as if he could see through the floor to their daughter's room. The furrows in his brow deepened. "She must be starving."

"I'll do it," Penny said. "I shouldn't have made the khichdi." She kissed Amit on his cheek. "You go and get back to your work. I know you have that meeting tomorrow. I'll clean up in here."

Penny piled the last of the dishes into the sink and rolled up her sleeves to get to work on washing them. She let the water run until it was almost scalding hot. A plume of steam rose up over the dishes. Kavi could wait just a little bit longer. It would be good for her.

Penny reached for the sponge. But as she did so, her gaze fell on the tattoo on her left forearm. It was still there, even after all these years, the skull red-brown against her coppery tan.

Penny felt a tightness in her chest, and this time, she was certain that Rakhi had nothing to do with it.

She turned off the tap, set the sponge aside, and tugged both sleeves back down.

—⚯—

A little while later, Penny was making her way upstairs with a grilled-cheese sandwich and some slices of apple fanned out beside it on a plate. She thought of her daughter—likely bleary-eyed, her cheeks streaked with tears, hunger gnawing at her—and took the last few steps a little more quickly.

As Penny approached her daughter's room, which was at the end of the hall, past the guest room and the bathroom, she became aware of voices, coming from that direction.

A few more steps, and Penny was certain that one of the voices was her daughter's and the other voice was a stranger's. A woman's voice—slow and languorous.

Penny stopped a short distance from her daughter's bedroom door, the plate shaking precipitously in her hands, her heart thudding, loud and persistent. With her breath bated, Penny took another step forward, and she listened, though she had a horrible, creeping suspicion of what she might hear.

THE BOYS

SCOTT FENTON

IN THE LOCKER ROOM, LUIS WATCHED the boys tug on their swimsuits, cherry-red trunks with the country club logo. The boys bent over, pulled their drawstrings tight. Adam's apples bulged in their throats.

They took turns in the shower—first Akaash, then Wade, then Patrick. Luis would go last. He would let them have the hot water. One by one the boys returned from the shower dripping wet, clutching folded towels. The boys shook themselves dry. On the ends of their hair, water droplets glistened like morning dew.

They were golden brown, the boys, the color of glazed donuts. Luis took credit for their tans. The boys never remembered to pack their own sunblock— not even Patrick, the head lifeguard. Instead, they borrowed from Luis. At the lockers, now, Luis said, "Hawaiian Tropic?" and Patrick took a handful and rubbed himself down. "Hey man, thanks, wow," he said, before turning to the others. "I love this guy. This guy always comes through."

The boys did whatever they wanted. The boys got away with it. If they'd had any supervision at the country club pool, they would have been fired. Today, Akaash loaded his squirt gun to shoot at sunbathers. Wade pushed Donica into the deep end, pulled her under. Patrick, sitting above the glittering green pool, laughed over the Walkie-Talkie. "I hope she drowns," he said. "I call mouth-to-mouth."

After the pool closed for the day, the boys gathered in the parking lot to figure out what trouble they might get into that night. Wade's parents were out of town, and they'd left a fully stocked refrigerator. "They won't care if we drink the shitty stuff," Wade said. The air, thick and wet. The asphalt shimmering in the heat. "You coming?" Patrick asked Luis, who was busy fingering the lock on his bike chain.

"Is there room?" Luis said. Wade's truck barely had three seats.

"It's a tight fit, but we'll squeeze," Patrick said. "Akaash can sit on my lap." He kept a straight face for a few suspended seconds before he burst into laughter, and Akaash said, "Yeah, ha ha, I bet you want me to. For real."

There was no wearing a seatbelt in Wade's truck. Thighs pressed warmly against thighs. Out on the highway, where the speed limit was sixty, Wade checked his phone and clicked away in response to what he found there.

"So Donica's all pissy now," Wade said. "She thinks I was seriously going to let her drown."

"It was a joke," Akaash said.

"Exactly!"

"You wouldn't do that to her if you didn't like her, you know?"

"That's what I was trying to say."

"She's not hot enough," Patrick said. "Not worth the drama." He dug his nails into the flesh of an orange. It hissed with each new strip he tore, juice dribbling down into his palm. "Vitamin C," he said, and tossed a fistful of peelings out the passenger side window.

"I can't take you anywhere," Wade said. "You're a barbarian."

"Okay, chill," Patrick said. "Shit's biodegradable." He wiped his hand on his shorts, threw an arm around Luis's shoulder. "You awake, man?" His arm was hairless. He shaved his body for swim team, everything below the neck. "Nodding off or something?"

"I'm awake," Luis said. "I'm here."

—◠◡◠—

The boys drove through Dairy De-Lite, the menu bright white against the blackening sky. Burgers and fries all around. A chocolate milkshake for Patrick, who craved something sweet. Wade sped off toward the pickup window before hearing the total. "He does this all the time," Patrick said to Luis. "Dine and dash. It's pretty funny." At the second window, the boys swore they didn't have the cash. It was an honest mistake. So sorry, wow—Wade must have left his wallet in the back pocket of some other pair of jeans. Could they possibly come back and pay later?

The cashier said, "Just take the food. Get out of here."

As they drove away, Patrick popped the lid off his shake and slurped it down. "Come on, man," he said. "Faster. I gotta take a piss, okay? I'm about to bust."

Akaash, meanwhile, buried his hand in the fast-food bag, searching for stray fries.

"Bitch, don't touch my fries," Wade said.

"What's mine is yours, motherfucker," Akaash said.

The boys spilled out of the truck and kicked off their shoes at Wade's front door one by one. Patrick's hula girl flip-flops, the hula girl quickly fading. Akaash's too-big tennis shoes, laces fraying at the ends. Patrick went to take a leak. Wade left in search of beer.

In Wade's bedroom, baseball trophies collected dust on the dresser next to Mountain Dew bottles, brown with tobacco spit. Luis sat on the bare mattress while Akaash lay on his back on the carpet, feeding himself french fries.

"Is there something, like, wrong with you? Mentally? Can you not talk?" Akaash readied another fry, dragged it through the ketchup, but the ketchup missed his mouth and landed square on his chin. "Sorry," he said. "That was offensive." He wiped away the sauce. Luis watched him lick it off his finger.

Patrick came into the bedroom still zipping himself up. "Ever take a piss that feels better than sex?" He landed next to Luis on Wade's mattress, where the Dairy De-Lite haul sat waiting for him.

"Don't be gross," Akaash said. "I'm eating, dude."

"The human body isn't gross. It's a miracle." Patrick's burger was so big he had to hold it with two hands. "The Monster," he said.

Akaash said, "The fries are better at Dairy De-Lite. I told you."

"But QuikBurger has the good dipping sauces," Patrick said. "That honey-roasted barbecue." The point, Luis learned, was moot—the boys weren't allowed at QuikBurger anymore. They'd already hit all three locations with their dine-and-dash scheme. At the Oceanside store, location number three, the manager caught onto their scam and threatened to call the police if the boys ever showed their faces at a QuikBurger again. He couldn't wait to see them in handcuffs, he'd said.

"That guy was fucking gay," Akaash said. "I bet he does want us in handcuffs."

Patrick had something to say, but his mouth was full, and he was going in for another bite. By the time Wade appeared with the six-pack he'd promised, Patrick's burger was gone. All that was left in the wrapper were the bits of lettuce he'd plucked off and the wet pink tomato.

"Bonfire at the Boneyard tonight," Wade said. "We going?" The answer didn't matter. Already he was rummaging through his dresser drawer. He pulled out cologne, the kind that came in an aerosol can, and sprayed a full five seconds of mist out into the bedroom before he stepped into it.

"Jesus," Akaash said. "Did you have to aim that right at my fries? I can't eat these. Trying to poison me. Thanks. The fuck."

Already, Patrick was double-fisting tallboys. "Who's going to be there?" he said.

"Some girls," Wade said. "Donica. Summer."

"Boring," Akaash said.

"Donica's nude was your wallpaper for like a month, though."

"It was not my wallpaper. I don't know where you got that."

"You're just pissy because Summer doesn't want to fuck you," Wade said.

"Yeah, well, she's probably racist," Akaash said. "I'm hot as fuck."

"And maybe she heard the chicken fingers story," Wade said.

"That never happened," Akaash said. "Fuck you. We don't talk about that."

"I want to know what this guy thinks," Patrick said. He scooted over on the mattress, wrapped an arm around Luis's waist. He pulled Luis close, so close Luis could feel the prickle of Patrick's stubble against his cheek. "My guy," Patrick said. He smelled like a deep fryer, like carnival food. "You with us, man? You good?"

"I'm good." Luis's beer was nearly empty. He hated the aftertaste, and the only way to make it go away once he'd started was to drink more.

"He's bored," Akaash said. "He's trying to figure out how to blow us off and go to some better party."

"Don't put him on blast like that," Wade said. "He just likes to take everything in. You know what he needs? A shot. We all need a shot."

There was raspberry vodka hidden in Wade's desk. Wade held the bottle by the neck. He could be delicate when he wanted to. He could pour carefully.

"This is the expensive shit," he said. "You're welcome."

The boys drank from little rinse-and-spit cups at Wade's bathroom sink. In the mirror, Akaash licked the shadow of mustache above his lip. Not a drop would be wasted.

"One more," Patrick said, "for the road?"

"Why do you always have to have two of everything, man?" Wade said. "Fine. But you owe me."

"Shit," Patrick said, patting himself down. "I must have left my cash in my other pants or something."

The vodka burned even after Luis swallowed.

———※———

On the drive out to the Boneyard, the boys decided tonight would be Akaash's night. They would suggest a game of truth or dare, and when Summer chose dare, they would make her follow Akaash into the woods. A boy and a girl went into those woods together and came back glazed with sweat, glowing. "In your case," Wade said, "she can think of it as an act of charity." Akaash didn't care what she thought of it. He'd been waiting all summer to get some. He called it a drought, but Patrick leaned in to Luis's ear and breathed the word *virgin*.

Luis had never seen the Boneyard in person before. Junked cars littered the open field, rust orange, thick bushes of moss feeding on their hoods. If you started digging out here, Wade said, you could find fossilized beer cans from the eighties, maybe earlier. In the woods, boys carved the names of their conquests into the trees, a tradition that went back decades. Megans. Brittanys. Wade swore he'd carved Donica's name just last week. "She's, like, barely a five, man," Patrick said. "A six if it's nighttime, I guess. But nothing to brag about." Patrick had lost count of how many girls he'd notched. He could recite the Js, at least, off the top of his head: Jenny, Julia, Jessica. At the Boneyard, Patrick carried a pocketknife with his condoms. Patrick came prepared.

The bonfire—growing and growing, spitting embers. Luis couldn't tell who was tending the fire, who'd started it, or who would stamp it out at the end of the night. He didn't know who hosted these parties. The busboys from the country club bar had just gotten off. Still in uniform, they threw wood into the fire that the fire didn't need, their sleeves rolled up, ties loosened. "What's up, Randy?" Wade said. Two different busboys turned around, answering to the same name.

The girls from the pool? Selfish, Luis thought them—Donica and Summer and the rest of the sunbathers arrived early every morning to claim chairs under the umbrellas even though they never opened them. The girls didn't need the shade, but they wouldn't let anyone else have it either. They fed the flames now with whatever they could find in the trunk of Summer's car. Beauty magazines. Her chemistry lab notebook. Proofs of last year's yearbook photo, her face melting in the heat. "I swear to God," Summer said, "that photographer gave Ava S. a second take. Where was my second take?"

A man with a big blue cooler watched the whole scene. He worked at the country club too, Luis realized—golf course maintenance, responsible for the greenness of the grass. Luis almost didn't recognize him without his standard-issue red polo. The flicker of his phone played over his face, a video of people sliding down banisters and getting hit in the nuts.

"This is good shit, man," he told Luis. He was in his twenties, but he hung out with the high schoolers. He could give them booze for a fair price. What could they ever give him? What would they ever want to? All day he drove from hole to hole in the maintenance golf cart, drinking forties out of paper bags and tossing the amber-colored bottles off the cart path and into the pond below. He was supposed to clean the pond, but every time Luis saw the water, it was scummed over.

"She's your girl?" the maintenance man asked Luis, and nodded his head in Donica's direction. Her fringe bikini top and cowboy boots meant she was trying too hard—Luis thought so anyway—but she had something the maintenance man wanted, something he hungered for.

"No, she's not."

"But you fuck her. Respect. I'll stand down. Let me know when you're done with her, though. I've had my eye on that girl since before the beginning of swimsuit season. What's her name?"

"I don't know," Luis said.

"Oh," the maintenance man said. "Right on. Keeping it casual. I feel."

—✺—

Luis watched the boys, and the boys watched the girls. Around the fire, Wade sniffed after the girls like a dog, Akaash close behind him. Sunglasses hung from their necks. Wade's shirt came off first—his always came first. His chest, sticky underneath. "My abs are solid for sure," he said to any girl who'd listen, "but I'm proudest of my quads." When Akaash saw Wade bare-chested, he took his shirt off too.

Summer said, "Did you bring your little squirt gun?"

"Little?" Akaash said. "It's eleven inches."

"I think you need a new ruler," Wade said.

Akaash said, "Let's play a game. Truth or dare?"

"Dare," Wade said.

"It's not your turn," Akaash said. "Ladies first."

"Hmmmm," Summer said. "Pass."

Akaash said, "Hey, my parents have a house on the beach. I'd love to take you out there sometime."

"Oh yeah?" Summer said.

"Yeah, it's got, like, a hot tub and all that shit," Akaash said.

"Quit lying," Wade said.

"You don't know," Akaash said. "Fuck. There's stuff you don't know about me."

Akaash dared Wade to investigate the inside of the wrecked school bus rotting in the overgrowth. Did you know, Wade said, a half dozen kids from East died inside that bus? It was a highway accident from a few years back. "Ladies' tennis team," Wade said. "They were en route to regionals. Michael says they were really good that year."

"Fuck," Akaash said. "Kinda tragic."

Luis remembered seeing the colorful wreaths on TV, adults wailing on the evening news. "Ghoooost busssss," Wade and Akaash said, dying laughing as they stomped through the weeds to the fading yellow. The windows that survived the impact had been painted black.

"I'll do any dare," Wade said. "You name it, I'll do it." He kicked the bus's folding door open now. He didn't need a countdown. He went up the stairs, thinking nothing of it, and disappeared into the dark. Wade was gone long enough that Akaash turned to Luis with a serious look on his face—"There could be, like, bats in there," he said, "fuckfuckfuck"—but then Wade came out, back into the firelight, carrying a stash of fireworks leftover from somebody's Fourth of July. Roman candles. Cherry bombs.

"What?" Wade said. "You were worried about me? That's sweet." He slid the sun-bleached box of cherry bombs open. "Dude, you can't even buy these in stores anymore." He rubbed the fuse between his thumb and his forefinger. "Dare me to light one?"

Patrick lounged in the bed of Wade's truck, his hand slipping absently into his shorts, the moonlight dark blue. He giggled when Luis came near. "He's sucking out there. Are you hearing this?" He pulled a can of Straw-Ber-Rita out of the six-pack ring. Softly, like he was picking fruit off a tree. "We call him chicken fingers," he said, "Akaash. It's funny. He took Jenny to the movies. Dark, empty theater, right? The nice one with the reclining chairs? She put his hand down her pants *for him*, and he still couldn't do it. It's like, what do you need to get the job done? Be creative, man. Butter works in a pinch. You've got that giant tub of popcorn right there."

Here was Donica, the fringe on her bikini an upturned mop. "That is not what happened," she said. "Jenny did *not* do that."

Patrick said, "I'm talking about Jenny F. You don't know her."

"Friedman, yeah, no. I know who you're talking about, asshole." Whatever she was drinking must have been almost empty. She had to tip back her red cup to finish.

Patrick flashed a sick smile. "Sweetheart, I'm sorry," he said, "but her name is all over those trees." He gestured toward the woods with his can. "Would you like me to show you?"

"You're disgusting."

"Coming from you," Patrick said, "that means a lot. Straw-Ber-Rita?" He plucked another can from the bunch and held it out to her. She stared at the offering, eyebrow cocked, letting him hold it there. When she finally reached for the can, Patrick pulled away. "You'll have to climb up here and get it," he said. "How bad do you want it?"

—⚹—

Patrick and Donica, sneaking off into the woods. Luis followed close behind them, darting from shadow to shadow. Donica was a craving Patrick needed to satisfy—Luis understood that—but for Patrick, it seemed the cravings didn't pass. Patrick was all appetite. Nothing would satisfy him. And what was Patrick to Donica? She hated him. As far as Luis could tell, she only talked to him because Patrick and Wade hung out together.

Luis watched from the underbrush, two dark shapes rubbing against each other beneath the pines. Patrick lost his shirt, and there, again, was that golden glow. *I made that,* Luis thought. *It's mine.* Luis was the one—in the daydream, he was!—who tugged Patrick's shorts down to his ankles. From the locker room, Luis knew what it looked like, Patrick's penis. Luis could conjure Patrick's penis vividly in his mind, and the pale blue boxer shorts at Patrick's feet, the ones with little sailboats on them. Patrick pushed Luis to the ground, and it was Luis's knees that scratched against the pine needles, not Donica's. Luis was Donica now. His head bobbing up and down. Patrick's penis tasted like sodapop. He had a certain fizz to him. *Mine mine mine.*

It would only ever be a daydream. Luis watched Patrick hold Donica's head in his hand like it was a cantaloupe at the supermarket and he was testing its weight. "You want it so bad," Patrick told Donica. "Take it." Afterward, he didn't pause to dress himself. He reached, instead, for his pocketknife.

—⚹—

The boys, like moths, drawn to firelight. The night was ending, and they could feel it. Akaash, pissing on the flames. Wade was six or seven beers deep and chugging another as a dare. He was drowning; he was choking on it. "Got a surprise for you," Wade said to Luis, wiping the foam from his mouth, sliding his hand into his pocket. The keys to his truck—he trusted Luis with the driver's seat. Luis was sober enough to handle the heavy equipment. He was the least drunk, anyway, of the four boys.

"You never let me drive your truck," Akaash said.

"Because you can only drink two beers before you're blitzed," Patrick said.

"I'm fucking phenomenal."

"You can't even piss straight," Wade said. "Your shorts are, like, wet right now."

"If I don't get any tonight, it's the curse of the ghost bus. Man, fuck ladies' tennis."

"How do you explain all the other nights?" Wade said.

"Ha ha, fuck off, man," Akaash said. "Seriously. Fuck yourself."

Akaash bent over and started vomiting. It was a chunky, wheat-colored mixture.

In a few hours, the boys would don their swimsuits again, cold and damp in the dark of their lockers, and sit high above the water surveying their kingdom. It was Luis's kingdom as much as it was theirs. He dressed with them, showered with them. His hair, too, was becoming blonder by the day.

The maintenance man was packing up his cooler, his column of red cups. Without the girls there to stare at, he had no business left at the Boneyard tonight. The girls knew how to leave somewhere before it went flat. The boys drank every last drop, even when the fizz was gone.

"Do you know what happened to Donica?" Wade asked Patrick.

"How would I know?" Patrick said. "She's your girl, man."

Luis had made it to the end of the night, to the truck ride home. The boys, his passengers, were someplace else. Akaash stared down at the floorboard. When he came to, he thrashed at the window. "If you throw up in my truck," Wade said, "I will slit your throat." Between Wade and Luis, Patrick snored. He slept as if he'd just feasted, a rope of drool hanging onto his lower lip. His head lolled, grazed Luis's shoulder.

Luis nudged him away.

One by one, Luis dropped the boys off at their brightly colored houses. Luis said, "Later, man," and each one of them said, "Night," somehow ignoring the blue light of morning. Luis watched the boys stumble up their driveways, trample over landscaping. The boys had been his. He watched their garage doors fall behind them quietly like curtains.

THE SIXTH DOOR

MEGAN GIDDINGS

GABBY RETURNS TO THIS MEMORY OFTEN. She is sitting in her bedroom, a copy of *Macbeth* triangled over her knee. Gabby put the book down to daydream about being rich enough to be someone whose entire life is travel. A plunge pool at sunset. The water and sky and glass of the pool so pastel she feels like candy. Being able to say which ramen stand in Tokyo has the best noodles, being able to say what are the best noodles. Going to Dar es Salaam and picking out octopus and fish to grill, cloth to buy. Even the exact daydreams are birthmarked on her brain. Her door swings open, and it's her older sister, Simone.

"Sometimes, when I think about our names, Simone and Gabrielle," Simone liked to say, "I think our parents wanted French poodles, not daughters." At the time, it never made Gabby laugh because some of the mean white kids at school would call her Poodle. The one time she told her mom that it hurt her feelings, her mom only shook her head and said they could be calling you so much worse. Poodle is cute. No one dies while being called Poodle. When she told Simone and her husband, James, they started calling her Poodle, elongating the word so it had a long, gushy ooh in the middle.

"Mom says you want to quit volleyball."

Gabby waits for her sister to say volleyball was the best thing she ever did in high school. That when she's an adult, she's going to long for the days when all she had to care about was jumping in the air and slapping a ball at the ground. To ask her why. Or to get mad and assert her I-am-your-big-sister-you-must-listen-to-me authority, the short shorts are not so bad. Instead, she gets into the bed next to Gabby. Reaches into her purse and pulls out a large candy bar. She opens it slowly, as if the wrapper was beautiful paper that she wanted to

175

smooth out to look at the design, and then breaks the bar in half. They eat the chocolate in silence.

This is the last time Gabby will ever see Simone. She spends some of it thinking her sister is an unusually loud chewer.

—⁓—

Eight years later, Gabby is drinking, alone, at Ginormous when someone touches her shoulder. Her first thought is *fuck it, I'm going to buy a gun*, and the thought is repulsive and hilarious, so there's a half smile on her face when she turns and sees James.

"What are you doing here?" Gabby hopes it sounds nice.

"It's near the anniversary. I just got in my car, and next thing I know, I'm here." He has grown a beard. She has forgotten how his hair was midnight: black, blue black, some whites near the temple. Gabby sips her Scotch, likes how it tastes like she is drinking lightly scorched earth.

"You're so old now, Poodle."

"That's a rude thing to say."

He is leaning toward her, the tip of his shoe almost touching hers. There's a look in James's eyes, as if he's trying to emulate how models look in perfume commercials: I smell incredible and I want to fuck you and isn't that worth one hundred fifty dollars? She thought about how her dad had never liked him. Her father has a theory—never trust a man named Michael who is too good to be a Mike for his friends, never trust a man named James who is too pretentious to be Jimmy for his grandma. Gabby's mom calls things like that his sea captain talk, weird aphorisms that seemed like only a man stuck alone at sea could make up.

Gabby's parents are in London. They are complaining about how expensive the food is. They say the city smells and is so damp. She wants to tell them the reason they're having no fun is that Simone is gone and they were dumb enough to think a trip would make them forget. Instead, Gabby asks for them to buy her some tea. It's the only London thing she can think of.

James buys her a drink. Another. They are telling stories about the past eight years. He remarried, but she died. A snorkeling accident. Gabby can't tell exactly how he feels. His voice is appropriately sad, but he drinks for a long time after saying it, as if he's trying to make sure there are no facial reactions for her to examine.

Gabby is drunk, so she's comfortable saying, "That's sketchy as fuck. First wife, missing. Second wife, died snorkeling. They're going to lifetime you."

"What?"

"They are going to make a movie about you on *Lifetime.*" She rolls her eyes. Another drink in her hands. And they are walking, the grass is somehow simultaneously blue and green. Gabby is telling a story even she can't follow. Another drink in a paper bag. It's hard to hold onto. Beer dribbles from the side of her lips to her chin. Down the street, someone is whistling, high and clear and loud, as if they are trying to will the entire world to feel cheerful. Gabby and James are sharing a cigarette. The moon is silver light behind clouds. James is holding her hand, but it doesn't feel like anything. She thinks she can see every bat in the world, hunting down moths, feeling so alive in the night. His hands brush her neck, and his lips are thin, his eyes are distant, and her brain says *he wants to hurt you*. But his hotel room bed is soft. There are luxury soaps in the shower. She brushes her teeth, drinks water. Poodle, he said at some point, maybe in the elevator, you seem so lost. And if it hadn't been the right thing to say, she would've laughed at how dumb the sentence sounded.

—⚬—

Simone's memorial service is more of a begging than a service. Every time someone speaks into a microphone, they can't help but say something like, *Simone, if you're out there, please come home.* She is everywhere, in the wood pews the attendees sit in, standing in a dark coat among the trees behind the church, lingering in a bathroom stall because she doesn't want to have to small talk in front of the mirror, have someone notice how long it takes for her to wash her hands.

James is patting Gabby's shoulder. Her mother and father have a hard time not touching her too. Even if she wasn't worrying about Simone, she still wouldn't be sleeping well. Multiple times a night, her parents open her bedroom door and stand in the doorway, watching her. And if not that, she hears them crying in the kitchen, walking around the house as if each cupboard and closet needs to be searched.

Some feel sorry for James. They bring him casseroles, can't imagine how this would happen.

Some are whispering he is already dating. They point to a blonde woman overdressed for the event. She is wearing platform heels and a tight black dress. Gabby sees her smile every time she sees James, but his only response is to nod once and look wary every other time.

—⚬—

James's house is beautiful. The outside is brick, red and brown. Gabby has always liked brick houses. The living room, dining room, downstairs bathroom,

library, game room, and guest room, all the places where company would feel
comfortable going, were lovely. Framed photographs of all the places James has
visited. Art that probably made people stop and consider it and how wealthy
its owner was. Large couches that hug asses and massage shoulders. Flattering
lighting. The upstairs is different. "There is the," James pauses, "our bedroom."
A study, another two bathrooms. And many tiny rooms he doesn't point out
but that Gabby notices are locked. Each probably three feet wide. Their doors
painted different shades of red.

"What are these?"

"Storage."

Gabby realizes she's told no one where she was.

She reminds herself that when Simone had colds, James would rub her feet,
make her homemade chicken soup. Gabby remembers how patient he was when
she was learning how to drive.

The next morning, James hands her a key ring with several keys.

"I have to go away on business," he says.

"Okay."

"I think it would be better if you didn't explore too much."

Gabby sips her coffee. She is wearing a white nightgown that makes her feel
like a ghost determined to be sexy.

"Is this reverse psychology? You tell me not to do it because you know then
I won't be able to resist?"

―⚭―

The woman James is marrying is named Melanie. Gabby thinks it's a terrible
name. Melanie, a name for someone's mom who wore Looney Tunes sweat-
shirts and thought *lol* meant *lots of love*. It's only been three years since Simone
disappeared. Gabby expects her mother to take the water glass she has in her
hands and throw it on the floor. Her father to tear up the wedding invitation,
set the RSVP card ablaze. Call James on the phone, set up a recorder, and say
this is proof you killed my daughter. Get him to confess to the whole thing. The
card is covered in roses and written in embossed gold ink. She forgot James's
middle name was Harlem. *What an asshole*, Gabby thinks.

"We'll get them a waffle maker," her mom says.

"Isn't it super weird he invited us?"

"It's nice. He loved your sister. He loves us."

―⚭―

The first day in the brick home Gabby spends watching TV and reading books.
She orders a pizza and eats it for lunch and dinner. James calls her at night but

doesn't ask about the house, the doors. The second morning, Gabby eats the last slice of pizza, takes the set of keys, and heads upstairs.

She expects to find a dead woman in each room. Each dressed in a different colored flattering silk dress. Diamond rings and silver bands glinting from their left ring fingers. Their bodies limp. Throats bruised with the pressure of James's hands crushing their lives out. Or maybe the walls painted with their blood, a dark shimmer. The expensive art of blood spray.

The first room has wedding portraits hanging on the walls. Simone and James embracing beneath a flowering cherry tree. James and Melanie seeing each other for the first time. Her dress, long and lacy. A woman and James toasting one another, their eyes exactly the same. James and a different woman sitting in a rowboat together, holding up a sign for a wedding date six months ago.

In the second room, there is a mannequin that looks like the same-eyed woman. She is dressed in a T-shirt and jeans. Another room, another mannequin. This one resembles the rowboat woman wearing a winter coat, a pom-pom hat on her plastic head. Her black hair in cutesy pigtails. Taped on the walls are printed-out emails. I had a dream I was walking on your penis, began one, and Gabby can't stop reading. The rowboat woman, if she was the email writer, loved thinking of herself as miniature. Giant penises, humongous hands. The fourth room has a mannequin of Melanie dressed in a bikini and wearing neon yellow flippers. The next, Simone. The mannequin's hair is her exact texture. It seems to Gabby as if it was Simone's hair, that somehow James had gotten it and made it into a wig. It is all so weird that Gabby laughs. She wonders if these are new additions. Put there to teach her some weird lesson about trust. Simone is wearing a version of her favorite black dress. Long sleeves, billowing out at the waist. The real version is hanging in Gabby's closet at her parents' home.

She opens the sixth door and inside is her. The mannequin is naked. Its breasts, Gabby thinks—and she is not being self-deprecating—are nicer than her own. Symmetrical, perky, no stray acne around the bra line. The mannequin Gabby has her left hand stretched out toward the real Gabby. Resting in its palm is a half-smoked cigarette. She realizes it was probably from the other night.

Is this a murder thing? Is it a sex thing? It's so confusing. Gabby locks all the doors and runs a bath. There is a container full of fancy bath things—salts, bombs, bubbles—and she pours in a cup of pink liquid without thinking. It becomes an over-the-top bubble bath. Gabby soaks and tries to think of what it could all mean. There are more doors to try. Gabby pulls her clothes back on, forgetting to dry off.

The seventh has nothing in it, but the eighth has a mannequin of James. Even the mannequin's hair and beard is black blue. It's wearing a suit as if it were about to go out dancing. Its eyes, strange. Gabby leans closer. They're made of sapphires. Real ones. Blue, but also transparent. All the women mannequins have dull plastic eyes.

There are footsteps downstairs.

Gabby notices the water she's dripped onto the floor, figures it will be evaporated by morning. She locks the door. Goes back to the bathroom and takes off her clothes. Wraps herself in a white silk robe and walks downstairs. James is in the kitchen, opening a bottle of wine.

"So," he says and looks up.

"That was the best bath of my entire life." Gabby is impressed by how good her lie sounds.

He tugs and the cork comes loose. James sniffs and then holds it out, still attached to the corkscrew, to Gabby.

"Why do people smell those? I can only always smell alcohol."

James sets the cork down.

"I know you went into the rooms."

"There was nothing that interesting in them."

He drums his left hand on the counter.

"I'm going to poison this glass of wine, and you're going to drink it all."

"Sure. And maybe if that doesn't work, you'll convince me to take up a dangerous hobby. I'll start wanting to run with bulls or go bungee jumping."

"I'll hire a man to start following you. People will tell you you're just being paranoid. And when I'm bored, Poodle, I'll have him kill you in the park." He points south, so Gabby would know exactly which park he was talking about.

"Very funny." She crosses her arms. Gabby feels as if she is growing. The words he says don't scare or titillate her. There is nothing he can do to make her small. Gabby sees him clearly. Even if he tries to hurt her, his fists would feel like someone tapping for her attention. She feels completely, wonderfully swallowed by the feeling.

James pulls out bleach from beneath the kitchen sink. He pours some of it in a wine glass with a golden rim. Splashes some wine in. The red wine slowly seeps into the bleach, and it looks pink.

"We're not even married," Gabby says.

"This is practice."

She takes his face in her hands and kisses him. Touches her tongue to his lower lips. Runs her fingers through his hair. When Gabby pulls away, James looks as if she slapped him on the nose.

"I thought you would be more exciting," Gabby says. She puts on her shoes and coat. Opens the front door. Doesn't care that she's leaving behind her clothes, some books. Gathers her purse.

"Where are you going?"

"Out."

The night is warmer than Gabby expects. She walks to the park where he threatened to have her killed. The leaves are falling. Two teenagers are making out on a bench. A woman is walking a collie and saying, "you're so good" to it in a low voice. She knows she will never see him again.

When Gabby tells people this story, they ask her how long James went to jail for, were they able to find her sister's remains, what did her parents think. She never answers those questions. Instead, she tells them what she did next.

Gabby maxes out her credit card on a trip to Chile. She eats seafood and drinks wine and speaks enough Spanish to be cute-friendly, not tourist-friendly. On her last day, she pays a man one hundred dollars to take her on a tour of a glacier park, gives him an extra two hundred dollars to take her inside a glacier.

It surprises her, still, how little people value their lives.

Inside the glacier, it's colder than Gabby has ever experienced. The sound of water hitting the sides is almost music. Like when someone rubs water on a crystal glass and plays a note. When Gabby looks up, she can see herself reflected from different angles. Her nose runs because of the cold. She knows if the glacier suddenly splits, the ice will crush her flat. Or if she falls into the water, there is no way to survive. Her heart beats faster. The man sneezes, and he jerks back. The boat sways and wobbles with his movements. Gabby grips the sides, forces the boat steady.

THE FISH IS GONE. BUT THE CAKE IS HERE.

BRIAN LEUNG

THE OLD DUDE CALLS FROM ACROSS the covered patio, "It's the Alps. You are here for trout!" His Slovene accent dominates a cool breeze. He's unshaven, but smiling and bright-eyed behind glasses with thick black frames, entirely clad in even blacker leather motorcycle garb, a helmet in the seat across from him as if it's a dining companion. In one hand he holds a slender, green paperback book, which he shakes at us in a way that's teacherly and menacing at once. Beyond him, the pine-laced mountain pass leads to a distant canvas of elevation. "Trout," he says again. Chaun and I have been torturing the waitress for a description of everything on the menu. I'm certain I'm getting the Three Meat plate. A safe choice. Plus, we are hungry and way off our intended route and not on purpose. Chaun's fault. It seems appropriate that this place is called Brunarica Slap because that's what I want to do to him. In two weeks, I'm downsized out of a job—a needed push, really, but with no prospects. Chaun insisted on this trip together anyway. Because we are one after all, Chaun and Gabe. Known in our circle as Chaun and Beefy Gabe or, more often, just "Chaungabe." It could be my passport, or the innkeeper who greets us individually by our first names, but something about Slovenia has reminded me that I like hearing my name apart from Chaun's.

But here we are, sitting side by side at a table covered by a red and white checkered cloth, the restaurant's only customers besides the old dude obsessed with our order. "The trout," Chaun asks the waitress, "is it whole?" The old dude chuckles as the waitress nods. "I'd like it headless," Chaun continues. More chuckling.

"I'm sorry," the waitress says earnestly, clearly having addressed this question from tourists countless times. "We cannot do this." She stands robust and upright in a white short- sleeved blouse and red apron tight around her waist. Chaun and I wait for an explanation, but none comes. Instead, she stares firmly at her pad, strong fingers keeping a pencil at the ready for a revised order. "Your decision?" she asks without looking up. I'm less bothered by the abruptness than her collective address, as if there were one decision to be made between the two of us.

More chuckling from our one-man audience who holds up two fingers and rattles off something in Slovene. Our waitress inspects us, then replies over her shoulder. Neither Chaun nor I speak the language, but when the man's tone becomes insistent, if not loud, and she shrugs her shoulders, leaving our table, I know what's happened. We're having trout.

"Did that just—" Chaun begins, but he's cut off by the old dude who approaches us with a beer and the helmet that holds his book.

"The Three Meat is good," the old dude says, plopping himself down across from us, "but I've ordered for you the trout." We begin to object, but the man raises a thick-fingered hand and smiles broadly, small gaps between each tooth. "I know. How dare I impose," he continues, puffing up his chest as if to mock his own bravado. "But it is what they are known for. My wife would slap my head for this. But as you see, she's not here."

There is something disarming in his honesty, and anyway, lost or not, it's a perfect day to sit in this covered patio surrounded by trees, a golden oak ceiling gleaming above as if it were the sun itself, though not the sun of the Florida Keys I'd have preferred. Chaun and I look at each other, exchanging silent permission to accept this adventure however it turns out. We've come to Slovenia for our tenth anniversary, five married. Chaun is a photographer and political poet, part of a loose group of Chicago writers called Queer Riot. So of course we've come to the land of the poets. This trip is a prelude to another, more important one. In five weeks, Chaun will visit his aging parents in Calgary. They know nothing about his poetry nor about me, which is why they are making one more try at matchmaking. Apparently, the unsuspecting woman is twenty-seven years old and from a wealthy Hong Kong family just like Chaun's parents were. I've insisted, at last, that at thirty-nine years old, it's time he tells them he's gay and has a husband. He's insisted that if he does, it will leave them childless and him without parents. "You have me," I said. He didn't reply, but the silence sounded like "you're not enough." I'm almost okay with that.

"I'll put some lettuce over the eyes or something," Chaun says about the trout. "I went through an entire childhood staring at fish heads and that was plenty."

"Yes, yes," the man says, clapping his hands together. "You are Chinese. Of course!" "Chinese-American," Chaun says.

The man laughs. "I've been to America many times. I know about your obsession with hyphens. I am Slovene. And you?" He looks me up and down. "I'm guessing you are about five or six hyphens. Typical white American. Yes?"

"He's got you pegged," Chaun laughs.

If typical is graying scruff and a little extra weight, I am indeed pegged. I love Chaun, though he insists I say this too often to him and declare it to too many people. Maybe I do this to remind myself that at first, he was the "hot Asian guy" at the gym my friends got tired of hearing about. I timed my workouts to what I figured were his. I'd enter the floor and look for his amazing shock of black hair and the crisply lined poison ivy tattoo trailing down from the back of his neck and into his tank top. I confessed to him on our fifth date that no matter where I was in my workout, if he finished and hit the showers, I was shortly behind. He rolled his eyes. "That's hardly news," he said. Occasionally he reminds me that was our fourth date, not the fifth, because the first time, he was standing at his car door in the gym parking lot, waiting for me. His hair was still damp, a black swoosh over one eye. We gave each other a chin-led 'sup as I passed, and then I looked back and it was on. He lived just two blocks away. Afterward, we exchanged numbers in case, well, definitely not to get coffee. Turns out you can hook up and get coffee.

"Matic," the man says, introducing himself. "I stop here every time I tour. Even with my wife."

My husband raises a finger. "Chaun, and Mr. Three Meat here is Gabe." Then he looks around. "Where is she? Your wife."

Matic shrugs, and his eyes widen at the sight of our water glasses. "Sparkling? You must have *beer* with trout. *This* trout anyway." He calls inside and gets a response from the waitress.

"Dark or light?" he asks us.

"We're cool," I say, giving Chaun an accusatory glance.

"Bah." Matic isn't having it and once again calls to the kitchen. "You will have half dark, half light." He holds up his near-empty glass. "I drink this in such good weather."

Chaun's not letting go. "You're traveling with your wife, and you don't know where she is?"

"Yes! Right. But I see my error. I believe when I say 'with,' Americans hear 'together.' I mean 'at the same time,' or—" he searches—"'simultaneous'? Yes. 'Simultaneous.'" He explains that he and his wife plan vacations and tours in proximity, but not necessarily with the same itinerary. Today she has ridden her motorcycle to Lake Bled.

"We're thinking about hitting that in a couple days," I say. It's an alpine lake, a brilliant green inset gem guarded by a medieval castle. Practically every brochure and website for Slovenia includes its image.

Chaun raises an eyebrow. "I don't remember that conversation."

"Right. *I* was thinking about it."

Matic sticks his tongue out. "Too many tourists, Gabe. The two of you, look at this." He gestures around us, though for a second, I fall behind because he's said my name. "Today I met you. You met me. We are having the right food. At Bled, they pretend for the tourists. Here I ask the woman to bring you trout, and she does because it's the right thing. You will tell your friends at home about this day. We sit in the cathedral of life." He points behind us at a picture bolted to the sloped ceiling. "And there is our Madonna." She's a black-booted woman astride a vintage motorcycle, clad in a leather bikini top, long black gloves, and a leather biker cap. Brando, double D.

Chaun laughs. Lake Bled has been dismissed. "Don't ever open a restaurant in Boys Town," he says to Matic, who clearly doesn't get the reference. "It's a gay neighborhood in Chicago. We're used to getting what we want."

"You two?" Matic is suddenly aware of the rings on our fingers, and I observe that he isn't wearing one. He nods his head and points to Chaun. "*You*, I understand. Asian men can be inclined this way, and you are very groomed. But this one! Gabe, you could lift my motorcycle."

Chaun's eyes are glazed in shock as he quickly stands. If Matic didn't notice us when we came in, I know he will be surprised by Chaun's height. It's all in his legs. "Did you fucking just say that?" Chaun says. I put my hand on his knee to calm him. He's heard some form of this insult for most of his adult life. He's told me that when he was younger, dating was a mess because every guy that asked him assumed he was a bottom. I did too, though I've never admitted that to him. "I'm going for a smoke," Chaun says. Maybe because his parents are on his mind, he's saving all his energy for that conflict, because it's clear he isn't taking Matic on. "Call me when our food comes out."

Matic places both hands flat on the table as Chaun walks away. "It was this Asian gay comment, wasn't it? I can apologize. I meant nothing by it."

I should be angry for Chaun, but I've never really worried about these assumptions and stereotypes. Fem or Masc. Top or bottom. Sub or Dom. Rice queen. Snow Queen. Whatever. I'm not political that way, but it's what Chaun writes about. He's been challenged far more often on these fronts than I have. He says my dispassion comes from white privilege, and I suppose he's right.

"Matic, that's a sore spot for sure," I muster. "Maybe you should go back to your table before my husband comes back." As I say this, the waitress brings out three beers, but Matic points to his original table where she delivers his glass.

"We were having such a nice time," Matic says.

My empathies in the moment are misplaced, I know it, but Matic sounds genuinely sorry, and I find myself unexpectedly happy with the scenario. One of us has bolted without the other. "It's a sensitive subject," I tell him.

"Of course," Matic says, gathering his helmet and standing. "In my twenties, I was with a man, Albin, for almost two years." His expression tightens as if calling the memory of this former lover forward in his mind. "He wanted me to come out, as you say. It was very difficult. I wasn't gay. I only loved *him*." Matic walks toward his table but turns before he makes it all the way. "The waitress says the trout is taking a little longer because they had to bring it up." He points over the railing, and then it's as if I've just walked in; there's an old dude at the rear of the patio in black leather motorcycle gear staring into a beer and sitting across from his bike helmet. I want to give Chaun the 'all clear,' but his posture across the narrow parking lot suggests that I give him a minute. He's leaning on the front of our rental, arms crossed, cigarette smoke gliding upward past his face.

I feel like an idiot sitting alone in the middle of the patio, so I walk with my beer to the railing. The half-light, half-dark beer is pretty good. There's a mountain stream just behind the restaurant and on the hillside, the terraced trout farm comprised of three rectangular ponds. Above these, six sheep with clotted wool sit beneath the shade of a tree. They are still enough to be statues.

The waitress sweeps behind me and places what looks like a slice of marble rye in front of Matic just as his phone rings. He speaks in Slovene for a few seconds, and then, clearly for my benefit, says loudly, "No, no. The fish is gone. But the cake is here. How is Lake Bled?"

Beyond him is that postcard view of pine forest and towering Alpine mountains pinned against a clear blue sky. I should be awed, but all I can think is, What the hell am I doing here? I could be on the beach in Key West with a rum and Coke, getting a little jealous at all the men and women ogling my shirtless husband, asking each other "What's he doing with *him*?" There are moments when I catch our reflections side by side and wonder the same thing.

That first day when we hooked up after the gym, and after a shower, Chaun surprised me. "I'm going to check out this show before it closes. Go with?" He handed me a one sheet from the Art Institute of Chicago advertising an exhibit on illustrated books of poetry. I didn't know anything about poetry and wasn't into art, but I'd just been fucked by the hottest guy of my life, a guy I'd obsessed over for months, and he was asking me out.

"Cool," I said, looking at the nasty gym clothes I'd put back on. "But . . ."

"It's not prom."

"There won't be dancing?"

Chaun smiled. "Hold on a second," he said, trotting off to the bedroom. When he came back, he was wearing his gym clothes as well. He stood in the door frame, cocked his head, and flung out his arm. "I doubt Miró cares what we wear." I laughed at the gesture and wracked my brain trying to think who the hell Miró was. My education was on.

Ten years later . . . our trout arrives. Chaun has been watching because he returns just as the waitress leaves our table. "Can you believe he said that?" He's still livid, but he keeps his voice down as he sits across from me.

"He feels bad. He had a boyfriend once. A lover, anyway."

Chaun slowly and silently mouths "whoa," offers a surprised expression, but is not ready to relent. "Let's just eat." The plates in front of us are indeed whole trout, fried golden, head to tail. Strangely, Matic ordered French fries for Chaun and a kind of fish salad for me. After the first bite of trout, Chaun and I look at each other. The flavor is so intense and savory that I see in Chaun's eyes it might have the power, if only for seconds, to wipe away homophobia and racism all at once.

"Okay," he says. "I'll give him props for this." Matic is watching, and I nod in appreciation. He gestures with his beer not so much in reply as in directing me to drink mine along with the fish. I comply, and if it's possible, the trout bursts with even more flavor.

"I think you should give our friend a chance to apologize."

"For saying out loud the things he actually thinks?"

"For saying out loud what he assumed *everyone* thinks." I stab my fork into one of Chaun's fries and slowly bring it to my mouth. "He *did* have a boyfriend," I quietly repeat before filling my mouth.

"Hard to believe," Chaun whispers.

"That's what he says."

"And Asian I suppose?" Chaun looks past me. Matic is texting, glasses propped on his forehead. "He's married." "*We're* married." "Not to women."

Chaun startles me, not even allowing a beat. "Hey, man," he calls. "That was bullshit what you said, but we're on vacation and I'm not going to spoil it by holding a grudge."

Matic smiles. "You're practically quoting our poet Tomaž Šalamun. He used to tell me I was full of shit all the time. And my wife. She says this too. You are in good company." He raises his nearly empty glass and speaks in Slovenian. "This is a saying that means something like even a fool can learn from his mistakes. I'm sorry for my offense."

"Okay," Chaun says. And for the record, I almost say, there wouldn't be so many people in China if the men were 'inclined that way.' But I rein it in. I want to call Chaun out for insinuating that gay men don't procreate, but an apology has been offered and accepted; the fish is good, the beer is good, so I let it go. And anyway, Chaun isn't done. "You mentioned Šalamun. I love his work. You knew him?"

"Tomaž? Of course. We set this world right many evenings."

I have no idea who these two are talking about, but I hear in Chaun's voice that the fire is out, though I've known him long enough he may be keeping an ember in storage. "*Poker*. I loved that book."

Matic laughs and, in a flash, he's back at the table next to us and calling out for another beer. "That was young Šalamun! Americans always mention this book. It's perhaps a bit loose for my taste. But the energy is there." The waitress sets a beer in front of each of us even though Chaun and I are barely halfway through our first. "I guess you are a poet then," Matic says. "Only a poet would know that book. And academics."

"I'd like to think I'm a poet," Chaun says. "I've published. But I pay the bills as a photographer."

Matic doesn't ask, but I offer anyway that I'm an executive director of a homeless shelter nonprofit, though not for much longer. I like to tell people about my job because it makes me sound like I'm a better person than I am. After all, I draw a salary, and it isn't my life's work.

Chaun knows this about me now, but early on, I wasn't quite so forthcoming about my ambivalence. There was a day when we planned to go to the dog park on Lake Michigan but I needed to stop by one of my shelters in Lincoln Park first. "Even on Saturdays?" Chaun asked. "Especially on Saturdays," I replied. He was impressed with my dedication to the homeless. I wasn't noble, and I didn't mention staff had been warned about being a little substance-groggy on weekend mornings. Then again, he failed to mention in those first few months that he was having sex with four other guys. I suppose I won.

Chaun is well into his trout as Matic holds forth on Slovenian poetry. He has a favorite, Kosovel somebody, and he mentions the godfather of poetry in this country, Prešeren. He takes a gulp of beer and looks to the ceiling. "And you must very much read Iztok Osojnik. This one is still alive. I think in Ljubljana." That is our anchor city while we're on this trip, which is why the mention of Prešeren comes as no surprise to me. There's a massive statue of him looming over the main square. In fact, we have seen no statues of generals or political leaders. Only poets.

Chaun types this information into his phone, asking for spelling. I say, "You know a lot about poetry."

"Of course. I'm Slovene."

"And your wife?"

"Maja? Does she know poetry? Yes, but this is a complicated question because she prefers women poets, which I respect, but this hasn't been the tradition. It has improved, but Maja likes your Elizabeth Bishop and—" He again searches the ceiling for words. "Castillo. Ana Castillo?"

Chaun looks impressed. "She's from Chicago."

"So," Matic says, pinching at his chin. "I am meeting an American poet and forgiving citizen. You are meeting a mountain guide." He corrects himself with a raised finger. "Former. And excuse me now for asking. Please tell me if this is a wrong question. A stereotype."

We're bracing.

"You two are what? 40. You're young. Slovenia is not exactly known as the destination for gays. I mean, Ljubljana has a pride parade, but you could fit in maybe two buses the number of people who walk."

I jump in. "This is Chaun's idea. I wanted Florida."

"And? Why aren't you there by yourself instead of here together? You're married, not shackled."

"Because I only get a couple weeks a year."

Matic shakes his head and laughs dubiously. "Tell me, boys. I assume you live in the same house. How many hours a day do you spend together?"

"Too many," Chaun says, smiling broadly.

"Maybe seven or eight. More on the weekends. A lot more."

"And the two weeks you have a year for vacation you want to spend even more time together? How do you make yourself new and interesting if you always experience the same things?"

Chaun nods at the proposal but now wears a skeptical expression, giving it full exposure by raking his hair away from his face. Using a thick fry as a pointer, he softly jabs toward Matic. "Who says new and interesting is the goal? What about comfortable?" This from the Queer Riot poet.

"Bah! Tonight, Maja and I will meet up at home, and I will tell her about you two and how I was offensive and friendly. And she will tell me that I don't learn. She will tell me about Lake Bled and probably some lost tourist she gave unwanted help to, and I will tell her she doesn't learn. We will have a drink, and it will be a good night. If it's a very good night, well." He winks. "We could not tell these stories if we are always together."

This strikes me both as a pernicious sentiment and something that makes entire sense. What if it were Chaun here alone at a trout restaurant with Matic, and I was thousands of miles away in Florida, I don't know, chatting with some similarly old dude ordering me drinks? What if we had stories to tell each other when we got back to Chicago? The waitress comes out and asks to remove the Jurassic mess of our plates, but we are still picking. Matic thanks her in English and adds something in Slovene.

"No more beer," I say.

He waves me off. "Of course not. You will be surprised." He stands and lifts his glasses to his forehead as if for the first time truly putting us in focus. "My new friends. I must be in Ljubljana tonight. It is fair to say that I have harmed and delighted you. Welcome to Slovenia!" We watch as he clomps out to his sparkling, blue-tanked motorcycle, slips on his helmet, and saddles up. Just before roaring off, he offers a two-finger "so long," which we return.

Chaun and I sit looking at each other, listening to the motorcycle trail off, but not saying anything. There is nothing remarkable about the brown of Chaun's eyes, yet, his black eyebrows and lashes, the whites, all seem set perfectly as if for a masquerade ball. We have been together a long time. Longer than I ever thought possible when I was teenager. Even in my early twenties. My parents have been married nearly fifty years, and Chaun's almost as long. We are supposed to become them. Isn't that what we fought for? In weeks I'll be out of a job, and Chaun may be disowned. The Queer Riot poet and his stay-at-home husband.

The waitress comes out to take our plates. "Matic," she volunteers, "he comes twice, maybe three times a season. But he usually stays at his table with a book. He likes you, I guess." I subtly elbow Chaun and check our waitress for insinuation, but she is all about clearing the table. "Have you ever met his wife?" I ask.

"Only a few times." She chuckles, hands full. "She tells *him* to order trout. But they laugh a lot and stay long. Once, two dinners." She turns, loaded down, and as she walks away, tosses back, "He's ordered for you our potica."

Chaun shakes his head, smiling begrudgingly. "Land of poetry," he says, and then, after a pause, "You might have stuck up for me when our friend was saying that racist, homophobic horseshit."

"I'm not sure about the homophobia." Chaun is incredulous, lifting a flat palm to my face. "And besides, if I intervened I'd just be confirming his stereotype that I'm the top in our marriage."

"Weak," Chaun says. "'So much that is weak has survived and lives out its long wondrous days with only the least of annoyance.' That's Greg Kuzma."

"Now that we've established I'm weak," I say as the waitress approaches with whatever Matic ordered for us, "I hope you feel better." We are not at an impasse. By the time we get back in the car, we will be talking about Matic and trout and our next destination, and we will know exactly what the other one is about to say because we do everything together. And at the right moment, maybe I'll slip in that I'm taking a trip, alone, to the Florida Keys. And that I want Chaun to go somewhere fabulous so that I can hear all about it.

"This is potica. Cake. Our version." The waitress sets two large brown and white swirled slices in front of us, the same stuff I thought was marble rye. Chaun asks for the check and makes a signature gesture with his right hand. "Americans always do this," the waitress says, half rolling her eyes. "Anyway, your check"—and here she mimics Chaun's gesture with a smile—"is paid."

After the waitress walks away, Chaun says, "This has been one fucking weird day. Wait 'til we tell Chuck and Shara."

"For sure," I say. "Exactly."

Chaun cuts into the potica with his fork and raises the piece as if to toast. "Shall we?" "I'm full," I say, which is absolutely not true. "And don't tempt me. Tell me about it later?"

Not eating cake might be the best part of the day, I decide. In front of us are the dozen or so rectangles of red and white checkered tablecloths and beyond that, the pine-filled pass and jagged silhouettes of gray mountains in the distance, the kind of view one wants to spend a long time describing to someone who's never been here.

THE MOON OVER WAPAKONETA

MICHAEL MARTONE

1.

There is the moon, full, over Wapakoneta, Ohio. Everybody I know has a sister or a brother, a cousin or an uncle living up there now. The moon is studded green in splotches, spots where the new atmospheres have stuck, mold on a marble.

2.

I'm drunk. I'm always drunk. Sitting in the dust of a field outside Wapakoneta, Ohio, I look up at the moon. The moon, obscured for a moment by a passing flock of migratory satellites flowing south in a dense black stream, has a halo pasted behind it. That meant something once, didn't it?

3.

When the moon is like it is now, hanging over Ohio, I come over to Wapakoneta from Indiana where I am from. I am legal in Ohio, and the near beer they can sell to minors is so near to the real thing it is the real thing. I told you I was drunk. The foam head of this beer glows white in the dull light like the white rubble of the moon bearing down from above. Over there, somewhere, is Indiana, a stone's throw away.

4.

Everybody I know has a brother or cousin or whoever on the moon, and I am using this pilsner for a telescope. Where is everybody? The old craters are percolating. They've been busy as bees up there. Every night a new green explosion, another detonation of air. This is where I make myself belch.

5.

The reflection of the moon over Wapakoneta sinks into each flat black solar panel of this field where I sit, a stone swallowed by a pond. In the fields, the collectors pivot slowly, tracking even the paler light of the moon across the black sky. There's this buzz. Cicada? Crickets? No. Voltage chirps, generated as the moon's weak light licks the sheets of glass.

6.

Let's power up my personal downlink. Where am I?—I ask by nudging the ergonomic toggle. Above me, but beneath the moon over Ohio, a satellite, then, perhaps, another peels away from its flock to answer my call. Let's leave it on. More satellites will cock their heads above my head, triangulating till the cows come home. But soft, the first report is in. Ohio, the dots spell out, Wapakoneta.

7.

What part of the moon is the backwater part? Maybe there, that green expanse inches from the edge where they are doing battle with the airless void generating atmosphere from some wrangling of biomass. Yeah, back there under the swirl of those new clouds, some kid after a hard day of—what?—making cheese, lies on his back and has a smoke consuming a mole of precious oxygen. He looks up at the earth through the whiffs of cloud and smoke and imagines some Podunk place where the slack-jawed inhabitants can't begin to imagine being pioneers, being heroes. There it is, Ohio.

8.

A pod of jalopies takes off from the pad of Mr. Entertainer's parking lot, racing back to Indiana where it's an hour earlier. The road is lined with Styrofoam crosses, white in the moonlight, and plastic flowers oxidized by the sunlight. X marks the spot where some hopped-up Hoosier goes airborne for a sec and then in a stupor remembers gravity and noses over into the ditch next to a field outside of Wapakoneta on the trailing edge of Ohio.

9.

They are launching their own satellites from the moon; a couple of dozen a day the paper says. Cheap in the negative gees. Gee. I look hard at the moon. I want to see the moons of the moon. The moon and its moons mooning me. In Ohio, I pull my pants down and moon the moon and its moons mooning me back. And then, I piss. I piss on the ground, my piss falling, falling to earth, falling to the earth lit up by the moon, my piss falling at the speed of light to the ground.

10.

I am on the move. I am moving. Drawn by the gravitational pull of Mr. Entertainer with its rings of neon, I am steering a course by the stars. Better check in. More of the little buzz bombs have taken up station above my head. Surprise! I am in Wapakoneta. I am in Wapakoneta, but I am moving. I am moving within the limits of Wapakoneta. I like to make all the numbers dance, the dots on the screen rearranging. X, Y, and Z, each axis scrolling, like snow in a snow dome. The solar panels in the field around me slowly track the moon as it moves through the night sky.

11.

Over there in Indiana, it's an hour earlier. Don't ask me why. You cross a road, State Line Road, and you step back in time. It can be done. Heading home, I get this gift, an extra hour to waste. But wait! I lost one someplace coming here. I shed it when I crossed the street, like sloughing skin. It must be somewhere, here at my feet. This pebble I nudge with my toe. Just what time is it? I consult my other wrist where the watch burbles, all its dials spinning, glowing softly, little moon. The laser beam it emits ricochets off my belt buckle, noses up to find its own string of satellites, bouncing around a bit, kicking the can, homing for home, an atomic clock on a mountaintop out west to check in on each millisecond of the passing parade, then, in a blink, it finds its way back to me here, makes a little beep. Beep! Here's the report: Closing Time.

12.

Mr. Entertainer is not very entertaining. It's powering down before my eyes, each neon sign flickers, sputters in each dark window. The whole advertised universe collapsing in on the extinguished constellation of letters. How the hell did that happen? I had my eye on things, and the moon over Wapakoneta hasn't moved as far as I can tell. The rubble of the bar is illuminated now by that soft indifferent dusty light diffused through the dust kicked up by the departed cars. The slabs of its walls fall into blue shadow; its edges, then, drift into a nebulous fuzz, a cloud floating just above the ground.

13.

What time is it on the moon? It's noon there now. It's noon on the moon. From the stoop of the extinct bar, I consider the moon's midday that lasts for days, lunch everlasting, amen. They must get drunk on the light. They must drink it up. They must have plenty to spare. The excess is spilling on me, pouring on me down here in Ohio, enough light for me, a heavenly body, to cast a shadow on the studded gravel galaxy of the empty parking lot, a kind of timepiece myself, the armature of an impromptu moon dial, the time ticking off as my celestial outline creeps from one cold stone to the next.

14.

Cars on the road are racing back to Indiana. I hear them dribbling the sound of their horns in front of them, leaking a smear of radio static in the exhaust. I am looking for my clunker. It's around here someplace. According to my uplink, I am still in Wapakoneta. A slow night for the satellites, they have been lining up to affirm that consensus, a baker's dozen have been cooking up coordinates. I punch a button on my car key releasing the ultrasonic hounds hot on the magnetic signature of my piece of shit. The nearby solar panels pivot toward me, sensing the valence of my reflection, hungering for the light I am emitting. Hark! Somewhere in the vast relative dark, the yodel of a treed automobile. I must calculate the vectors for my approach.

15.

Later, in Indiana, which is now earlier, I will remember back to this time, this time that is happening now, as I navigate by means of sonic boom to the bleat of my Mother Ship supposedly fastened to the edge of some solar panel field out there somewhere in the dark. But the sound is reverberating, gone doppler, bouncing off the copse of antennae to the right, the bank of blooming TV dishes to the left. The night air has become acoustic, dampening the reports. I am getting mixed signals, and it seems my car is moving around me. That may be the case. Perhaps I left it in autopilot. It's nosing toward home this very minute, sniffing the buried wire, or perhaps it's just playing games with me, its own guidance system on some feedback loop as it orbits under the influence of an ancient cruising pattern programmed long ago for the high school drag in Fort Wayne. My guardian satellites, whispering to each other, hover above my head, shaking theirs, "Lost, poor soul, in Ohio, in the holy city of Wapakoneta."

16.

Everybody I know has a sister or a brother, a mom or a dad setting up house-keeping in some low-rent crater of the moon. I intercept postcards—low-gain transmissions of the half of earth in the black sky and a digital tweet weeping "Wish You Were Here!"—when I eavesdrop on the neighborhood's mail. On nights like this, with the moon radiating a whole spectrum of sunny missives, I want to broadcast a wide band of my own billet-doux banged out with a stick on any handy piece of corrugated steel in the ancient language of killing time.

17.

I fall into the ditch or what I think is the ditch. Flat on my back, I stare up at the moon, canvas, sailing above this pleasant seat, my bishopric, and find myself thinking of my kith and kin again and again. The starlight scope is in the car. I hear its honk still, a goose somewhere in the marsh night asking the tower for permission to land. If I had the goggles now, I could see where I've landed but would, more likely, be blinded by this moonlight boosted by the sensitive optics. Night would be day, and the moon over Wapakoneta would be more like the sun over Wapakoneta. I might see some real sun soon if I just close my unaided eyes for a bit and let the whole Ptolemaic contraption overhead wheel and deal.

18.

But the watch I wear is still turned on and on the lookout for pulses of light angling back this way from the fibrillating isotopes atop Pikes Peak. The watch's microprinted works synthesize a "bleep" a second, a steady erosion to my will to doze. At the top of each hour, it drops a drip, and this absence more than the regular tolling pricks me to a semiconducted alertness. The solar panels at the lip of the ditch chirp their chirp, Wapakoneta's moon, a dilated pupil centered in each dark iris. And there's the car's snarled sound still hoping to be found. So much for silent night, holy night. Lo, a rocket off yonder rips the raw cloth of night.

19.

At that moment I open my eyes, and in the ditch with me is the big ol' moon its ownself half buried in the mud. Hold on there! There is the moon, the moon over Wapakoneta. It's there up above, where it should be. It's there over this other moon mired in the mud of Wapakoneta. My eyes adjust to the light. O! I'm not in the ditch but on the berm below the old moon museum, the building's geodesic concrete dome, teed up on a dimple in a hummock in Ohio, mocking the moon overhead. The real moon rises above the arching horizon of this fallen fake.

20.

Armstrong hailed from these Wapakonetish parts. Got drunk here on near beer, I suppose. Contemplated the strobing codes of lightning bugs down by the river. The river caught the moon's pale and silent reflection. Pitched a little woo too. Looked up at the moon, very same moon I spy with my little eye. First guy to go there. Got a pile of rocks marking the spot there. I've seen pictures. "Wish you were here!" Down here, they keep the moon rocks he brought back under glass in the hollowed-out moon building before me. The school kids, on field trips, herd by the cases of rocks. The little rocks. The big rocks. Big deal! The kids have got a brother or sister, uncles and aunts, sweeping the dust together into neat piles upstairs. Here's to the first man on the moon from the last person on earth.

21.

The earth is slowing down. Friction as it twirls. When the moon untucks the oceans, makes the tides bulge, it's like holding your hand out the car window as you race toward Indiana, a drag against the cool night air, skidding to a halt. Long time coming. Every once in awhile, they throw in a leap second or two to bring the world back up to speed. Another cipher of silence at the top of the hour to keep the whole thing in tune. One day the earth will creep to a crawl, and one side will always be facing the face of the moon always facing me. A slow spinning dance around the sun. My watch skips a beat. The silence stretches on and on.

22.

At twelve o'clock high, a huge flock of satellites float in formation, veiling the moon. They are migrating north. The swallows returning to Capistrano. A new season? Reconnoitering to be done by morning? Who knows. My own orbiting dovecot coos to me still, homing, homing. You are in Ohio, in Wapakoneta, in Ohio. I release them just like that. The blank LED goes white in the moonlight. They disperse, disappear, kids playing hide and seek in the dark.

23.

At my feet are rocks painted blue by the moon's light. I pick one up out of the dust and launch it into space at the moon hanging over Ohio. I lose sight of it, swallowed up in the intense glare I am aiming at. Sure thing! I've chucked it beyond the bounds of earth. It's slipped into space on the grease of its own inertia. But I hear its reentry, splashing into the ocean of solar panels yards away, the light we've all been staring at turning solid. I heave another sputnik into orbit, hoping to even up the gross mass of the planets, which is all out of whack in this binary system. I'm a run-of-the-mill vandal, my slight buzz waning. But soft! A frog jumps into a pond. It makes that sound a frog makes when it jumps into a pond.

24.

Didn't I tell you? It is an hour earlier in Indiana. The moon over Wapakoneta is gaining on me here as I race along the section roads toward home, all of its imaginable phases caught by the thousands and thousands of black reflections in their tropic glass panels. The moon waxes on all the mirrored surfaces, silent, a skipping stone skipping. Yes, I'll catch it tonight as it sets, embrace it, a burned-out pebble, in my empty backyard.

GLOSSOLALIA

KYLE MINOR

"ARE YOU INTERESTED IN ME BECAUSE I'm a girl or because I love Jesus?"

"I am interested in you because I like you."

"But if I didn't love Jesus, would you still be interested in me?"

"I would like to think I would be interested in you no matter what."

"But if I didn't love Jesus, I don't think I would be the same person."

"If you didn't love Jesus, I think in some ways you would be the same person."

"But I wouldn't see the world the same way; I wouldn't read the same things; I wouldn't make the same choices; I wouldn't be around the same people."

"But I think you would still like a lot of the same things. You would still be a ski instructor in the winter. You would still spend the summer here on the beach. You would still run. You would still bodysurf. You would still be physically very beautiful. You still would be a person who cares about other people, and you still, probably, would have taught me to bodyboard."

"But I used to be a person who didn't love Jesus. I used to make different choices. Like when I was a freshman in college, there was this older guy, and he used to come into my room and sleep in my bed, and he knew how to do things with his hands and his mouth. He knew how to make me feel things."

"You didn't have sex with him even though you didn't yet love Jesus."

"I didn't have sex with him because I had an idea of Jesus, but I didn't yet really know Jesus. I thought I did, but I didn't."

"But you prayed to Jesus, didn't you?"

"I did pray to Jesus, but not in tongues."

"When did you start to pray in tongues?"

"When I was filled up with the Holy Spirit."

"Is that when you stopped messing around with this guy?"

"No. It was later. There were other guys. In Madrid, this one guy took me to an R.E.M. concert."

"Did it make you feel dirty to mess around with him?"

"No. It made me feel good. But I still felt empty inside."

"How did you learn how to pray in tongues?"

"I prayed to be filled up with the Holy Spirit, and then I was given the gift."

"Can you do it on command?"

"I can do it anytime, if that's what you mean."

"Can I hear you do it?"

"Would you like to pray with me?"

"Will you do it if I pray with you?"

"When I pray, I do it. It comes naturally."

"How do you know what it is you are saying if you are speaking a language you don't know?"

"I don't know what I am saying. It is my spirit that knows what I am saying. My spirit is communing directly with God's spirit. I can't explain it, but I can feel it, like this energy pulsing through me."

"If I held your hand, could I feel the energy too?"

"I feel like you are being glib."

"I am not being glib. I just feel like this is something I don't understand, but I really do want to understand. I want to be a person who is open-minded to new experiences."

"Take my hand. Here. Take my other hand. Let's pray."

—⁑—

"What did you think just now, when I was speaking in tongues?"

"I thought a lot of the sounds were repeated and there were a lot of consonant clusters. I heard maybe some sounds that sounded like German and some sounds that sounded like Hebrew or Arabic maybe. There were also a lot of sounds that you don't make when you speak in English, like rolling your Rs and flattening out your O sounds."

"That's true. I have noticed those things too."

"Do you ever try to think about recording what you say when you say it? Like, maybe you could do some code-breaking and make a dictionary."

"Again, I feel like maybe you are being glib."

"Hear me out. I'm being serious. The idea is you are speaking a language that people don't speak on earth, except people who speak the language of angels. So consequently, if you follow the logic, it's a real language. So wouldn't it have the things a real language has, like grammar and syntax and vocabulary? And if that's so, couldn't you study it just like you could study any other language?"

"That's movie stuff. That's like something starring Patricia Arquette."

"Why not, though? There's people who do this for a living. They go over to Papua New Guinea or wherever, and they spend time around a language, and then they reconstruct it, even though when they first get there, they don't know the first thing about it."

"That's missing the whole point."

"Why?"

"Because if you knew the language, then the purity of the communication would be lost. You'd start crafting all the words instead of the spirit that indwells in you crafting the words.

"But—and here I'm not being glib, I'm just trying to understand—don't you want to know what it is you are speaking to Jesus or the angels or whatever?"

"You don't pray to angels."

"But it's an angel language, right?"

"The idea is that you're not in control. You're giving yourself over to it."

"Is that why you jerk your body to the left when you pray in tongues?"

"That's a manifestation."

"Why do you do it?"

"I don't do it. It comes over me when I give myself over to the Spirit."

"Does it happen to everyone who speaks in tongues?"

"Some people fall down like they are dead."

"That's slain in the Spirit."

"Right. Some people fall into fits of laughter. Some people bark like dogs, but not too many people. I don't want to judge, but I think sometimes when that happens a lot of it can be for show. But I don't know."

"That's something that worries me. It's a little bit frightening, don't you think, like on TV, when a lot of people are doing it all around, and there's this ungodly cacophony?"

"That's the fear of the Lord you're feeling."

"How can you be sure?"

"How can you be sure of anything? You know. I know. I know that I know that I know."

"Here, this stuff is at odds with logic, maybe, I think."

"I think that's a wrong way to think about it, but tell me what you're thinking."

"I took this philosophy class. Dr. Willard Reed. He was talking about the distinction between belief and knowledge. He said knowledge is problematic. You can't really know stuff that isn't somehow verifiable. Like you didn't see it with your own eyes or experience it yourself or there hasn't been some kind of consensus among the people who study the thing. And even then, there's problems. How do you know you aren't fooling yourself? Or how do you know the consensus might not be wrong? Like the consensus used to be that the earth was flat. And on top of that, how do you know that the universe didn't just begin two seconds ago? After a while, everything starts to be belief."

"I don't guess it matters much which is which, then, if it's all so slippery."

"I don't guess it does."

"But what kind of way is that to live? Walking around not being sure of anything. Everything tentative. No place for boldness. No place for meaning. Wouldn't that just throw you into some kind of paralytic feedback loop or something? Wouldn't you just be staring at your navel forever?"

"Not necessarily, but I don't know. You just described a lot of the way I think a lot of the time."

"That's why you have to let go control. That's what praying in the Spirit is. You're letting go of that control and giving yourself over to your creator. It's an act of faith in the unseen. Although, I have to tell you, there are things I have seen."

"What kinds of things?"

"Visions. Gold dust."

"Gold dust?"

"There have been meetings where the Spirit of God has come down, and the manifestation was gold dust that began to appear on everyone's shoulders."

"Manifestations, like the jerking to the left."

"I'm not going to say anymore if you're going to mock everything."

"Honestly, I'm not mocking. I really want to know. Tell me about the visions."

"Once I was praying in the Spirit, and I had a vision of a golden vessel."

"Like a ship?"

"Like a vase or a container. It was on a cloth of purple silk. There was an angel there, and he was holding out his hands."

"What did the vision mean?"

"For a long time, I didn't know what the vision meant. But then my friend who is a prophetess—quietly, quietly a prophetess, like, literally, hardly anybody knows—said it was a message about being a vessel for the Spirit, and about a royal calling, but I had to give myself to it."

"That's why you write the magazine articles?"

"That's why I'm writing the books. That's why I'm traveling around so much. To speak into people's hearts and lives."

"But you like it too. You're good at it. You don't want to work at a desk job."

"That's true. I don't want to be chained to a desk. I was made this way for a reason."

"Any other visions?"

"Yes."

"Tell me."

"Another time. Later."

"All right. It's a lot to risk, right? Telling me all these things?"

"It's nothing to risk. I already have given myself over to all of it."

"I can wait. I want to get to know you."

"Would you hold me now?"

"Yes."

"Don't come over here inside my blanket. You stay inside your blanket and I'll stay inside my blanket, and you can hold me that way, with the separate blankets."

—⁂—

"Do you like it here?"

"I'm uncomfortable here."

"Why?"

"I don't like the cold, and I don't like all the soldiers in their uniforms, and I don't like all the military songs. I think I might be a pacifist. But these are the men and women who give their lives to keep us free."

"I like watching the football game, and I don't mind cheering for Air Force, but I am uncomfortable with the whole martial atmosphere. It seems to me to have a lot to do with death and killing."

"But sacrificial death and killing, don't you think? Not death or killing that anyone wants to do."

"I don't know if that's true. That's what basic training is for, I think. To break down the part of a person's conscience where they have this inhibition against killing, so they can want to kill, so they can kill at will, to save their lives or save their buddy or fulfill their mission."

"I think that's a selfish way to think about it. Because it's because of these guys and gals here that you have the freedom to say something like that."

"I can't deny it. I know that's true. That complicates the way I feel about it."

"You are shivering. Here, let's combine our blankets."

"Can we put them under our legs, too, because these bleachers are so cold?"

"You know, if you moved out here with me, I wonder if you could take the cold all winter, if this is what it does to you."

"Are you really here for good? I mean, you were in Florida, and now you're here, and you've been back and forth. But maybe you would just end up back in Florida."

"I don't want to be anchored anyplace. I want to be free to move around. But I like cold places. I wouldn't mind moving to Alaska. My aunt has a hotel in Alaska. I like the idea of spending some time there with her, helping her run it for a while."

"What if you—even we—had children? Wouldn't you want to stay put for a while, for the sake of stability?"

"I don't want to have children ever. I mean, I love children. I think I would be an okay mother. But the things I'm meant to do with my life would, I think, make it very difficult to have children."

"I didn't know this about you, that you wouldn't want children. It surprises me."

"This is why it's good, I think, you came out here. We need to sort these things out. We need to find out if we love each other."

"I feel like you're holding some things back."

"That's true, but here we are, and I want to watch this football game since I paid forty bucks each for the tickets."

—⚏—

"Is it okay with you if I put my hand on your knee while I drive?"

"Yes. I'm very happy that you put your hand on my knee."

"It's interesting, you know. Whenever I relate to you in a physical way, you respond very positively. But whenever I relate to you in a spiritual way, it gets complicated, and I don't know how to read you, exactly."

"I feel like in some ways they are different issues."

"I don't think they are in any way separable."

"I feel like the physical expressions of love are very important, and they mean something."

"I don't disagree. That's why I won't let you kiss me."

"But it's strange. You will let me do other things that seem to me to be more intimate than kissing is."

"I feel like if you and me were kissing, I would be giving myself over to you in a way that I'm not ready to do."

"Why is that?"

"Because I think that spiritually we are in very different places. I think you're open to spiritual things, but I don't think that you are really very far along. And I can't tell if you are open to them because you really desire them or if you are just open to them because you want to be closer to me."

"That's a fair question to raise. I don't know either sometimes. There's a lot of things going on very quickly, and it can be confusing to me."

"Also, I don't know if I love you."

"Do you think love is some kind of lightning flash? Like it strikes you and then the reverberations just ring out forever?"

"That's how love is with God, I think. And I think that's one thing you haven't really entered into the fullness of."

"I think that maybe love is a choice people make."

"That's not very romantic."

"I don't know what good romance is sometimes. I mean, it's good to be romantic, and it's good to have feelings. But I've had feelings for people before, and they've had feelings for me, but what was lacking, I think, was a choice to make a life together. A commitment."

"It's very scary to me to hear you speak that way. Because it seems very mechanical to me. It seems in keeping with many of the things that seem cold about you, to me. Everything seems so reasoned, so calculated. It makes me think that everything about the way you approach me must be some kind of calculation."

"If that were true, though, wouldn't I just tell you everything you wanted to hear all the time? It seems to me evidence of good faith that we have these kinds of conversations all the time, and that we have these, for lack of a better word, arguments or disagreements."

"I don't enjoy arguing or disagreeing."

"Me either."

"I'm just going to keep my hand on your leg here, except when I have to shift gears, until we get up to the top of the mountain, okay? I just want to enjoy the ride and enjoy you and enjoy this kind of closeness while we look at the mountains and enjoy the creation and all its wonder. It's not a slight to you. It's just something I need right now, if it's all right with you. But I want to keep my hand on your leg, okay?"

"Of course. I love that you have your hand on my leg. It is really nice."

—⋘—

"That right there is called Witch's Titty."

"Why?"

"Because look at it. It looks like a Witch's Titty."

"Yeah. I guess it does.

"You know what I think whenever I pass this place?"

"Tell me."

"There was this dance in high school, and there was this boy, let's call him Bob; he asked me to this dance. He was a senior, and I was a freshman. I got all dressed up, and he got me a corsage. When you go with a senior and you're a freshman, it's exciting, you know, because he picked you. You're the one he picked, and he passed over older girls to pick you. And before I left, my dad told him he could keep me out until midnight but no later. And he kissed me on the cheek, my dad, and he said I love you and we trust you, me and your mother. So we went to this dance, and it was all right. There was music, there was food, there was dancing. And afterward, I wanted this guy, Bob, to kiss me. It was something I really wanted. I had built it up big time in my mind. He drove me out to this park I'm going to take you to later, out by the ski lifts. It was the place where all the kids went to sit in their cars and make out. We had to drive past Witch's Titty to get there. And I knew that was why we were going to this park, and it was okay with me. But when we got there, this guy, Bob, he started acting really nervous. He was staring straight ahead, and he started sweating at his forehead. I felt sorry for him because I could tell he was very nervous. Then he said, like he was apologizing, 'This is just something I really have to do.' And he leaned toward me, and I thought he was going to kiss me. But then he put his hands up my dress. I wanted to say no to him, but I was so surprised I guess my voice caught in my throat. And then I put my hand down there to push his hand away, and he grabbed my wrist and held it so hard it bruised a ring around my wrist where he was holding it. Then he put his hand in my panties, and he stuck his finger up inside me and poked around. It didn't hurt. It didn't feel good, either, but it didn't hurt. Then he just held his finger in there like that for a while and moved it around. Then he drove me home."

"What did you do?"

"I didn't do anything. I went inside and went to bed and stared at the ceiling for a long time. It wasn't until a lot later that I cried."

"So nothing happened to him?"

"He's still around. We became friends again later. I forgave him."

"I don't forgive him."

"You don't have to. But that's something you'll have to work on. Unforgiveness. Like the things you sometimes say about your mother."

"I just feel protective of you. I don't like it that for him there were no consequences."

"You carry the consequences around inside yourself, don't you?"

"Me or him?"

"Something about you reminds me of him sometimes."

"That makes me feel terrible that you would say that."

"I just think there's things you should know about me if we are really going to think about being together."

"Is that what we're doing?"

"It's just something I thought of because we were driving by Witch's Titty. That's all."

—⚇—

"When a long time passes like this and you're so quiet, I wonder what you're thinking."

"Do you think you have the right to know what I'm thinking?"

"I had a girlfriend in college one time who used to say things like that. She used to say, 'You know what I like about my thoughts? They're mine. I don't have to share them with you.'"

"Did she say that after you were prying at her to give up her thoughts?"

"Usually, yes."

"All right. What do you want to know?"

"So many things."

"You choose one thing. Any one thing. I'll tell you."

"One thing. Okay, the visions. You told me one time you would tell me more about the visions."

"You see this here?"

"What? The road? The mountains? The sky?"

"The motion, through space. Through time too. Once I was driving this road, and I had a vision of motion through space and through time."

"While you were driving?"

"I saw all of creation as though it were a liquid, and we were swimming through it. Me, and all the creatures, land creatures and water creatures too. The water was a deep blue, sparkling, but also translucent. You could see through it. And the rock faces were shimmering like precious jewels."

"Was this a distraction while you were driving?"

"It was almost as if I were no longer driving anymore. I had given up control and although in the physical world my hands were on the wheel, and even though in the vision I was moving through a space not unlike the one we are moving through right now, and even though I had given up control, and even though there was that drop-off there just out your window, a couple thousand feet, maybe, I wasn't afraid. What I was mostly was in awe."

"Was it like you imagined seeing these things, or was it like you actually were moving through these things."

"It was physically real. I could even smell the perfume of it."

"What did it smell like?"

"There was a sweetness to it. There was a honey and almond quality to it."

"Was the car moving through it too?"

"The car went away. It was just my body being carried forward on the current of it."

"Sometimes when you talk about these things, I want to believe you, and I want to understand, because I do believe you, but it is very hard to believe you, and it is very hard to try to know how to understand."

"Because you aren't yet seeing with the eyes of the Spirit."

"Because I haven't had experiences like this, and I've never known anyone else who has. There is a certain light that gets in your eyes when you talk about them, and it is a little bit frightening to me."

"That's something you have to let go of."

"Maybe so, but I don't know how."

"You do it by doing it."

"That's easy to say, but if it were easy to do, wouldn't many other people do it? If nothing else, to speak the tongues of angels and harvest the gold dust and sell it at market rate?"

"When you speak of it that way, it makes me angry."

"I don't mean to make you angry, and I am not making fun. I like you and possibly want to love you. I'm just trying to look at what you're saying from all different directions and turn it over in my mind that way."

"That's not letting go. That's holding onto control."

"I don't know what to say."

"Maybe it would be better not to say anything else for a while."

"Okay. All right. Okay."

—◦—

"Rise and shine."

"I'm so tired."

"It's morning."

"It's dark."

"The idea is to hit the slopes early."

"Really, I'm wiped. I'm sorry."

"I'm turning on the light."

"Please don't. Really. I don't know if it's the altitude or the nonstop going or just maybe general emotional exhaustion. I'm not trying to bail out on you. I'm still willing to ski. But my body doesn't want to get up so early right now, and I feel like I should listen to it so I don't get sick."

"It smells like sickness in here. Your breath has a sinus quality to it."

"That's what I'm talking about."

"The only way out is through. Please, get up. Let's ski."

"You know people there. Why don't you go on without me, and let me catch up with you this afternoon."

"Really?"

"Please understand."

"Really? This is really the choice you are making?"

"Please?"

—◊—

"There are many ways in which I feel more like your mother than like a person with whom you might be falling in love."

"This is because I didn't go skiing this morning."

"It's so many things. You are, I have come to believe, a fundamentally passive person."

"What do you mean?"

"Like it was me who drove all the way here from Colorado Springs."

"I can't drive a stick shift."

"I offered to teach you."

"Don't you think it would be horrible to try to learn while driving up the steepest mountains in the whole country?"

"Those are in Alaska."

"Those drop-offs, though."

"But that's a spirit of fear."

"That's a spirit of safety. I want to be safe. I want you to be safe. I don't mind learning to drive a stick, but I want to learn in a parking lot."

"I have to ask you to clean up after I make dinner, or to do the dishes."

"We're staying in all these houses where friends of yours are out of town for the winter. I don't know what I should and shouldn't be touching or when it is an imposition to take the initiative. It's a situation where I feel like you're in the driver's seat, and I'm mostly taking my cues from you."

"I'm thinking about gender roles here. It seems to me like the man should be taking the leadership roles in a relationship. But you are always taking your cues from me. I am the de facto leader, even though I am a woman."

"There have been many instances where I have tried to take the lead, but you have made it clear that you don't like the choice I make."

"That's, what I mean by passive. You just concede the high ground to me."

"I don't think you would respond well to being strong-armed."

"With love you have to do it. With love."

"To me, the more loving thing would be more of a give and take. More of a partnering kind of thing."

"I feel like because you are so passive that one day the anger is going to come spilling out. I feel like you don't tell me when you are really angry."

"I have only one time been angry, but I knew it wasn't right to be angry, so I didn't say anything about it to you."

"When?"

"When you were still living in Florida and you went to visit that guy in North Carolina and you rode on the back of his motorcycle and you called me and told me what a good time you were having there on the back of his motorcycle."

"That's true. That was fun. Really, truly fun. I loved visiting him, and I loved going for a ride on his motorcycle."

"That made me angry, but I didn't say anything because I didn't feel like I had the right to say anything because I don't own you, we aren't committed, and you have the right to make your own choices."

"So why get angry?"

"Because I wanted you to be having fun with me and not that guy on that motorcycle."

"You don't own a motorcycle."

"I don't even like motorcycles. People I knew kept getting killed on motorcycles."

"So you were worried about me getting killed?"

"No, I was mostly worried about you having fun. And one other thing."

"What?"

"I know some women who had orgasms from riding motorcycles. I had a picture of you with your arms around his waist, riding those mountain roads, holding onto him, having an orgasm."

"So you weren't concerned about whether I was going to get killed?"

"Did you have an orgasm?"

"Of all of the questions you should never have asked, this is the number one question you never should have asked."

—m—

"Your flight leaves in six hours, so I think we ought to leave in three. That gives us an hour to get to the airport and an hour for security and baggage and another hour cushion in case we hit bad traffic."

"Let me finish packing my things, and then do you want to have dinner together before I leave?"

"You can have dinner at the airport, and it's too early anyway, don't you think? I don't think I'll be hungry until much later."

"The reason I was thinking dinner was I have a feeling that after today we may not keep seeing each other anymore."

"I haven't decided about that yet."

"If that is what happens, I want to spend one last nice time with you and let you know that I cared about you and that I care about you."

"That's something I want too. I'm going into the bedroom and lie down while you finish packing. I'm tired, and I know you're tired. When you're done packing, why don't you come into the bedroom and lie down and rest?"

—⚬—

"I love holding you."

"Shh."

"I mean it. This is something I will take with me when I leave."

"Shh."

—⚬—

"The reason I can't let you kiss me is the same reason as always. Even though right now I want you to kiss me. Do you understand?"

"I don't understand."

"I want you to understand. I don't want you to be hurt."

"I will be hurt, but let's not talk about it right now and interrupt what is nice."

"Will you do one thing for me? When we get to the airport?"

"Yes?"

"When you go through the gate, and you want to turn around and look at me, don't look back."

"I know what it means, for you to say that to me now."

"Shh. Put your face against mine. Touch your face to mine."

"I don't know what to say."

"Don't say anything. Just put your face against my face."

"Language fails."

"Just close your eyes and let go for a while. Let's be together. Let's be."

"But what does it mean?"

"You don't have to understand what it means. I don't understand what it means. It's not less beautiful if you don't understand it."

"I want it to mean when we get to the gate I'm going to turn around and take one last look at you."

"Shh."

"So I can remember you until the next time I see you."

"Shh."

"I love the way it feels, being so close to you."

"No more words."

A DEATH FORETOLD

XAVIER NAVARRO AQUINO

ABUELA DOESN'T WANT TO DIE. SHE'S still holding on to life for the stubbornness of it. And on one of the worst days to head down the mountainside, Ma and Pa decided to drag Diego and me to see her.

A hurricane snuck up on us. The news was predicting all sorts of trajectories on their spaghetti maps hoping to confuse María toward a different path. All wishful thinking. María slammed us so hard we felt the asses of the trees bending through the concrete walls. When it rains that much on our mountain, the creeks turn to tsunamis grinding through the jungle, knocking down trees, and snapping bamboos against utility posts. The power would be gone with the wind postapocalypse. María stir-fried our shit pretty nasty.

We drove down the road in our Buick wagon that blended into the red dirt of the melting hillside. The shoulders were almost impossible to see through the thick rain, and Pa had to drive viejita pace to keep us from sliding off the face of the mountain. I asked him why on such a day he would want to go see Abuela, and he ignored me. As if the answer was clear.

When we arrived at the nursing home, María was looming overhead, yet to impose her will. The home was a bright orange with metal bars over every window that made it look like a concrete prison. A ramp ascended from the foot of the building to the entrance. The people inside, the old idle men and women, wore faces of abandonment—forgotten by their families that stopped visiting, forgotten by the world, and tended to by complete strangers. I overheard Ma and Pa talking once—shortly after Abuela got sick—about how they wanted to take care of her, but we didn't have a spare room and they didn't want her to sleep on the couch. There was no way we could make space. We didn't have money to feed ourselves. We barely spared crumbs for the mice living in our cabinets. But the owners of the nursing home offered a major discount to care for Abuela. It weighed on both Ma and Pa, their decision to stick Abuela in a home, because that wasn't what we were supposed to do. That wasn't our custom.

Abuela was one of those types who survived the 1985 landslide in Mameyes. She used to tell us about this whenever it poured heavy on our barrio. She'd sit us on her lap and recite from her memory, recollecting the mud that crushed through the buildings, remembering the immediate yells, then the silence. Diego wouldn't remember those stories. He was barely a couple of years old. But I did. Abuela wore that survival like a badge.

Now she was part of the newly petrified, the ones that spend their last days encased in a different kind of shell. Lethargy lingers heavy in nursing homes. And the mind tends to wander off, creating stories about the old, trying to figure out how they ended up there. I often wondered why the elderly are forgotten. Maybe it was that they became irrelevant to the new generation. Maybe it was because their moment of dreaming or holding on to that tiny flame was extinguishing. But still, I hoped that Abuela was different.

She was thin. The tubes that probed inside her made her look mechanical. Her receding hairline bore her large forehead. The string of silver hair that was left on her scalp was pushed to the side. She had no breasts. Her skin looked fragile and compressed over her bones, as if you'd taken a vacuum and sucked all of her out.

Ma stepped toward her in silence—her footsteps echoing in the bare room. She bent over Abuela and spoke softly in her ear, petting her brow as Abuela mumbled noises. Ma whispered in her ear, telling her we'd come to visit. That it had been a week since our last visit, but we were back and that we were healthy. She emphasized the weather and its constant change. That so much was changing lately.

Diego and Pa stood next to each other. Diego had spent the entirety of the car ride working on his Rubik's Cube that he got from Pa. He worked hard trying to decipher the code, but the cast from his broken hand troubled his movements, and you'd see him shaking the cube as if it would shake itself into six solid-colored sides. I could feel Ma growing impatient as she continued to talk to Abuela. She sat—at first—next to her in a white plastic chair, then moved between the corners of Abuela's bed, tightening the sheets and patting down the pillows. We just stared at the vegetable sprouting its roots on the bed.

Routinely, the nurse who tended to Abuela would walk in and check the tubes and needles on the surface of her skin—brushing them with iodine and pulling them out in such a mechanical method. She would then smear the remainder of the iodine on Abuela's bruised arms and try reinserting the IV drip into her collapsing veins.

Ma watched the nurse as she worked on retrieving the vein duct that seemed to twist with every attempt.

"Can't you be a bit gentler?" Ma scolded. "Miss. Please. Stop that!"

Ma quickly stomped next to the nurse.

"I need to get this in. Please, back off a minute," she said. Abuela shuffled her skeleton frame. Movement. I don't think I'd ever seen her move during her entire stay in the home. It must have taken the greatest effort for her to showcase her pain. Ma grabbed the nurse and tossed her to the concrete floor. Pa ran over and struggled to help up the nurse, who clung to the bedpost, crying. Her knees were split and blood streamed down her shin. Ma offered her hand in an attempt to help.

"I'm sorry. Let me—"

"Get away," the nurse said. She ran off.

Ma stood there, then started pacing. She tried cleaning up the floor and straightening the bed sheets. Ma wasn't the violent type, but something snapped that morning. As if all her guilt billowed out for everyone to see: everything about Abuela made her sick. Unable to distract herself, she left the room.

"Hijos, pay your respects," Pa said to us as his eyes trailed Ma out of the room.

Diego shyly moved to the skeleton on the bed. I walked behind him.

"Migue, what do I say to her?" he asked me.

"Tell her about school," Pa whispered to me. "About the pitching you've been doing all summer. The games you'll start. Anything, mano."

Diego said nothing to Abuela. He just stood before her, looking down at his Rubik's Cube, fiddling with the moving sides.

"Hola, Abu," I finally said. I placed my hand on her clammy palm. She kept garbling words to herself, her eyes shut. I talked to her. Told her about Diego, how old he was. I told her about how I'd been showing him how to throw a ball and that I was graduating high school, the first to do so. But I got no response.

"Diego, say something to her," Pa scolded as he snatched the cube from his hands.

"It's not like she's going to say anything," Diego said. Pa glared at us. The ceiling fan clicked softly above.

"Go to the car, you two. Now!" Pa said.

We filed out of the room and left the home. The rain outside started falling again. We rushed to the car and got into the back seats. Ma was in the passenger seat with her window down, letting the drops pelt against her cheeks. She said nothing to us as she stared absently through the rain.

When we arrived home, we saw the wind had picked up and dropped tree branches and logs onto the road. I rushed Diego to the front porch and waited as Pa and Ma locked the car doors. The rain hurt my skin as it fell. We hadn't bought plywood to board up the windows because the ferretería had run out of lumber and supplies. I joked to Ma that praying wasn't going to stop the winds from blasting the windows or tearing the roof off. She wasn't amused and smacked me across the back of the head.

Before Abuela got sick, she had told me about a time when the news didn't accurately warn the public about natural disasters. The intel they received was crap shot. So she'd resort to prayer in order to "prepare" for incoming storms. Often saying things like "our ancestors would deter the rains," "Yukiyú is our guardian and will defeat Jura cán." I didn't believe it. I argued with her about Mameyes and the disaster, whether those old religions and superstitions could've warned everyone when the ground was melting under their feet, if that would've saved all her friends. She laughed and said all belief is superstition. That it didn't hurt to believe.

—⁂—

The thunder kept bashing outside, the wind turning, the long drag of María continuing from the afternoon into the night, enveloping everything with water, the house shaking around us. Diego and I moved into our bedroom and hid under the covers for most of the evening while Pa and Ma sat quietly in the living room, listening in case we needed to flee into the bathroom because of a blown window or the roof splintering.

We spent the entirety of the hurricane watching the ants creep on the walls. When we got really bored, we watched snails crawl from under our doorway. Diego would sprinkle salt on their backs and watch as they helplessly sizzled before dying. When that didn't entertain him anymore, he'd curl up next to me on my bunk and start flailing like a fish. I'd shove him and punch him on his shoulder, demanding he stop. He'd fart as I pushed him off my bed, then tear back into it laughing.

The night went on with an underlying fear that we'd be stirred out of sleep. So we slept shallow. Trees snapped with the lightning pops, and by the time dawn peeked over the horizon, our house was drowned under so many loosened branches the door was almost impossible to shove open.

Ma was asleep on the sofa with the blanket Abuela made for her just before she got sick. Pa had ventured out into the madness on the street. I followed Pa, slivering my way past most of the carnage, and stood next to him as we both gazed in sync at the disaster. The hurricane had taken our cars and tossed them down the side of the mountain. I started to worry about Abuela and the home. Wondered how long it would be until the power returned. There was no way it could be out for more than a month or two tops.

Pa and me climbed our way out of the debris and onto the main road. So many people from our barrio were surveying the landscape too, some even letting their toddlers walk alongside them, diapers and all, everything looking like a Night of the Living Dead redux. Many of our neighbors lost their roofs, some their entire homes. We were lucky. We pushed through until we ran into Thomas, the gringo from the US and charlatan of our block. He often stalked our house, standing in the dead of night looking in from the street corner, his silhouette outlined under one of the light posts. No one knew where he lived, just that he drifted. He surprisingly survived the night. Must've hidden in one of the nearby caves.

Thomas was sunburnt. His skin always carrying that perpetual red, the white ends of his hands like lobster claws. Thomas "el tomate," Diego and I called him.

"Damn news, they never get nothing right," Thomas said as he pushed through some of the bamboo stumps.

"They got this one right, if you paid attention."

"Y la Doña, how's she?" he asked with a thick accent.

"Don't know. We won't know for a while. From the looks of things, we aren't getting down anytime soon. We visited yesterday and she seemed—"

"I meant Nadia. How's she?"

"Nadia?"

"Haven't seen her around since—"

"I wasn't aware you were supposed to be seeing her." Pa puffed his chest out.

"Easy, man. Easy. Just checking in."

"Everyone's fine. That's what matters."

"Mándale un saludo."

"Mjm," Pa said.

Thomas always pushed Pa. I think what Pa hated the most about him was that pseudosympathy shit he pulled on everyone. And Ma fell for it every time. I grew suspicious at times that maybe they had a thing. It would've explained Pa's outbursts.

Ma had been taking in people like stray dogs ever since we put Abuela in the home. Our house at one point became known as the buzzing gas station. Gente would drop in and out, Ma offering up food we didn't have or couldn't afford.

She'd make Diego and me split our meals with those strangers, with the likes of Thomas. Between the two of us, we must've lost twenty-something pounds. She'd even let them use the bathroom. All while Pa was off at work. Might as well have been luxury suites with bayside windows and a fancy Jacuzzi pool. Ma got sappy and sentimental whenever she materialized a success story. Especially when it came down to the older ones. Whenever we supplied the goods to los viejitos, Ma pride-padded the fuck out of her labor of love. I guess it made up for her guilt that she abandoned Abuela in a home.

Thomas was Ma's favorite of the bunch. He was one of those classic drifters, the likable kind who stayed clear of the needle but not the rum. He'd lost his wife and kids in a shipwreck off the coast of Loíza—current sucked the family below water one by one as he watched dizzily under the baking sun. Apparently, in his tourist fever pitch, he had a dozen tragos of Bacardí before setting offshore and hitting a reef. Since then, pobre Thomas lived inside the bottle. He somehow drifted toward our mountain, far from the coast and the hotels. Said the city was cruel to people in need. Nature and those from it were kinder, gentler in their care. And Ma tried her hardest to help clean him up.

I suspected that Ma and Pa were headed to a shipwreck themselves. And it was only a matter of time before the shit exploded like a cohete on New Year's.

—∞—

Pa was binging on his usual Ojeda rants, listening in on his radio to pass the nights after María. He was convinced he'd be able to catch news about help that would come to our barrio, that we'd soon be airlifted out to safety to a place where there was clean water, power, and food.

Ojeda seethed through the speakers about the debt on the island, how Americans were coming in and trying to invest, cryptocurrency, pyramid schemes, and the "works" of colonialism, as Pa liked to call it. All reasons why the aftermath of María hurt and sustained for so long.

"Thomas came by today," Ma interrupted, cutting into Ojeda's soliloquy.

"So?"

"Started talking up this investment group that is looking to acquire land around here. Says it would be a good opportunity for us to consider."

"Pal carajo all of that. Now? He comes to you to pitch you on schemes after all this?"

"We were just passing time, Ernesto. Better than being glued to your radio."

"Mjm."

"It sounds like a good idea. He explained it all to me."

"That's all bullshit. Don't believe it."

"I'm telling you, Ernesto. It sounds like something we should think—"

"Cállate ya. It's all nonsense."

"It's a way to reinvest in the land. He said it could help fund some independent projects that would create turismo. More money. More opportunities."

"None of those things work. Ask Pedro if he's retired already. He pitched that same garbage about Herbalife a year ago. Said he'd make 100k each month. That fucker is still living out of his mom's house. Eating all her food. Working en la Puma pumping gas."

"It's not Herbalife."

"It's garbage."

"Okay then, Ernesto. You're right. We can continue starving."

"Starving because you keep giving everything we buy away. I know what you've been doing when I'm out. I'm not stupid, mujer."

"That's not the point. Last week he came by—"

"Last week? How many times is he going to keep dropping in—"

"He's been coming around a lot lately," I said without thinking. I knew I'd hit a sour note because everything fell silent. Pa just stared at Ma until he snapped.

"You screwing around with him?" Pa yelled.

"Just leave it," Ma whispered as she sat knitting the hole in Abuela's blanket.

"Tell me the fucking truth."

But Ma never responded to his barking. Pa tossed kitchen plates on the floor and banged his chest like an angry monster. Ma didn't move. She waited for him to stop.

"What's it going to be then, Ernesto? You want us to sit around here eating up Ojeda's propaganda? We can't live off that."

"Better than nursing the damn gringo you fuck with."

"You're not fond of los gringos? What about your job at the factory? Dime. That's an American company, Ernesto."

"That's not the same, Nadia—"

"It's not? You can lash out all you want. Right now, what's paying our bills is your primo, Uncle Sam."

"I'm using it for now. As soon as we're able to get out from under it, we won't need it anymore—"

"That's your excuse, Ernesto. All I said was maybe we consider investing in something. That's all."

"Listening to Thomas, right? That's the best you got. Please, that won't lead but to a dead—"

"End? Because your party is so productive, Ernesto?"

And they kept at it. For the entire evening, they went back and forth. I couldn't listen to it. I went off to my bedroom and found Diego sitting on his bunk trying to read with a flashlight. He wore his Clemente jersey and was reading through Gutiérrez's La Habana trilogy.

"That's not your reading level, mano. If Ma and Pa catch you reading that filth, they'll slap you hard."

"It's crazy scandalous. Makes me think of the freedom they have with fucking. Are all Cubans screwing each other that way? They sound so happy for it, mano. They're doing something right."

"That's just one dude. He's trying to be like Bukowski."

"Bukowski?"

"Never mind, mano. Be sure they don't catch you. Ma would never let you hear the end of it."

"At least they got freedom there. Cuba libre! Like the drink, Migue!"

"That's not the point, mano. You're missing it."

"Maybe you are, cabrón."

"Whatever."

I closed the bedroom door behind me and sat on the desk, thinking about Abuela, thinking about Thomas, until I fell asleep.

—⁂—

The next morning Ma and Pa were barking at each other again in the kitchen. I heard a metal pot thrown and some of our glass cups shatter against the tile. Diego was sitting up on his bunk wrapped in his blanket, hugging his knees.

"Wait here. Don't come out until I get back, okay?"

"They're really going at it."

"Wait here."

I crept to the kitchen. Pa's knuckles were bleeding. Ma sat on the sofa covering her face from exhaustion. I wanted to rush toward her to see how she was. It boiled up inside of me until it nearly overfilled, and I felt paralyzed. I watched them there but couldn't move.

"You know it's people like Thomas that own the property where Mami is staying?" Ma said.

"Don Paulo owns that house! It's on a good foundation. He wouldn't cut corners."

"No, pendejo. Don Paulo doesn't own the house. He rents the house cheap. It's an older gringo couple."

"Where are you getting that—"

"Thomas told me—"

"Thomas!" he let out a loud cackle. "That's where you got that garbage. You must be crazy to think ese borrachón is telling you the truth. It benefits him not to be honest."

Ma didn't entertain him. She dabbed her hand against her forehead, trying to hold back her whimpering. So Pa kept rambling. Ma let him have that moment.

"That's the truth, Nadia. Everything's fine! I'm telling you he's lying. He's lying. Because if not—" Pa started pacing around the kitchen looking for more plates to throw. "If what he said is true, I'm going to cuadrar cuenta. Ese cabrón. This is on you, Nadia. This is on you."

Pa went up to Ma and shoved her before storming out the front door.

"Cabrón!" I yelled to him, trying to chase him, but Ma grabbed my arm and pulled me back inside. I tried to pull away, but she insisted.

"What happened? Ma, what did he do?"

"Tu Abuela, mijo. Thomas came by an hour ago. He tried reaching Abuela's house. The mountain came. The house . . ."

"Ma?"

"I'm sorry, Migue. So sorry; it's my fault."

"Ese tomate is lying, Ma. We were just there. She was just fine."

"No, mijo. No."

"Ma . . ."

I wanted to assure her in that moment, but the only thing that came to me was Abuela's conversation about superstitions, about belief.

"Don't worry, Ma. Believe she's all right. We'll believe." I locked her hands in mine and smiled, hoping we could wish things into existence.

THE WARHOL GIRL

SUSAN NEVILLE

THE SOUND OF A LEAF BLOWER. Everywhere that high shrill scream. The homes, small cottages with English gardens. No visible places of employment. A high school but no children playing. No gravestones in the graveyard. No jet trails in the sky. An iron bridge over a picturesque river, connecting one state to another. No one passing either way since he himself crossed over. He was early for the appointment and hoped to get his bearings. The wind!

She had said the house was second from the corner, a simple brown cape with a rectangular dormer over the front porch. He found it easily. The gardens had been cut back for the winter. Pine needles piled underneath the rhododendrons. Leaves falling en masse from a linden tree in the front yard, like they were being poured from a bucket. Could he walk from the car to the house? What had possessed him to make this appointment?

He could. He walked. Head down. The wind. Yesterday he had buzzed his hair like it was in Iraq. He had ironed his clothes. He looked unfamiliar to himself. He smelled of soap. There were times he thought it might be easier to navigate this world now if he had a cane.

The leaves! The reflections of leaves on the blue windows of his car seemed less frenetic than on the trees where the branches were frantically shaking off the dead. Which image was the real one? The reflected ones were only bobbing, bobbing. The disconnect made him feel seasick.

He tells himself he won't look back at the car, but he looks back to make sure it is still there as he'd left it.

And there is a crash test dummy sitting, staring forward, in the driver's seat.

He turns fully around and stares at the dummy's staring. It only takes a second to realize it is the shadowed headrest. Still. In that beat, he thinks he sees the head move toward him. He thinks he sees the dummy blink. The silvered reflection of the leaves in the blue-green glass give it mirrored glasses. The back seat belt looks like the back of the dummy's suit. The seat itself looks like his chest. Perhaps it was the accumulation of fumes. Years of fumes. They've widened the perceptual beat, that weird hallucinatory space only the artist and the mad were destined, it seemed, to consciously account for. Which one was he? Both, he was afraid. Had always been that. Afraid.

—⁓—

He rang the front bell and waited for the woman inside to answer. The wind. He needed to be inside the house. He was familiar with the house from the photographs she'd sent him. When women sent him pictures of their houses, there was always a ghost image of the camera-pointing woman somewhere in one of the photographs: in a mirror, most often, in the glass covering a photograph or a metal knickknack or even an appliance. It was difficult to take an interior photograph without, at some point, getting a reflection of yourself taking the photograph. And so the woman who opened the door was not completely unfamiliar to him. A blessing. She had been wearing a loose dress in the reflection. The camera had been covering her face in the image she'd sent, of course, but she was dressed in the simple way of a woman who has always been beautiful. He could tell a lot of things from the way her hands held the camera.

Are you the carpenter? she asked him. She put her right hand up to shade her eyes as though she were looking out the front door directly into the sun, but today there wasn't a sun. He couldn't see her face in the mix of gloom and hand.

He said that yes, he was. He stood waiting. What else did she want him to tell her? I've brought the samples, he said when she didn't ask him in and just continued squinting out the door at him. To turn around in the daylight, to walk back to the car, to make it across the bridge and then home was impossible at this moment, but right now making it across the threshold seemed equally impossible.

He reminded her he was there so she could check the wood and stain since the table would be made particularly for her space. This was of course a lie. A copy of a copy, Amish made, it was already in his workshop, waiting for him to apply the stain. You asked me to come, he said.

She backed up into the front hallway and motioned him in. From the photographs she had sent him, he expected light and air. There were floor-to-ceiling cottage windows in the living room and dining room, but today the shutters were shut as though the woman was preparing for a hurricane or burial.

They were at least five hundred miles from the sea in any direction, 6,624 miles from Fallujah. A relatively safe place, this. The center of the country.

The walls were painted, as he knew, a glossy deep green with white trim. The dark paint did not, in photographs, appear dark as in dreary. But with the shutters closed and the lamps turned off, it was in fact dreary.

The woman closed the door behind him. I hope you don't mind the dark, she said, and she pressed her hands against her temples. I think I may be sick, she said, and she walked down a step into the living room.

The floors were slick with shine. For a second he was afraid to step down. It was water, endless and dark. It is a floor, he told himself. It will hold you. Take a step and walk. He walked. The danger was of course that at any step it might turn again to water.

The woman lay back on the couch. How trustful she was. He recognized the couch from the photographs. She picked up what looked like a wet cloth from the floor in front of the couch, where his coffee table would soon be, and she laid it across her eyes. He worried about the damp cloth on the hardwood. Despite everything, he still loved the grain of wood.

There was a round black circle in one corner where a plant had obviously been. That stain would bother him. He would sand it out or replace the boards. He would suggest this. He would suggest painting the room a more cheerful color.

The tasks would add up, if she would have him. He had just enough energy to make it through a series of odd jobs before he hit bottom again. Perhaps she would care. Perhaps she had a spare bedroom. She would feed him and make the bed with clean sheets.

It will just take a minute, she said. So sorry, she said. This happens rarely.

Migraine? he asked.

She lifted her hand and made a limp motion that seemed to indicate yes.

It's the wind, he said.

He'd never had a migraine, but he recognized the signs. And it seemed like migraine weather.

She made another motion with her hand, again an affirmative motion.

Her legs were long and so were her fingers.

There was a piano in the corner of the room. An old Steinway grand. The black wood shone and reflected greenly from the wall. It was like he'd come in from the dying tones of a Midwestern autumn to something verdant. There were magazines and books all around the room, notebooks and pencils. There was a long window seat that served as a bookcase. He counted each breath. He closed his eyes and looked for the red spot that helped him meditate. It was there.

Perhaps I should come back at another time, he said.

She made a motion that seemed like no, though he wasn't sure which question she was answering.

Her hair was thick and long. There were strands of it across the couch pillow, like an arm. There was something seaweed-like to her hair. Perhaps that too was the green. Was it gold or silver, the hair? It had been hard to tell in the silver reflection, and it was hard to tell now. He hadn't noticed at the door. Her skin was a bit green as well. The color of mint. From an illness? He had been wrong about the floor. It wouldn't hold him.

Breathe, he told himself. Silver and mercury glass urns and vases filled a bookcase on one wall. That's where he'd seen her image, multiplied in the photograph. They appeared to be old, not reproductions. He wondered if mercury glass had ever been made from mercury. When he was a child, he liked nothing better than sick days when the thermometer would fall and break on the kitchen floor.

The balls of quicksilver would roll together and form amoebas of silver. Quicksilver. How was it stored when it wasn't in glass? In some type of bladder. Like eye drops. Wine. A miraculous substance, quicksilver, but poison.

Outside the windows, the leaf blowers continued their alarm. When you took the photo of the room, he said, you had the shutters open. The windows.

She nodded.

Do you have auras? he asked.

No answer.

With the migraines, he said. He didn't know what else to say. I have auras, he added. He was of course lying.

Her hand said yes. His hands were shaking.

I have the ones that look like a fortress, he said.

Where had he read this? Was this an odd thing to say?

She didn't seem to take it as odd. She had no reason to trust him, but she seemed to trust him. He had sent her many photos of his work. His student work. She had called him a true artist.

She took a deep breath. He could see her chest rise. Tea, she said. In the kitchen, she said. Would you? she asked. The caffeine. She had mentioned it in her email. You'll come for tea.

He made his way across the watery floor.

The kitchen was painted a lighter tone, but still that minty green. There was a thermos on the countertop and two cups. He opened the top of the thermos. He breathed in the steam, felt it warm his face. He screwed the top back on. The shutters above the sink and in the breakfast nook were closed against the wind and light, and there was more of the mercury glass mixed with polished silver on a sideboard. It was everywhere. On top of the refrigerator, on top of the stove, in the doorless cabinets. Enough to kill a person.

Above the sideboard was what looked like a Warhol print. He had noticed one like it in the living room. He was close enough to this one to see that it was signed. He walked carefully around the table to the sideboard to examine it. The colors were bright, pink and red, sharp colors against the dull green of the woman's walls. 1968. The year his parents graduated from high school. He was struck by the mouth and hair of the model, a silhouette. The aristocratic nose and chin of the woman in the living room. He wondered if she'd paid for the portrait or if he'd asked her to model for him. Then again, how old was the woman in the living room? Whose choice, the woman's or Warhol's? Was the model for this print a daughter or mother or sister or the woman herself?

A Warhol girl. What had he thought of Warhol, back when he thought about such things. Art school. Before Iraq. He'd envied Warhol, surely. The life he'd had. The freedom, the notoriety. The confidence. And hated him.

The door next to the sideboard was closed. Cautiously, he opened it. On the other side of the door was a white room. Too vivid. Spare. A south and west exposure, floor-to-ceiling windows, obviously a room built on and then closed off. A bed against one wall, bookcases against another, and outside the uncovered windows a ginkgo tree, still yellow with leaves. Two sugar maples, red. Black-and-white photos on the wall. The same face. Something pulled him into the room. He walked quietly. Every one was an image of the girl from the Warhol print, or someone who looked exactly like her, at different ages but always with a famous man. Some of them he recognized from school or thought he did. Men of genius. A theologian, an architect, several poets, a novelist. There was a senator and a governor. There were men he didn't recognize, but they had a familiar look. Scientists or literary men. In every photograph, the Warhol girl wore her hair in a simple bob. She was beautiful in every pose, in any light. In any era, she would be beautiful. It was clear in the photos that she wasn't simply a decorative woman. She was in charge of the event. Intelligent. The men were looking at her but also listening. She was giving them ideas, and they were adjusting their own ideas in light of them, though they would never say so. No one would ever know this about her. She would be erased, of course. A woman who slept with men as they passed through. Muse. Siren. A wealthy woman with connections.

The largest photo was of the Warhol girl herself, arms uplifted, in a room filled with pillow-shaped silver balloons: Mylar or something similar, on the ground and floating near the ceiling and everywhere in between. It was an installation. There was a framed article beside the photo. Silver Clouds, by Andy Warhol. The Museum of Contemporary Religious Art. The balloons were kept moving by some unseen source of wind.

But it was the theologian's face that appeared most often in this gallery. He had read all the theologian's books when he was an art student. Art had been his ultimate concern then, and that ultimate concern, the theologian had led him to believe, was sacred. The theologian made him believe that he believed in God even though he said he didn't. It had comforted him all these years. Something to hold in Iraq, something solid. He'd joined the reserve for money while in school. And she, the Warhol girl, had talked to the man. And now she was talking to him perhaps. Here, in the pocket of nowhere.

He closed the door as quietly as he could and poured the strong tea into the two white cups. He walked back to the living room. He took a breath when he reached the glossy floor. It will hold you, he said to himself. In his imagination, he could see the coffee table she would hire him to make and it was as real and solid to him as the woman or the silver vases, so he walked carefully through the space where it would be. He half expected the imagined table to bump against his leg. He put his cup on a coaster on a table next to a side chair. He couldn't see where she might set hers, so he held the scalding cup in his left hand and held the handle out toward her. Your tea, he said, and she held up the talking hand to reach the handle. He helped the two meet. The hand was papery. Was she blind? Thank you, she said.

I couldn't help but notice, he started to say, but she'd begun to drink the tea. He sat down on the piano bench and waited. He knew he couldn't make it easily from the house back to the car.

In the quiet, he pondered the girl in the print. A '60s hippie girl, she was at the center of the world for a time. She had left the Midwest. She hadn't been afraid. She had met the beautiful people, the brilliant glittering people. Her life had been filled with spangly silver things and white teeth in black lights and with drugs and anorexic longing. She was beautiful and fragile and fragrant and lovely and smart. He discerned that from the photos. And the collection of silver, like the clouds, the stars, spinning, reflecting light.

Was the Warhol girl the same girl as the one in the photographs and was she lying there on the couch in front of him? How old would that make her now? Did he hate or love her? It was too dark to tell.

He had wanted to be someplace like that once, to be that high with art and life, the way he had been in art school.

Yes, for a while he had been like that! The tea was doing some kind of mojo on him. He wondered, not for the first time, if his madness was nothing more than fear of madness. No, it had almost killed him.

After the military, he had come back here for good, here in the center of the country. Less dangerous.

I was an artist once, he said to the woman, gesturing to the lithograph. I was, in fact, very good at what I did. For a time, he said. I was very good.

He put his hand over his mouth to stop himself from talking, but he kept on talking through his hand. Was he talking out loud so she could hear or just talking in his head?

For a while I painted houses, he said. To make money while I did my own work.

There is nothing more intimate, he thought, than the relationship between a painter and the woman whose house he is painting.

And then he started woodworking until he realized he could get furniture just as cheaply from other craftsmen and put all his energy into selling. I'm a sculptor, he added. Or was, he added, truthfully.

But you're still an artist, the woman said. Her voice was melodic, haunting, like a poet's.

Oh no, he said. At some point, I realized I will never have my work in a museum. I would not be in the canon of artists. As the styles change, my tables will end up in landfills, no matter how much time I spend on them.

Why did he feel the need to disparage his own work to this woman? He had made the originals in the photos she sent him, even if he sold copies when he could get away with it. She wouldn't buy anything from him now. But he felt that, with her, he could go back to his true work. It seemed that he had fallen in love with her photograph. This was not good. It was never a good sign when he felt himself falling in love. He was in real danger now. He had never made a single true thing, however, unless he was in love.

But that arc upward that came with love would not stop with the thing made. It was an explosion that continued past the planets and the stars, to the edges of the universe until it fell back in upon itself, destroying the thing he'd made so carefully and leaving him shivering in the heat.

Was it Andy Warhol, he said, who convinced us that marketing is everything?

But that is not true, she said.

Perhaps I could have made more of my life, he said through his fingers.

She waved her hand. Quiet. He shushed himself. He would wait. What was her story?

Perhaps the Warhol girl had a baby before she left for the city. The baby was now in her thirties. She was as beautiful as her mother had been. Her mother was dead. The Warhol girl's daughter inherited the picture. She had it on the wall in her kitchen and this other in the living room. She collected silver and glass. How did she make her own money? She came from money. There were oil wells on her property. The woman on the couch, the one he now loves, is the Warhol girl's daughter, a trust fund girl. He had never known a trust fund girl.

Warhol sent her the silkscreens in memory of her beautiful hippie mother. She wanted to be an artist as well. Perhaps she was Warhol's soul mate. But art frightened her because of its connection with her mother.

I have fallen in love with a photograph, he thought. You mustn't be afraid of art, the Warhol girl whispered to him. You mustn't be.

So he had spoken aloud after all. He got up bravely, he thought, took the measurements of the room and the empty space on the floor. He had to leave. He left her with his business card. He ran. The memory of the Warhol girl got him through the next dark months.

—⁓—

Five months after the first visit, he returned to the woman's house with a table. She had been so patient. He had worked and reworked it. It was an original. The copy of the copy would go to someone else. He had wrapped this special table in cloth and tape. He made it across the bridge again, drove into the pocket town.

It was spring and there had been a flood. There were sandbags along the river.

This time when she met him at the door her eyes were clear, and she didn't cover them with a cloth. Her hair was quite clearly silver, not mint green. The eyes were a soft gray blue. Clouded. She both was and was not the Warhol model. He calculated quickly. She could have been the woman in the photographs but not the Warhol girl. She was probably the Warhol girl's mother. For five months she had been his muse.

He unwrapped the table carefully, like he was unwrapping chocolate, a holy relic. She had a trash bag ready for the covering. It felt like a winding sheet. All the leaves were long down, and they'd been whisked away to the leaf crematorium. They'd been replaced by crisp green. She had the top half of the living room shutters open to let in the pale light. There were thin lines on her face. She was in her seventies, perhaps even early eighties, several decades older than he originally thought.

She wore a blue duster. Old woman clothes. Still, she was quite beautiful in her old woman way. He would care for her if she would let him. Was it his only chance?

The shutters were open. She had already made the thermos of tea and had it waiting with the cups on a silver tray. There was something disjointed about the juxtaposition of thermos and silver and translucent white cups. The inside of a thermos tends to darken and chip like the mercury glass she was so fond of. That occurred to him.

He had put a sort of obsession with her into every turn of the lathe when he made the table legs. He sealed the burled wood with layer after layer of oil. It was the most beautiful piece of furniture he had ever made. Soon some factory in China would be turning out copies, but not one of them would ever be like this one.

She was suitably impressed. She lingered over the burls, the grain.

She had been gardening before his arrival. After admiring the table, she put on a large-brimmed hat. Straw. She took him out to the garden. The roses were uncovered. Soon they would bloom. What he thought had been her backyard was simply an antechamber. She took him through an arched wooden gate. On the other side of the gate, there was a hosta garden and an arrangement of pear trees planted so the spaces between them were gothic arches. Through this garden, there was another garden and beyond that the confluence of the Wabash and the Ohio rivers. It was a sunstruck day. The river glistened like the blade of a knife.

I've never seen the Midwest more beautiful, she said, than during the flood. All the fields were mirrored with rain. The barns were in the middle of an ocean.

Did you know Warhol? he asked. It wasn't necessarily the question he'd been waiting to ask her, but it was the one he asked.

My daughter knew him better, she said. I introduced them.

Is that her portrait in the kitchen and the living room?

It is, she said. This garden is in her memory, she said. My little house as well.

So her daughter had been the Warhol girl.

The mercury glass and silver?

The silver clouds, she said.

It felt like joy to me, she said. Silver balloons. The Pentecost.

But bruised, he said.

Yes, bruised. Still, she said. They were something a young girl would love.

In this, he saw the influence of the theologian.

What did her father think?

My husband, she said.

Of Warhol?

Of all of it.

I have a house separate from his. This is the house I live in. He lives in another house in another state. My daughter's ashes are scattered here.

Why did you stay?

Her ashes are scattered here.

Why did your husband leave?

Her ashes are scattered here.

How did she die? he asked.

She was a fragile girl.

Was she always fragile?

She was always fragile, but she was never afraid.

The mother of the Warhol girl walked through the garden and out the gate. He followed her. She pointed to the river.

Last night, she said, the Wabash was streaked with such bright silver it looked like you could mine it. The silver was the real thing and it went on, depths upon depths. If I had placed my hand in it, she said, I truly believe it would have come out glazed. And to the north, it looked as though someone had placed a painted scrim of gold and fresh green fields along the edge of the river; it was that surreal in its perfection.

That type of vision frightened him. It was too much for him. Like an explosion. It would knock him so hard he would never be able to stand up.

You don't think this place is beautiful, she said, but it is extremely beautiful. When you make something out of what you're given, you help justify man's ways to God.

The pear trees in her gated garden, trees usually so flame-like, had been trimmed to form a gothic arch between them, an explosion of arches that formed paper-thin waxed blue cathedral windows out of the night sky. The garden rested against her home as the daughter might have rested against her mother's arm.

They walk together through the town, the crazed woodworker and the Warhol girl's mother. He begins to see things he hadn't seen before. There are sculptures and small gardens, a stone labyrinth. This was the site, she explains, of two nineteenth-century utopias. And the art? he asked. I invited the artists here, she said. They felt that this place was a holy place.

Everything he sees is singing. Everything chimes, in pattern and variation of that pattern. The screens in the doors are gold and they glow and harmonize with the gates and an iron flock of birds chimes with the flocks of very real birds and they inscribe complicated figures of light in the air, like a figure skater on ice, and all around him, the sudden glimpse of a brooding monk or child or woman or fallen angel—the mind's first draft—that makes him look again to see that no, it's no monk, no crying child or grieving mother, but a piece of carved stone. Too much. Too much.

This woman with the beautiful translucent skin, the extraordinary radiance, made this. She made this. Trust fund girl. Did you sleep with him? By this he meant, and she understood he meant, the theologian.

He must know. He believed he knew already. She was the muse to famous men. She slept with them of course. She slept with all of them. Slut, he thought. Slut. The word gave him comfort. It made the place stop whirling, the gates and stones stop shouting. Slut, he thought again. She was now his muse. Perhaps he would make his own great art, his great ideas, if he could keep his balance. Slut. No. Tamp that down, something in him said. Please do not fly off, he said to himself. Do not ruin this, he said to himself. Be content with making copies, and do not try ever again to become a little god.

He never embraced me, she said, never tried to embrace me. But he had that response to women that you felt that he understood you, he had that empathy. We were important friends to one another. It made his wife jealous of course, she said.

Once I was sitting with him at dinner, she went on, and we had just picked raspberries and I offered him a bowl of fresh raspberries and he said that his doctor told him he couldn't eat anything with seeds.

In the garden, she holds the imaginary bowl of raspberries in front of her, and they seem real. She takes a deep breath to smell them.

I said to him that he should just inhale their essence, and it would be like it will be in the next world where we have no need of eating but we experience the essence of everything good.

We talked, she said. He wrote. I wrote. We made this place together.

My daughter believed the stories about us of course. That's when she went to New York. She was angry with me.

But the memory of a life, she said, like the house of art, has many rooms. We fill them one by one and century by century. Most of them are locked shut most of the time, dust-covered. Make one true and honest thing, and it will live there even as it's forgotten. Now and then, someone will open a door and flip on a light. That someone will discover some indescribable hidden-away beauty. That moment, too, will be forgotten.

They walked back through the garden and into the green living room. The mother of the Warhol girl picked up the tea service and started to put it on the table. This is where the service will go, she said. Let me take a photo first, he said. She sat down on the couch, behind the table. He took the photograph. He would take it home with him and work with it. He would add shadows and sources of light. He would carefully remove any images of human beings from the reflections. He would Photoshop the woman out of the image. He would sell thousands upon thousands of this particular table. It was gorgeous in that setting. The emerald green of the walls, the white wainscoting, the light.

ICICLE PEOPLE, OR THE LAKE EFFECT SNOW QUEEN

JASMINE SAWERS

I DIG MYSELF OUT OF MY house to start my patrol. When I emerge, the path I've made is already filling back in with fat, wet snow, blowing in all directions. It is ever trying to buffet me about, to billow me to the edge of town, to strike me snow-blind and wind-deaf so I lose my way, but I got my snow legs a long time ago. The flakes come quick and steady in clumps that smell of sugar glass about to break. Once, I might have made a snowball, a snowman, a snow fort. Once, it might have seemed beautiful. Today, I trudge through it until I find my first extraction.

It's an Accord with its nose in a ditch, ass end raised high in the wind with the back tires spinning slowly. The snow piles higher, shoves the car deeper into a groove that may once have been earth but is now only ice, only soiled run-off snow. I get to work shoveling one side before the car is buried entirely.

Inside is a woman who has left middle age behind. She is wedged against her steering wheel, and the only thing keeping gravity from grinding her against it and stealing her breath away is the integrity of her seatbelt. With shaking hands, she clutches the rosary hanging from her rearview.

"Mother Mary?" she gasps when I kick open the passenger's side window.

"I'm Gerda," I say. Everyone knows it's only me out here, but still she chants the name of a saint instead. "Can you crawl over to me?"

"Thank you, Lord," she says. "Thank you, Jesus."

Spat from the car like gristle, the erstwhile driver gets a fleece and a heat pack and some soup. She is bundled into another neighbor's house to wait for a doctor on a snowmobile. I give her half a nod when I brace myself against the gale and take my leave. Low but not low enough, the others say, *Don't mind her—remote people, those Orientals, but they're hard workers.*

Blizzards used to be monumental events. The kind of thing you could build befores and afters around. A good reliable "where were you when." What did you do when The Big One stormed through in '77, old-timers might ask. How about that Beast with Teeth in '92? Yeah, I haven't heard anyone say that shit in ten years at least.

The first bad one I remember was The October Storm in '06. I was eight. It was so early in the season, the leaves hadn't fallen from their branches, and so the weight of the ice and snow brought trees down across Western New York, across roads and electrical lines and roofs and cars. The whole neighborhood was without electricity for a week. "Come stay with us," said Kai's mother, the only other Thai on the street—the only other Thai in the village—but Grandpa just threw some wood into the fireplace, and alone we hunkered down to wait. Kai and I built a snow tunnel between our two houses and called it a palace. There was much courtly intrigue. We mourned when proper autumn weather melted it away.

The next extraction has been buried in several days' snow. Snow steals sight, steals sound. Others might call this dampening a peace, but I know gray washed into gray. I know the price of stillness. The world glitters under its blanket of snow, beguiling, but if there's magic there, I've lost the eyes to see it. I set to work shoveling the car free. In time, it reveals itself as a Subaru.

With the blow torch I used for dinner party crème brûlée in a different life, I melt the ice that's frozen the doors shut. There's a family inside. A dad lies slumped over the steering wheel, and two toddlers, so safe in their backward-facing seats, occupy the back. Dad struck his head on the windshield and bled out. The children, lilac blue without a mark on them, froze to death.

I take off my gloves and lay my palms on the head of first one baby and then the next. Some icicle people, you can bring them back. Some icicle people, they're not dead until they're warm and dead. But one baby's ear falls off in my hand, and the other loses her nose. Buddhism teaches us not of souls but of flames, and these flames have been snuffed by a relentless winter.

I am not the praying type. I radio for the snowmobile coroner.

More than twenty-five years after our palace melted, the blizzards come one on top of the other in an unremitting cascade. No more clever names. No more springtime thaw. They all bleed together into a single ongoing trial. The government, having shirked its civil duties long ago, issues toothless travel advisories, and then toothless travel bans, but still cars crash and pile up on the 90, still people must be sprung from ditches by the kindness of their neighbors, still we wake to the news that someone else has frozen to death while carrying out any given fool's errand.

Thus the burden of care has fallen to us. Frank with his three-driver fleet of pickup trucks, industrial plow blades mounted to each front, salt spreaders under each tailgate. Tammy and Bob keeping the lights on at the corner store 24/7. A handful of rescuers on the ground, all equipped with radios and thermal layers and politically incorrect seal skin parkas with chinchilla fur hoods. But I'm the only one in my neighborhood. I'm the only one canvassing Harvest Glen, hoping to find a live one.

So every day I suit up and set out with the rucksack on my back. Kitty litter, bottled water, steaming soup in a thermos, single-use heat packs, scarves and mittens and fleece blankets. Flashlight, matches, lighters, blow torch, kindling. A five-gallon gas can tightly sealed and lashed to the outside of the pack, ice cleats on my boots, a couple of trekking poles with ice tips. A shovel tied across my shoulders. The early morning light, a trick of the eye.

The snow slows. The quality of the light tells me it's late afternoon. One more sweep along the borders of Harvest Glen and I'll be making my way home in the dark by muscle memory, but that suits me fine. I come upon a car not yet buried, still puffing out its exhaust, wheels spinning in place. It roars like a lion furious to find himself caged.

I approach the driver's side and knock. A wild-eyed man startles and tries to roll the window down, but it's frozen. I set my pack down and rummage inside for the kitty litter and hold it up for him. His expression blooms into one of befuddled wonder, and that's when I know him.

"Kai," I say. His brows knit and his mouth quirks against the syllables of my name. I swallow past the dryness in my throat. "Stop revving," I say. "Let me put this down." He nods and lets off the gas, hands raised as if in surrender.

Kai stopped speaking to me in high school. He got in with cooler kids, which in our school meant the kids with steady access to weed and beer. That they were all white goes almost without saying, but I've got a different perspective of whiteness these days.

He forgot our garden games, secrets passed from tongue to ear in the dark, summer days whiled away under a willow tree. He forgot my grandma's kuey teow, his mother's ribbons in my hair, his family tied with mine. He forgot me.

I pack the kitty litter tight under the tires. I rap my knuckles on the trunk and sidestep into the snowbank. Kai hits the gas, and the car, a Camry near as old as we are, rocks in its effort. Kitty litter flies up into the air and exhaust coughs out in thick black sputters. Finally, it lurches forward and skids free with a squeal. I thought Kai would peel off, fishtailing in his haste to leave me, but he stops some twenty feet away and gets out of the car.

He jogs toward me, chanting my name as if there were anyone else he could possibly be addressing out here, where we've been abandoned by heaven, our neighbors, and the indifferent weather.

"Do you need a ride?" he asks when he reaches me, panting. "Where are you living these days?"

He's skinny and not dressed for the cold. I can see the knobs of his wrist bones pressing tight against thin brown skin. He has great dark circles under his eyes, which are rheumy and watery. He doesn't look like himself, but he smiles like the boy I once knew, the one with a million magical ideas and the hand around my wrist, forever pulling me into his far-off worlds. I turn my face away.

"Same place," I say, shoving the kitty litter back into my pack.

"Seriously?"

I sling my rucksack back on and cross the shovel over my shoulders. I point my feet toward home. He's scurrying along beside me, saying *wait, wait*.

"Come on," he says, "I'll give you a ride. It'll be dark soon. It'll take like an hour to get home walking."

An hour and a half, more like, and that's if I don't find anyone else who needs me to lead them out of the oppression of all this snow.

"You should get snow tires and all-wheel drive," I tell him. "Then maybe I'll think about catching a ride from you."

"I knew the damn tires were bald," Kai says. "I'm so fucking stupid."

He's fallen into step beside me like we're kids again, like it's 2010 and we don't know how the world's gonna smother our flames into embers, like he never told Matt Buchanan *sure Gerda's a dork, but she'll do anything I tell her to*.

"How's your grandma?" he asks. "How's your grandpa?"

"If they were alive, they would be over a hundred years old."

"Oh."

"Go back to your car, man," I say. "Go home."

"I'm really sorry about them," Kai says. "They were the best."

I plant my trekking poles and face him. He looks like the moon: pale and wan, a reflection of something else's light.

"What do you want, Kai?"

He hitches his shoulders up, shoving his fists into his armpits. I wipe the snow gathering in my lashes as he bounces from foot to foot. The shape of my breath merges with his.

"Kai."

"Come sit in the car with me," he says in a rush. "Get warm a minute, even if you don't want a ride."

I am not the nostalgic type, but history bears me back into his car—all that's between us and the elusive memory of sunshine.

I used to like autumn best of all. The kaleidoscope of changing leaves. The way everything smelled like something new was about to be born of clean rain. Kai's mother always made her special pumpkin pie from scratch—rendered the lard, scooped out the pumpkins and kabocha squash, ground fresh spices from the Asian grocery store in the city. No one made a pie like hers. That last September, we took turns blowing hot steam from his mother's pie out of our noses like sleepy dragons.

The Camry's heating system is not prepared for the lake effect life. I crack a heat pack and set it on the console between us. Kai rubs his hands together briskly and puffs hot breath into the cup of his palms.

"I've missed you," Kai says after a while. "I didn't realize how much 'til I saw you."

"Still working on object permanence, I guess."

"Huh?"

I shake my head and stare out the windshield into the vast howl of snow.

"Remember that tree down on Lake Bluff?" he says. "That was supposed to take us to the giant's house if we climbed high enough."

"You fell out of that tree."

Kai wriggles out of his coat and rolls up his right sleeve. He shows me the scar on the inside of his elbow. What was a pink smile when we were kids has faded into a white crescent barely raised.

"How about that shack we found way into the woods behind the old Hoffsheimer place?"

"We both needed tetanus shots."

"Yeah, but before that."

Me and Kai, dragons and chain mail and princesses to save. Endless days waving our swords and jumping the creek and digging for treasure/gnomes/China. In real life, it was a long-forgotten storage shed full of rusty farm equipment older than my grandparents, an infestation of termites, and black mold crawling up the walls and into our lungs. That shack was spankings when we came home scratched and infected, peering into each other's windows after dark, passing notes in our own invented alphabet.

"Not really," I say.

"What about jumping off the falls at Zoar valley?"

Hold my hand, and we'll go at the same time, he said. *Are you ready?* My hand in his. *One. Two. Three!* That perfect, weightless ecstasy in the moment before we hit the water.

"Where?"

Kai scoffs. Of course—I'm tiresome and joyless, taking away his fun. As usual.

"What happened to you, man?" he asks.

"What happened to you?"

Kai lays his forehead against the steering wheel. I should open the door and start the long trudge back home. I should leave him to whatever it is he does and get back to my fireplace. My grandma's bonsais. My grandpa's crosswords. My solitude.

Kai raises his head again and casts his eyes up to the sky. Beyond the spiral of whipping snow, it's an endless steel gray that saps all the hope from your heart. I have a dim flame these days, and suddenly I can see Kai's is just the same.

"God," he says. "Can you even remember the last time it was summer?"

We used to catch pollywogs in the creek. Everything smelling like fresh-cut grass. Freckles blazing like a constellation through the sunburn across his nose. Scraped knees. In and out of each other's houses like we owned them both. The world rendered orange and purple by an infinite dusk. Sparklers leaving trails of firelight when the sun finally set.

"Do you ever think about leaving Buffalo?" Kai asks. "I try and I try, but it's always something. Someone calls me needing help. I wake up to find my ass tumbled off the wagon in the night and I don't know how. My car gets stuck in the snow on the outskirts of town." He looks at me, and he is six years old. Eight. Twelve. Thirty-five. He looks at me and says my name.

I want to weep into his cloudy eyes. I want to sob into his splintered heart. But I am not the crying type.

VERSUS THE BROWN SOCKS

PABLO PIÑERO STILLMANN

I SPENT THE FIRST FEW MONTHS of my parents' divorce alone, mostly in front of the television. Whereas my father already lived with his new girlfriend, my mother was busy with work, visits to the psychiatrist (some of them emergencies), meetings with her lawyer, and coffee dates with friends to update them on the comings and goings of the legal process. Nieves, a robust and grumpy housekeeper, made me lunch every day and looked after me until my mother got home at night.

I spent those afternoons watching all sorts of kids' shows. One was a Bulgarian series about a magician named Zslorya who saved children from dangerous situations. The rescue always involved a magic trick, and at the end of the episode the magician would explain the trick to the viewers. I also watched lots of baseball because Frecuencia 8, for some reason, showed all the Cleveland Indians' home games. After all this time, I still haven't been able to forget some names from that mediocre squad: Carlos Baerga, Keith Hernandez, Sandy Alomar, Greg Swindell.

But my favorite show, the one I never missed, was *Buenas Tardes con Omar*. Remembering that show is like remembering a dream: hazy, confusing, and saturated with emotions. When it came on, five or six p.m., I'd move from the upstairs television downstairs to my mother's room. I shouted to Nieves that I was going to do my homework, but she didn't care; she was watching her own programming on the kitchen set, an old contraption with knobs that used to belong to my great-aunt. I watched *Buenas Tardes con Omar* in my mother's room, with the door locked, because, at nine years old, I was embarrassed to watch a show that was, in my opinion, aimed at little kids.

Omar, a bald man in a sky-blue sweater vest over a white shirt and black tie, sat behind a table covered with toys. I don't really remember a lot of what he did. He sang, read viewer mail, maybe told riddles.

What kept me tuning in to that show religiously was "The Adventures of Débora and Gastón." Débora was a white sock puppet on Omar's right hand, and Gastón a red sock puppet on his left. Débora and Gastón were orphans. Or they were trying to find their parents. Something like that. The important thing was that these two socks traveled the world and had all sorts of adventures. The villains were represented by other hands that showed up from both sides of the screen wearing brown and tan socks, the type of socks only worn by adults who've given up on life. So every day, Débora and Gastón were stuck atop the Eiffel Tower, or had mistakenly boarded a boat headed for Senegal, or needed to deliver a package to the Japanese emperor.

I can still feel the excitement of watching those socks come to life. There was a tingle in my hands, a knot in my stomach. As soon as the segment began, I was no longer in my sad existence but transported into an inflatable kayak on Lake Peipus or a hot air balloon over Mount Kanchenjunga. Débora and Gastón felt to me more human than my parents, my teachers, or my classmates.

Besides being a peerless broadcaster, Omar was a phenomenal writer. While shows of that era (e.g., Zslorya's) consisted of standalone episodes, "The Adventures..." was serialized. At the end of Monday's segment, one had no idea how the siblings would escape their troubles until the start of Tuesday's segment. Each adventure was a puzzle. During the twenty-four hours between Omar's shows, or seventy-two from Friday to Monday, I, along with tens of thousands of other children, racked my brain thinking of how my favorite socks would wiggle out of their latest imbroglio. If a brown sock had trapped them under the Sphinx of Giza, then I'd spend a lot of my school day—at a corner desk, so my classmates and teacher wouldn't catch on—writing the script of Gastón and Débora's escape from the Sphinx of Giza. My solutions never held a candle to Omar's.

"The Adventures..." really hit its stride toward February of '91. The structure of the episodes changed: instead of lasting one tight six-minute segment, sometimes the socks would eat up two or three segments of *Buenas Tardes con Omar*. I became even more obsessed with these stories, even though some of the time I had no idea what was happening. (I didn't understand this as a boy, but "The Adventures..." had adopted the abstract quality of real life.) How was it that Gastón and Débora were in the Gunnuhver hot springs if we'd last seen them eating pupusas in Cuscatlán? In one episode, our protagonists stole a time machine from an independent scientist's illegal laboratory. This allowed the socks to travel to Ancient Greece and also to witness the implantation of Christianity in the Roman Empire. They also attempted, without luck, to thwart Ivan the Terrible's massacre at Novgorod. By then, Omar had forgotten about scripts—maybe also about the audience and the cameras—and would now solely improvise.

Without a doubt, the best plotline of "The Adventures . . ." came during this jazz age of the show. A tan sock stole a Vermeer painting, *The Allegory of Faith*, from a New York museum, sold it, and, with the money, hired a group of mercenaries to time-travel with him to the Haitian revolution to quell the slave uprising. Gastón and Débora, of course, went after him.

Although Omar's story was peppered with fantasy—Vermeer, for example, who died in the 1600s, showed up in eighteenth-century Haiti armed with knives to kill a landowner and burn his papaya farm—to this day I know more about the Haitian revolution than about the one that took place in my own country.

In one of the Haitian plotline's many climaxes, Gastón and Débora were tied to the trunk of a palm tree while the mercenaries danced, sang, and doused them in gasoline. They couldn't yet burn them alive because Captain Beaulieu, who was on his way by horse, had the matches.

Then there was a commercial break. Let's say the first ad was for cookies. The next one for powdered milk. After that, maybe, there was an ad for whole wheat bread, which was all the rage back then. Then came an ad for kids' toothpaste. My love for television had turned me into a commercial break expert. I knew that during *Buenas Tardes con Omar* the breaks were made up of between three and four ads lasting thirty seconds each. After the last ad came a fifteen-second ID. And just as expected, the toothpaste ad was followed by the station's logo accompanied by a deep voice that said, *Telecapital: Honored to be in your home.* But after that came another ad. I sat up. Then came a station ID in which Telecapital wished its viewers a merry Christmas. In March? And another, this one congratulating President Batoner on his successful fifth year in office. Then an ad for a doll that needed its diaper changed. Then one for instant coffee. Then, again, an ad for a doll that needed its diaper changed. Then another one for the instant coffee. *Telecapital: Honored to be in your home.* Then . . .

The commercials lasted until the beginning of the next show. I had one of those anxiety attacks I'd seen my mother get: dry mouth, brain reeling, body unable to stay put. For a moment, I thought of asking Nieves what she thought had happened with Omar, but I hated her and, more importantly, I was certain she hated me too. (Nieves and I rarely spoke, and sometimes I would catch her glaring at me.) I wasn't actually worried about Omar, though. He was omnipotent. What terrified me was that I would never know how (or even if!) Gastón and Débora escaped from the Haitian palm tree.

My mother would get home at night, exhausted, and immediately run a bath. I remember that night as the only one in which I looked forward to her arrival. In complete hysterics, I'd already looked up Telecapital in the phone book and called to demand an explanation. The receptionist hung up on me. I hadn't changed the channel, certain that Omar would eventually show up to assure us, his disciples, that all was well in his kingdom. But Omar never did, so I hoped that my mother would be able to explain the never-ending commercial break. Maybe it was something very common in television and I had nothing to worry about.

I heard the front door open and my mother exchanging a few words with Nieves, who then left. I would've run to her, but I didn't want to lose sight of the screen. When my mother finally appeared, she looked haggard: disheveled hair and smeared makeup. She sat on the bed.

"Hug me," she said. Then she began to cry.

I did as she said, all the while not taking my eyes off the screen, feeling the warm tears accumulate on my right shoulder.

Once she stopped crying, my mother went into the bathroom to run her bath. I stayed on her bed waiting for Omar. The room filled with the smell of Marlboros. Every once in a while, I heard my mother's sobs bouncing against the tile. I stayed that way, hooked to Telecapital until I fell asleep under the exhaustion of so much anxiety.

The next day in school, not able to talk to my classmates about Omar's mysterious disappearance, I spent all classes writing scripts in my notebook. Each one was crazier than the next, probably as a tribute to my hero. The math teacher called me up to the board, but I refused to obey. He insisted. I called him a tyrant—an insult I'd heard Débora hurl at Charles Leclerc—and ended up at the vice principal's office.

Of course, that afternoon when it came time for *Buenas Tardes con Omar*, I ran down to my mother's room, locked the door, and turned on the television. I couldn't believe my eyes. Instead of my favorite show, there was a cartoon starring a mermaid.

I never found out what happened to Omar. Things were very different back then. If a media company as powerful as Telecapital didn't want people to know something—it could be as serious as the murder of a political activist or as banal as a reason for a show's cancellation—then the people didn't know and that was that. Sometimes I'll bring his name up at dinner parties, just as a fishing expedition, but those who were fans of Omar usually just repeat the same old rumors, most violent or sexual in nature, none confirmed.

For weeks, every day at five or six p.m., I turned on the television, just in case. I'd never hated anyone like I hated that stupid mermaid. I now thought of Gastón and Débora more than ever. Then came the apocalyptic rains of 1991, the ones people still talk about with quivering voices. I was just a kid, had no sense of the meaning of either danger or loss. In fact, I celebrated the second deluge, the one in which more than fifty people lost their lives, because it led to schools being shut down for a week.

I spent the first two days of that impromptu vacation lying on the sofa watching television. I didn't shower or brush my teeth, and I peed on the potted tree next to the window from where I could continue watching Zslorya or the Cleveland Indians. I would've gladly stayed in my pajamas the whole week, but the judge in charge of my parents' case, seizing on the school shutdowns, summoned me to testify on Wednesday.

That morning my mother dressed me in a corduroy jacket and a clip-on tie. She parted my hair down the middle, which was, according to Omar, how Captain Beaulieu did his hair. In the car ride over, my mother coached me on how to respond to the judge's questions. *Tell him we eat lunch together every day. Tell him I check your homework after dinner. Tell him I'm tough but fair. Tell him you love Nieves like a second mother.* At stoplights, she'd apply her makeup.

My father was waiting for us at the bottom of the stairs that led to the courthouse. As always, he had on a suit and a bowtie and held his briefcase in his left hand.

I hadn't seen the man since he'd left and couldn't bear to look him in the eyes.

"You're not going to say hello to me?" he said. It made me feel as if it were my fault that he'd been taken away from important things—meetings, conferences, long-distance calls—to go to the courthouse.

My parents left me in a drab waiting room along with the other children. Apparently, all the judges had called in the sons and daughters of broken homes during those days of no school.

There were no more free chairs, so I sat on the floor. From there I noticed that the men who worked at the courthouse all wore brown or tan socks, the women brown or tan stockings.

It was beginning to make me angry that my mother hadn't thought of telling me to bring the sports section of the newspaper or something to keep me entertained when I heard a high-pitched voice call my name. It was Danila, a girl from my class. Danila never spoke to me in school, she was pretty and popular, but that day she had no choice. There was, magically, an empty chair next to her where she invited me to sit.

"Are your parents getting a divorce?" she said. She was wearing a red velvet dress and white ballet shoes.

"Yours too?"

"I already testified," said Danila. "It's not a big deal."

"Why are you still here?"

She pointed to a teenager in a black sweatshirt playing with a handheld console. "Just waiting for my brother."

Danila and I talked for a long time. She even laughed when I impersonated our English teacher, a hunchback with a conspicuous hearing aid. Danila and I played hangman using crayons and paper the courthouse placed on a table to accommodate the children. The crayons were all broken, and the paper was thick. Every once in a while, a woman with dyed auburn hair walked in to call a child. *Lemmy Vila, Rogeli. Rojano Obregón, María.*

I was so happy with Danila that I never wanted to be called. Sure, she'd been forced to hang out with me, but maybe now she saw how funny and smart I was and would also be my friend at school. Maybe she could even be my girlfriend.

After a round of hangman, Danila squinted toward the corner opposite us and smiled.

"Look," she said, "Carlos is here too."

Carlos Gama was in our grade but not in our class. All I knew of him was that he'd been a finalist in a regional geography contest. The principal had called him up during a school assembly to congratulate him. Carlos had a sheaf of papers on his lap and drew with great concentration, switching crayons often.

I was disappointed when Danila suggested we go over to say hello, as I wanted her all to myself, playing hangman until the end of time. Why had Carlos's parents also decided to get a divorce?

"Be quiet when we go over," said Danila. "I want to scare him."

We left our things on the chairs and walked slowly to Carlos. He didn't see us coming, and once we were a meter or so away, I noticed what he was drawing: two oblong figures, one white and one red, both with googly eyes, who were crying because they were tied to a palm tree. Captain Beaulieu stood to the side holding a flaming torch.

Carlos became startled when he finally saw us and rushed to cover the drawing with both hands. "What are you doing here?" he said.

"Our parents are all getting divorced," said Danila.

I asked Carlos what he was drawing.

"Nothing," he said crumpling the paper.

In the only telepathic experience I've had—probably the only one I will ever have—Danila's brain linked to mine. The information wasn't transmitted in words but in images. I saw her hiding in her basement watching Omar on a small television. I'm sure I transmitted an image to her as well. The connection didn't last more than a second.

"We're over there playing hangman if you want to join us," said Danila.

Carlos's face turned beet red.

A few minutes later, the woman with the auburn hair yelled my name.

SAYING GOODBYE TO YANG

ALEXANDER WEINSTEIN

WE'RE SITTING AROUND THE TABLE EATING Cheerios—my wife sipping tea, Mika playing with her spoon, me suggesting apple picking over the weekend—when Yang slams his head into his cereal bowl. It's a sudden mechanical movement, and it splashes cereal and milk all over the table. Yang rises, looking as though nothing odd just occurred, and then he slams his face into the bowl again. Mika thinks this is hysterical. She starts mimicking Yang, bending over to dunk her own face in the milk, but Kyra's pulling her away from the table and whisking her out of the kitchen so I can take care of Yang.

At times like these, I'm not the most clearheaded. I stand in my kitchen, my chair knocked over behind me, at a total loss. Shut him down, call the company? Shut him down, call the company? By now the bowl is empty, milk dripping off the table, Cheerios all over the goddamned place, and Yang has a red ring on his forehead from where his face has been striking the bowl. A bit of skin has pulled away from his skull over his left eyelid. I decide I need to shut him down; the company can walk me through the reboot. I get behind Yang and untuck his shirt from his pants as he jerks forward, then I push the release button on his back panel. The thing's screwed shut and won't pop open.

"Kyra," I say loudly, turning toward the doorway to the living room. No answer, just the sound of Mika upstairs, crying to see her brother, and the concussive thuds of Yang hitting his head against the table. "Kyra!"

"What is it?" she yells back. *Thud.*

"I need a Phillips head!"

"What?" *Thud.*

"A screwdriver!"

"I can't get it! Mika's having a tantrum!" *Thud.*

"Great, thanks!"

Kyra and I aren't usually like this. We're a good couple, communicative and caring, but moments of crisis bring out the worst in us. The skin above Yang's left eye has completely split, revealing the white membrane beneath. There's no time for me to run to the basement for my toolbox. I grab a butter knife from the table and attempt to use the tip as a screwdriver. The edge, however, is too wide, completely useless against the small metal cross of the screw, so I jam the knife into the back panel and pull hard. There's a cracking noise, and a piece of flesh-colored Bioplastic skids across the linoleum as I rip open Yang's panel. I push the power button and wait for the dim blue light to shut off. With alarming stillness, Yang sits upright in his chair, as though something is amiss, and cocks his head toward the window. Outside, a cardinal takes off from the branch where it was sitting. Then, with an internal sigh, Yang slumps forward, chin dropping to his chest. The illumination beneath his skin extinguishes, giving his features a sickly ashen hue.

I hear Kyra coming down the stairs with Mika.

"Is Yang okay?"

"Don't come in here!"

"Mika wants to see her brother."

"Stay out of the kitchen! Yang's not doing well!" The kitchen wall echoes with the muffled footsteps of my wife and daughter returning upstairs.

"Fuck," I say under my breath. Not doing well? Yang's a piece of crap, and I just destroyed his back panel. God knows how much those cost. I get out my cell and call Brothers & Sisters Inc. for help.

—⚉—

When we adopted Mika three years ago, it seemed like the progressive thing to do. We considered it our one small strike against cloning. Kyra and I are both white, middle class, and have lived an easy and privileged life; we figured it was time to give something back to the world. It was Kyra who suggested she be Chinese. The earthquake had left thousands of orphans in its wake, Mika among them. It was hard not to agree. My main concern—one I voiced to Kyra privately, and quite vocally to the adoption agency during our interview—was the cultural differences. The most I knew about China came from the photos and "Learn Chinese" translations on the place mats at Golden Dragon. The adoption agency suggested purchasing Yang.

"He's a Big Brother, babysitter, and storehouse of cultural knowledge all in one," the woman explained. She handed us a colorful pamphlet—*China!*

it announced in red dragon-shaped letters—and said we should consider. We considered. Kyra was putting in forty hours a week at Crate & Barrel, and I was still managing double shifts at Whole Foods. It was true, we were going to need someone to take care of Mika, and there was no way we were going to use some clone from the neighborhood. Kyra and I weren't egocentric enough to consider ourselves worth replicating, nor did we want our neighbors' *perfect* kids making our daughter feel insecure. In addition, Yang came with a breadth of cultural knowledge that Kyra and I could never match. He was programmed with grades K through college and had an in-depth understanding of national Chinese holidays like flag-raising ceremonies and Ghost Festivals. He knew about moon cakes and sky lanterns. For two hundred more, we could upgrade to a model that would teach Mika tai chi and acupressure when she got older. I thought about it. "I could learn Mandarin," I said as we lay in bed that night. "Come on," Kyra said, "there's no fucking way that's happening." So I squeezed her hand and said, "Okay, it'll be two kids then."

—⚒—

He came to us fully programmed; there wasn't a baseball game, pizza slice, bicycle ride, or movie that I could introduce him to. Early on, I attempted such outings to create a sense of companionship, as though Yang were a foreign exchange student in our home. I took him to see the Tigers play in Comerica Park. He sat and ate peanuts with me, and when he saw me cheer, he followed suit and put his hands in the air, but there was no sense that he was enjoying the experience. Ultimately, these attempts at camaraderie, from visiting haunted houses to tossing a football around the backyard, felt awkward—as though Yang were humoring me—and so, after a couple months, I gave up. He lived with us, ate food, privately dumped his stomach canister, brushed his teeth, read Mika goodnight stories, and went to sleep when we shut off the lights.

All the same, he was an important addition to our lives. You could always count on him to keep conversation going with some fact about China that none of us knew. I remember driving with him, listening to *World Drum* on NPR, when he said from the backseat, "This song utilizes the xun, an ancient Chinese instrument organized around minor third intervals." Other times, he'd tell us Fun Facts. Like one afternoon, when we'd all gotten ice cream at Old World Creamery, he turned to Mika and said, "Did you know ice cream was invented in China over four thousand years ago?" His delivery of this info was a bit mechanical—a linguistic trait we attempted to keep Mika from adopting. There was a lack of passion to his statements, as though he wasn't interested in the facts. But Kyra and I understood this to be the result of his being an early model, and when one considered the moments when he'd turn to Mika and say, "I love you, little sister," there was no way to deny what an integral part of our family he was.

—〰—

Twenty minutes of hold time later, I'm informed that Brothers & Sisters Inc. isn't going to replace Yang. My warranty ran out eight months ago, which means I've got a broken Yang, and if I want telephone technical support, it's going to cost me thirty dollars a minute now that I'm post-warranty. I hang up. Yang is still slumped with his chin on his chest. I go over and push the power button on his back, hoping all he needed was to be restarted. Nothing. There's no blue light, no sound of his body warming up.

Shit, I think. There goes eight thousand dollars.

"Can we come down yet?" Kyra yells.

"Hold on a minute!" I pull Yang's chair out and place my arms around his waist. It's the first time I've actually embraced Yang, and the coldness of his skin surprises me. While he has lived with us almost as long as Mika, I don't think anyone besides her has ever hugged or kissed him. There have been times when, as a joke, one of us might nudge Yang with an elbow and say something humorous like, "Lighten up, Yang!" but that's been the extent of our contact. I hold him close to me now, bracing my feet solidly beneath my body, and lift. He's heavier than I imagined, his weight that of the eighteen-year-old boy he's designed to be. I hoist him onto my shoulder and carry him through the living room out to the car.

My neighbor, George, is next door raking leaves. George is a friendly enough guy, but completely unlike us. Both his children are clones, and he drives a hybrid with a bumper sticker that reads IF I WANTED TO GO SOLAR; I'D GET A TAN. He looks up as I pop the trunk. "That Yang?" he asks, leaning against his rake.

"Yeah," I say and lower Yang into the trunk.

"No shit. What's wrong with him?"

"Don't know. One moment we're sitting having breakfast, the next he's going haywire. I had to shut him down, and he won't start up again."

"Jeez. You okay?"

"Yeah, I'm fine," I say instinctively, though as I answer, I realize that I'm not. My legs feel wobbly, and the sky above us seems thinner, as though there's less air. Still, I'm glad I answered as I did. A man who paints his face for Super Bowl games isn't the type of guy to open your heart to.

"You got a technician?" George asks.

"Actually, no. I was going to take him over to Quick Fix and see—"

"Don't take him there. I've got a good technician, took Tiger there when he wouldn't fetch. The guy's in Kalamazoo, but it's worth the drive." George takes a card from his wallet. "He'll check Yang out and fix him for a third of what those guys at Q-Fix will charge you. Tell Russ I sent you."

—⚏—

Russ Goodman's Tech Repair Shop is located two miles off the highway amid a row of industrial warehouses. The place is wedged between Mike's Muffler Repair and a storefront called Stacey's Second Times—a cluttered thrift store displaying old rifles, iPods, and steel bear traps in its front window. Two men in caps and oil-stained plaid shirts are standing in front smoking cigarettes. As I park alongside the rusted mufflers and oil drums of Mike's, they eye my solar car like they would a flea-ridden dog.

"Hi there, I'm looking for Russ Goodman," I say as I get out. "I called earlier."

The taller of the two, a middle-aged man with gray stubble and weathered skin, nods to the other guy to end their conversation. "That'd be me," he says. I'm ready to shake his hand, but he just takes a drag from his cigarette stub and says, "Let's see what you got," so I pop the trunk instead. Yang is lying alongside my jumper cables and windshield-washing fluid with his legs folded beneath him. His head is twisted at an unnatural angle, as though he were trying to turn his chin onto the other side of his shoulder. Russ stands next to me, with his thick forearms and a smell of tobacco, and lets out a sigh. "You brought a Korean." He says this as a statement of fact. Russ is the type of person I've made a point to avoid in my life: a guy that probably has a WE CLONE OUR OWN sticker on the back of his truck.

"He's Chinese," I say.

"Same thing," Russ says. He looks up and gives the other man a shake of his head. "Well," he says heavily, "bring him inside, I'll see what's wrong with him." He shakes his head again as he walks away and enters his shop.

Russ's shop consists of a main desk with a telephone and cash register, across from which stands a table with a coffeemaker, Styrofoam cups, and powdered creamer. Two vinyl chairs sit by a table with magazines on it. The door to the workroom is open. "Bring him back here," Russ says. Carrying Yang over my shoulder, I follow him into the back room.

The work space is full of body parts, switchboards, cables, and tools. Along the wall hang disjointed arms, a couple of knees, legs of different sizes, and the head of a young girl, about seventeen, with long red hair. There's a workable cluttered with patches of skin and a Pyrex box full of female hands. All the skin tones are Caucasian. In the middle of the room is an old massage table streaked with grease. Probably something Russ got from Stacey's Seconds. "Go 'head and lay him down there," Russ says. I place Yang down on his stomach and position his head in the small circular face rest at the top of the table.

"I don't know what happened to him," I say. "He's always been fine, then this morning he started malfunctioning. He was slamming his head onto the table over and over." Russ doesn't say anything. "I'm wondering if it might be a problem with his hard drive," I say, feeling like an idiot. I've got no clue what's wrong with him; it's just something George mentioned I should check out. I should have gone to Quick Fix. The young techies with their polished manners always make me feel more at ease. Russ still hasn't spoken. He takes a mallet from the wall and a Phillips head screwdriver. "Do you think it's fixable?"

"We'll see. I don't work on imports," he says, meeting my eyes for the first time since I've arrived, "but, since you know George, I'll open him up and take a look. Go 'head and take a seat out there."

"How long do you think it'll take?"

"Won't know till I get him opened up," Russ says, wiping his hands on his jeans.

"Okay," I say meekly and leave Yang in Russ's hands.

In the waiting room, I pour myself a cup of coffee and stir in some creamer. I set my cup on the coffee table and look through the magazines. There's *Guns & Ammo, Tech Repair, Brothers & Sisters Digest*—I put the magazines back down. The wall behind the desk is cluttered with photos of Russ and his kids, all of whom look exactly like him, and, buried among these, a small sign with an American flag on it and the message THERE AIN'T NO YELLOW IN THE RED, WHITE, AND BLUE.

"Pssh," I say instinctually, letting out an annoyed breath of air. This was the kind of crap that came out during the invasion of North Korea, back when the nation changed the color of its ribbons from yellow to blue. Ann Arbor's a progressive city, but even there, when Kyra and I would go out with Yang and Mika in public, there were many who avoided eye contact. Stop the War activists weren't any different. It was that first Christmas, as Kyra, Yang, Mika, and I were at the airport being individually searched, that I realized Chinese, Japanese, South Korean didn't matter anymore; they'd all become threats in the eyes of Americans. I decide not to sit here looking at Russ's racist propaganda and leave to check out the bear traps at Stacey's.

—⟶⟶—

"He's dead," Russ tells me. "I can replace his insides, more or less build him back from scratch, but that's gonna cost you about as much as a used one."

I stand looking at Yang, who's lying on the massage table with a tangle of red and green wires protruding from his back. Even though his skin has lost its vibrant color, it still looks soft, like when he first came to our home. "Isn't there anything else you can do?"

"His voice box and language system are still running. If you want, I'll take it out for you. He'll be able to talk to her, there just won't be any face attached. Cost you sixty bucks." Russ is wiping his hands on a rag, avoiding my eyes. I think of the sign hanging in the other room. Sure, I think, I can just imagine the pleasure Russ will take in cutting up Yang.

"No, that's all right. I'll just take him home. What do I owe you?"

"Nothing," Russ says. I look up at him. "You know George," he says as explanation. "Besides, I can't fix him for you."

—◊—

On the ride home, I call Kyra. She picks up on the second ring.

"Hello?"

"Hey, it's me." My voice is ragged.

"Are you okay?"

"Yeah," I say, then add, "Actually, no."

"What's the matter? How's Yang?"

"I don't know. The tech I took him to says he's dead, but I don't believe him—the guy had a thing against Asians. I'm thinking about taking Yang over to Quick Fix." There's silence on the other end of the line. "How's Mika?" I ask.

"She keeps asking if Yang's okay. I put a movie on for her.... Dead?" she asks. "Are you positive?"

"No, I'm not sure. I don't know. I'm not ready to give up on him yet. Look," I say, glancing at the dash clock, "it's only three. I'm going to suck it up and take him to Quick Fix. I'm sure if I drop enough cash they can do something."

"What will we do if he's dead?" Kyra asks. "I've got work on Monday."

"We'll figure it out," I say. "Let's just wait until I get a second opinion."

Kyra tells me she loves me, and I return my love, and we hang up. It's as my Bluetooth goes dead that I feel the tears coming. I remember last fall when Kyra was watching Mika. I was in the garage taking down the rake when, from behind me, I heard Yang. He stood awkwardly in the doorway, as though he was uncertain what to do while Mika was being taken care of. "Can I help you?" he asked.

On that chilly late afternoon, with the red and orange leaves falling around us—me in my vest, and Yang in the black suit he came with—Yang and I quietly raked leaves into large piles on the flat earth until the backyard looked like a village of leaf huts. Then Yang held open the bag, I scooped the piles in, and we carried them to the curb.

"You want a beer?" I asked, wiping the sweat from my forehead.

"Okay," Yang said. I went inside and got two cold ones from the fridge, and we sat together, on the splintering cedar of the back deck, watching the sun fall behind the trees and the first stars blink to life above us.

"Can't beat a cold beer," I said, taking a swig.

"Yes," Yang said. He followed my lead and took a long drink. I could hear the liquid sloshing down into his stomach canister.

"This is what men do for the family," I said, gesturing with my beer to the leafless yard. Without realizing it, I had slipped into thinking of Yang as my son, imagining that one day he'd be raking leaves for his own wife and children. It occurred to me then that Yang's time with us was limited. Eventually, he'd be shut down and stored in the basement—an antique Mika would have no use for when she had children of her own. At that moment, I wanted to put my arm around Yang. Instead I said, "I'm glad you came out and worked with me."

"Me too," Yang said and took another sip of his beer, looking exactly like me in the way he brought the bottle to his lips.

—⁂—

The kid at Quick Fix makes me feel much more at ease than Russ. He's wearing a bright red vest with a clean white shirt under it and a name tag that reads HI, I'M RONNIE! The kid's probably not even twenty-one. He's friendly, though, and when I tell him about Yang, he says, "Whoa, that's no good," which is at least a little sympathetic. He tells me they're backed up for an hour. So much for quick, I think. I put Yang on the counter and give my name. "We'll page you once he's ready," Ronnie says.

I spend the time wandering the store. They've got a demo station of *Championship Boxing*, so I put on the jacket and glasses and take on a guy named Vance, who's playing in California. I can't figure out how to dodge or block though, and when I throw out my hand, my guy on the screen just wipes his nose with his glove. Vance beats the shit out of me, so I put the glasses and vest back on the rack and go look at other equipment. I'm playing with one of the new ThoughtPhones when I hear my name paged over the loudspeaker, so I head back to the Repair counter.

"Fried," the kid tells me. "Honestly, it's probably good he bit it. He's a really outdated model." Ronnie is rocking back and forth on his heels as though impatient to get on to his next job.

"Isn't there anything you can do?" I ask. "He's my daughter's Big Brother."

"The language system is fully functional. If you want, I can separate the head for you."

"*Are you kidding?* I'm not giving my daughter her brother's head to play with."

"Oh," the kid says. "Well, um, we could remove the voice box for you. And we can recycle the body and give you twenty dollars off any digital camera."

"How much is all this going to cost?"

"It's ninety-five for the checkup, thirty-five for disposal, and voice box removal will be another hundred and fifty. You're probably looking at about three hundred after labor and taxes."

I think about taking him back to Russ, but there's no way. When he'd told me Yang was beyond saving, I gave him a look of distrust that anyone could read loud and clear. "Go ahead and remove the voice box," I say, "but no recycling. I want to keep the body."

—◊—

George is outside throwing a football around with his identical twins when I pull in. He raises his hand to his kids to stop them from throwing the ball and comes over to the low hedge that separates our driveways. "Hey, how'd it go with Russ?" he asks as I get out of the car.

"Not good." I tell him about Yang, getting a second opinion, how I've got his voice box in the backseat, his body in a large Quick Fix bag in the trunk. I tell him all this with as little emotion as possible. "What can you expect from electronics?" I say, attempting to appear nonchalant.

"Man, I'm really sorry for you," George says, his voice quieter than I've ever heard it. "Yang was a good kid. I remember the day he came over to help Dana carry in the groceries. The kids still talk about that fortune-telling thing he showed them with the three coins."

"Yeah," I say, looking at the bushes. I can feel the tears starting again. "Anyhow, it's no big deal. Don't let me keep you from your game. We'll figure it out." Which is a complete lie. I have no clue how we're going to figure anything out. We needed Yang, and there's no way we can afford another model.

"Hey, listen," George says. "If you guys need help, let us know. You know, if you need a day sitter or something. I'll talk to Dana—I'm sure she'd be up for taking Mika." George reaches out across the hedge, his large hand coming straight at me. For a moment I flash back to *Championship Boxing* and think he's going to hit me. Instead he pats me on the shoulder. "I'm really sorry, Jim," he says.

—◊—

That night, I lie with Mika in bed and read her *Goodnight Moon*. It's the first time I've read to her in months. The last time was when we visited Kyra's folks and had to shut Yang down for the weekend. Mika's asleep by the time I reach the last page. I give her a kiss on her head and turn out the lights. Kyra's in bed reading.

"I guess I'm going to start digging now," I say.

"Come here," she says, putting her book down. I cross the room and lie across our bed, my head on her belly.

"Do you miss him too?" I ask.

"Mm-hm," she says. She puts her hand on my head and runs her fingers through my hair. "I think saying goodbye tomorrow is a good idea. Are you sure it's okay to have him buried out there?"

"Yeah. There's no organic matter in him. The guys at Quick Fix dumped his stomach canister." I look up at our ceiling, the way our lamp casts a circle of light and then a dark shadow. "I don't know how we're going to make it without him."

"Shhh." Kyra strokes my hair. "We'll figure it out. I spoke with Tina Matthew after you called me today. You remember her daughter, Lauren?"

"The clone?"

"Yes. She's home this semester; college wasn't working for her. Tina said Lauren could watch Mika if we need her to."

I turn my head to look at Kyra. "I thought we didn't want Mika raised by a clone."

"We're doing what we have to do. Besides, Lauren is a nice girl."

"She's got that glassy-eyed apathetic look. She's exactly like her mother," I say. Kyra doesn't say anything. She knows I'm being irrational, and so do I. I sigh. "I just really hoped we could keep clones out of our lives."

"For how long? Your brother and Margaret are planning on cloning this summer. You're going to be an uncle soon enough."

"Yeah," I say quietly.

Ever since I was handed Yang's voice box, time has slowed down. The light of the setting sun had stretched across the wood floors of our home for what seemed an eternity. Sounds have become crisper as well, as though, until now, I'd been living with earplugs. I think about the way Mika's eyelids fluttered as she slept, the feel of George's hand against my arm. I sit up, turn toward Kyra, and kiss her. The softness of her lips makes me remember the first time we kissed. Kyra squeezes my hand. "You better start digging so I can comfort you tonight," she says. I smile and ease myself off the bed. "Don't worry," Kyra says, "it'll be a good funeral."

In the hallway, on my way toward the staircase, the cracked door of Yang's room stops me. Instead of going down, I walk across the carpeting to his door, push it open, and flick on the light switch. There's his bed, perfectly made with the corners tucked in, a writing desk, a heavy oak dresser, and a closet full of black suits. On the wall is a poster of China that Brothers & Sisters Inc. sent us and a pennant from the Tigers game I took Yang to. There's little in the minimalism of his décor to remind me of him. There is, however, a baseball glove on the shelf by his bed. This was a present Yang bought for himself with the small allowance we provided him. We were at Toys 'R Us when Yang placed the glove in the shopping cart. We didn't ask him about it, and he didn't mention why he was buying it. When he came home, he put it on the shelf near his Tigers pennant, and there it sat untouched.

Along the windowsill, Yang's collection of dead moths and butterflies looks as though they're ready to take flight. He collected them from beneath our bug zapper during the summer and placed their powdery bodies by the window. I walk over and examine the collection. There's the great winged luna moth, with its two mock eyes staring at me, the mosaic of a monarch's wing, and a collection of smaller nondescript brown and silvery gray moths. Kyra once asked him about his insects. Yang's face illuminated momentarily, the lights beneath his cheeks burning extra brightly, and he'd said, "They're very beautiful, don't you think?" Then, as though suddenly embarrassed, he segued to a Fun Fact regarding the brush-footed butterfly of China.

What arrests me, though, are the objects on his writing desk. Small matchboxes are stacked in a pile on the center of the table, the matchsticks spread across the expanse like tiny logs. In a corner is an orange-capped bottle of Elmer's that I recognize as the one from my toolbox. What was Yang up to? A log cabin? A city of small wooden men and women? Maybe this was Yang's attempt at art—one that, unlike the calligraphy he was programmed to know, was entirely his own. Tomorrow I'll bag his suits, donate them to Goodwill, and throw out the Brothers & Sisters poster, but these matchboxes, the butterflies, and the baseball glove, I'll save. They're the only traces of the boy Yang might have been.

—⁂—

The funeral goes well. It's a beautiful October day, the sky thin and blue, and the sun lights up the trees, bringing out the ocher and amber of the season. I imagine what the three of us must look like to the neighbors. A bunch of kooks burying their electronic equipment like pagans. I don't care. When I think about Yang being ripped apart in a recycling plant or stuffing him into our plastic garbage can and setting him out with the trash, I know this is the right decision. Standing together as a family, in the corner of our backyard, I say a couple of parting words. I thank Yang for all the joy he brought to our lives. Then Mika and Kyra say goodbye. Mika begins to cry, and Kyra and I bend down and put our arms around her, and we stay there, holding one another in the early morning sunlight.

When it's all over, we go back inside to have breakfast. We're eating our cereal when the doorbell rings. I get up and answer it. On our doorstep is a glass vase filled with orchids and white lilies. A small card is attached. I kneel down and open it. *Didn't want to disturb you guys. Just wanted to give you these. We're all very sorry for your loss—George, Dana, and the twins.* Amazing, I think. This from a guy who paints his face for Super Bowl games.

"Hey, look what we got," I say, carrying the flowers into the kitchen. "They're from George."

"They're beautiful," Kyra says. "Come, Mika, let's go put those in the living room by your brother's picture." Kyra helps Mika out of her chair, and we walk into the other room together.

It was Kyra's idea to put the voice box behind the photograph. The photo is a picture from our trip to China last summer. In it, Mika and Yang are playing at the gate of a park. Mika stands at the port, holding the two large iron gates together. From the other side, Yang looks through the hole of the gates at the camera. His head is slightly cocked, as though wondering who we all are. He has a placid nonsmile/nonfrown, the expression we came to identify as Yang at his happiest.

"You can talk to him," I say to Mika as I place the flowers next to the photograph.

"Goodbye, Yang," Mika says.

"Goodbye?" the voice box asks. "But, little sister, where are we going?"

Mika smiles at the sound of her Big Brother's voice and looks up at me for instruction. It's an awkward moment. I'm not about to tell Yang that the rest of him is buried in the backyard.

"Nowhere," I answer. "We're all here together." There's a pause as though Yang's thinking about something. Then, quietly, he asks, "Did you know over two million workers died during the building of the Great Wall of China?" Kyra and I exchange a look regarding the odd coincidence of this Fun Fact, but neither of us says anything. Then Yang's voice starts up again. "The Great Wall is over ten thousand *li* long. A *li* is a standardized Chinese unit of measurement that is equivalent to one thousand six hundred and forty feet."

"Wow, that's amazing," Kyra says, and I stand next to her, looking at the flowers George sent, acknowledging how little I truly know about this world.

NIGHT SHIFT

TESSA YANG

THESE DAYS, ISABELLE'S EXHAUSTION ANCHORS ITSELF in strange places. She feels it in her sagging wrists and the top of her head. As warm static at her fingertips. An oil slick in the gut. She's been the night attendant at the Speedway for seven and a half years. Never before has daytime sleep eluded her with such persistence.

What's changed? Nothing: Not the thickness of her blackout curtains. Not the quality of her pink foam earplugs. Not the volume of the neighbors who rent the apartment downstairs (retired couple, bird watchers, porch full of wind chimes and prayer flags). Yet at noon, Isabelle invariably finds herself lying in bed as a tiny marching band blasts its horns between her ears. Or as old, idiotic riddles cartwheel through her brain on repeat.

What has four eyes but can't see?
Mississippi!
What can you catch but not throw?
A cold!

Her daughter, Lynn, recommends yoga and meditation. But what does she know? Lynn is an attorney for a makeup company called All Natural Beauty that recently came under fire for testing its products on guinea pigs. (*"Allegedly* testing," Lynn barks whenever Isabelle mentions the lawsuit.) She carries her stress like a war banner. Her back is a pretzel of knots. It's a point of pride with her that she inherited Victor's mania for long hours. "Daddy was such a hard worker," she'll sigh, gazing into her vast weed-choked backyard during their weekly lunches, and Isabelle will stab her fork into her salad and wish, as usual, that she had not come.

The Speedway manager, Baran, recommends valerian-root tea. "The ancient Greeks used it to relax. It smells like an asshole," he says, "but it does the trick." Baran stops by once a month, as Isabelle's shift begins, to "touch base" and confirm that the little red pepper spray canister remains intact and ready for action beneath the register. His idea, not hers. Baran is twenty-six and feels bad about leaving an old lady defenseless.

After he leaves, Isabelle slouches forward and rests her cheek on the counter, inhaling the smell of Lysol. She likes the night shift—its mystery, its quiet. She likes how glossy and promising the snack packages look beneath the white fluorescence, so much so that she suffers a sense of letdown when she walks back to her car each dawn. Always she thinks there will be more mystery. *More* promise. When Baran drops by, she wants celestial fireworks and angelic fanfare to mark this glorious union between the forces of Management and Labor. Instead she gets a discussion about asshole tea. Why would she want her mouth to smell like an asshole? Anyway, she needs something a lot harder than ancient Greek flowers. One of those tranquilizer darts they use on escaped animals at the zoo would be good. A sharp prick in the butt, a rubbery heat spreading to her fingers and toes, and she would be out for hours.

The bell jingles as the door flies open. Isabelle stays where she is, watching impassively as a kid in glasses and cargo pants hurries past the glowing wall of beverages. At the counter, he halts, panting. A white triangular stud gleams in his left ear. His T-shirt reads, "Tacos for President."

"I need ten dollars' worth of gas. Number four."

Isabelle sighs. Her breath makes a little smog on the Formica. With great effort she lifts herself off the counter and prods the register awake.

"Thing is," says the kid. He grimaces. "I don't *have* ten dollars."

She blinks at him. She lifts her hand from the register and sets it on the counter, drumming her fingers.

"Look," he says. He lowers into a kind of half squat so they're eye to eye. "I ran out of the house without my wallet. Please? It's an emergency. My wife's going into labor and I—"

"Try again," says Isabelle.

He pauses. "My little brother got into a car accident, and I've got to get to the hospital before—"

"*Eeeeeehhhn,*" says Isabelle, mimicking the noise of a buzzer. "You can do better than that."

He looks flustered. "I don't know what you want to hear."

"How about the truth?"

The kid chews the inside of his cheek. He could be nineteen, early twenties. He jiggles his leg, and the keys clipped to his belt sway and jangle. "I think my boyfriend's cheating on me," he blurts at last. "Tyler texted me to say he saw Nick coming out of a bar with some girl."

"Well, if Tyler said it," remarks Isabelle, "it must be true."

He seems not to hear. He licks his lips, patches of which are bright red and fresh looking, as though he picked at them on the drive over.

"I just gotta know, you know? I gotta see for myself. I thought I'd try and get over there as fast as I could and catch them in the act."

"Then what?"

His forehead crinkles. "Well, I—I hadn't really gotten that far. But I'll think of something. I'll know what to do. Please." The frantic, beseeching expression returns. "You can have whatever you want. My watch—" He sets it on the counter, a clunky digital thing, the inside of the leather strap faded from age and sweat. He begins to empty his many pockets. A crushed piece of Trident sugarless gum. A baggie with three green pills. A rubber band. The spring from a broken pen. A wad of tissues. Another rubber band. "You can have it all. I've got to get over there. My gas light's been on since yesterday. There's no way I'll make it without—"

"What are these?" asks Isabelle, nudging the baggie of pills with her fingertip.

He looks shifty. "Vitamins."

Isabelle considers the mess of him scattered across the countertop, everything he can afford to give. "All right. You leave these here as collateral, I'll let you fill the tank. Then you come back once your quest has ended. Pay what you owe. Our transaction will be complete."

She taps the register again. The kid looks a little dazed, like he can't believe his paltry bargaining actually worked. He runs out of the building without saying thank you. Isabelle watches him fill the old Ford parked at pump number four. She doesn't suppose she'll ever see him again. The register will come up ten dollars short, but Baran will find someone else to blame. Phil, the gawky teenager. Danica, who comes in to replace Isabelle at dawn.

—◊—

She resumes her slouch across the counter. Around one, a taxi driver walks in, looking for change. Then an exhausted-looking girl in pink scrubs, blonde hair a frizzy halo, purchases a pack of cigarettes and a Diet Coke. Isabelle mops the floor. She eats her lunch: a plastic cube of Kroger potato salad and a raspberry

Snapple snatched from the back of one of the refrigerators. It's a quarter to three. The kid has not returned. She claws around under the counter for his baggie of pills, takes one, pops it into her mouth, and washes it down with a swallow of tea.

She waits for something to happen.

She and Victor used to get stoned when Lynn was at summer camp, but it's been a long time. She goes to make the coffee, wobbling a little on the still-damp floors. She divorced Victor after he cheated on her twice—first with their real estate agent and then with the high school librarian. Later he got pancreatic cancer, and she had to endure Lynn's dewy-eyed proclamations about how brave he was, right up until he died in a bed at Bethesda North.

The coffee steams and hisses. Isabelle sips from her cup too quickly. The liquid scalds her tongue and brings tears to her eyes. She never got to catch Victor in the act. The first time he came out and told her. The second time she guessed, and he didn't deny it. He was bizarrely honorable like that. No excuses, no entreating her to take him back, not even when he was dying and the librarian had abandoned him for a healthy man.

If she *had* caught him in the act? Isabelle tries to imagine her response. Crying? Hurling shoes and picture frames? No: she's always been too dignified to admit when she gets hurt.

The floors are dry now. Still, she continues to wobble. Her thighs feel like they're eight miles from her feet. She can't figure out how to bend her knees. Through a series of awkward lurches, she makes it back behind the register. She's so thirsty. The fluorescent lights emit a low organ melody. How has she never noticed it before? She closes her eyes, just for a second. When she wakes up, she's lying on the floor, and a tiny green dragon is hovering above her navel, its wings beating a shimmering blur like a hummingbird's.

"Oh, boo hoo," says the dragon. "Poor Isabelle. Poor you. So lonely. So cold. No one's got it harder than Isabelle. Lowest of the low."

She touches the back of her head to ensure she didn't crack it on her way to the floor. Everything seems to be in order. She sits up. The dragon settles on the edge of the countertop, peers down at her through crazy purple eyes.

"Who are you?" asks Isabelle.

"Take away my first letter," says the dragon. "And I remain the same. Take away my last letter, and I'm still the same. Even take away the letter in my middle, and I won't know the difference. Who am I?"

Isabelle thinks for a moment. "Empty," she says. "You're Empty."

"No, you are." The dragon cackles. It's a sound of destruction, like pages being ripped from a book. Isabelle shuts her eyes again, but when she opens them, the dragon's still there, flying in tight circles around the rack of lighters and gum.

"I have a stomach," says Isabelle. "I have intestines and blood and lungs and bones—"

"You know that's not what I mean."

She does know. But she doesn't want to face it: the cavernous waste that finds her sweaty and sleepless at midday, that tempts her to its lip with its siren song of *regret, regret, regret.*

The door opens. A boy trots inside and yanks a six-pack of Dos Equis from the fridge. He's almost certainly too young to be buying beer, but Isabelle rings him up without carding him. She no longer hears the organ melody. She can't hear much of anything. It's as if her head's been packed with steel wool. It takes all her concentration to navigate the register's touch screen. The boy flashes her a grin and races outside to his truck. Isabelle sees a girl in the passenger seat with a long ponytail, a tank top strap sliding off one shoulder.

The dragon floats to the window and shakes his tiny head in disgust. "Young love is so uninspiring."

"I never said that," says Isabelle.

"I'm saying it right now, crazy pants. They don't know what's waiting for them. Abandonment, dejection. Or, if they're really unlucky, they'll get the long slow melt toward hatred."

"I didn't hate Victor."

"No. You loved him. You used to sneak out to the hospital and feed him ice chips at night. Never told Lynn, though, did you? Far better to go on acting vengeful and wronged. You know she's never forgiven you for how you treated him at the end. Her daddy dearest, Papa of the Year . . ."

"What can you easily break," asks Isabelle, "but never touch?" She's desperate to make the dragon shut up and has the feeling that if she can stump him with a really tough one, he'll go away. The dragon cackles again. "That's easy. A promise."

"What three letters change a girl into a woman?"

"Age."

"Everybody is attracted to me, and everybody falls for me. What am I?"

"Oh puh-*leeze*," says the dragon. "At least give me a challenge. You're gravity."

Isabelle feels feverish. She stumbles to the nearest refrigerator, grabs a bottle of water, and untwists the cap. Her blurry reflection hovers over the colorful ranks of beverages. The dragon is no longer speaking, but she can still hear him. *Mama*, goes the voice from inside her head. It's the voice of an aggrieved

eight-year-old Lynn, begging for a Wonder Woman comic at the bookstore—
though as the word repeats, *MamaMamaMama*, it becomes untethered from
its origin, and Isabelle realizes her daughter could be asking for any number of
things she never received.

After the divorce, Isabelle cut herself off from the world. She drew Lynn
into her self-exile. Wouldn't let her stay after school or go out with friends.
Forbade sleepovers, birthday parties, homecoming, prom. They lived like filthy
hermits, takeout containers spilling off the arms of the sofa. The TV was always
on, even when Isabelle stopped paying the cable bill and the screen glowed a
harsh, empty blue. That was the start of all Lynn's neuroses. She threw herself
into her studies. She picked at her eyebrows and chewed the ends of her hair.
Crescents of shed fingernails gathered beneath the kitchen table. The only reason Lynn had survived those years, Isabelle knew, was the weekends she spent
with her father. Victor of the normal house and steady job. Victor, who went
on doling out child support and alimony, never saying a single word against
Isabelle, never threatening to take away custody, even though Lynn must have
complained and he could see the yard falling into ruin, the wisteria vines snak-
ing over the windows and sealing the house in darkness.

It is this silence that Isabelle resents the most. He was too polite, and she was
too proud, and Lynn had suffered from their refusal to have it out with each
other, get angry, throw shoes. It's twenty years later, and she and Lynn still
can't step outside their perfunctory script. They talk about groceries, politics,
the weather, Lynn's job. Isabelle had always thought time would ease things
between them. She sees now it has only frozen them back there, before that
glowing blue screen.

Isabelle sinks to the floor with her back to the cold refrigerator door, but
it feels more like flying, like a giant hand has bundled her into a slingshot,
drawn back the leather pocket, and sent her wheeling and flailing toward some
unimaginable target.

"Hey," says the dragon. "Hey. Lady. Hello?"

It's not the dragon. It's Tacos for President. He's crouched next to her, waving
a palm in front of her face. Isabelle slaps his hand away. Her eyeballs feel like
they've outgrown their sockets. The kid takes hold of her arm and helps her to
her feet. Outside, the parking lot fills with the weird gray light of almost-dawn.
An enormous crow perches on the ice bin. Isabelle staggers to the counter
and leans against it for support. She flexes her fingers, curls them slowly and
deliberately into a fist.

"Lady, you are high as all fuck," declares the kid.

"I saw a tiny dragon," Isabelle admits.

"Oh, him. He's the worst. Here." He hands her a crumpled ten-dollar bill. Isabelle smooths it against the counter and presses it flat against her cheek.

"Your quest?" she asks.

The kid shuffles his sneakers. "Nick was sleeping when I got there. Alone. He'd just got off the late shift at Walmart. Turns out Tyler's sort of a liar. I guess he's, like, jealous of me or something?"

Isabelle slips the ten into the register and begins blearily to count out the drawer. She's having trouble with the numbers. She keeps looking around for the dragon. She can feel herself coming down, a sick settling, like a dirty bottle sinking to the bottom of a pond. The crow in the parking lot caws once, twice. The door jingles, and Danica waltzes into the building clutching a purple thermos. She's in her late thirties, a dreamy girl with heavy wood jewelry and big headphones that she slides down around her neck when she asks Isabelle how her shift went.

"Usual," says Isabelle. She's afraid if she utters one more word, she might throw up. She shuts the cash drawer. On a whim, she sweeps the baggie of pills and the rest of the kid's stuff from under the counter into her purse before she walks out. She lost track of him while she was struggling with the drawer, but he's still in the parking lot, sitting on the hood of the Ford with his heels propped on the bumper, looking shiny and unspoiled in the day's first light.

"You got someone to drive you home?" he asks.

"I'll manage," says Isabelle.

"You shouldn't drive in your state. Let me take you."

She studies his features, the lines of muscle standing out on his young arms, and her thoughts leap briefly to the pepper spray taped under the counter. But she's tired and sick, and for the first time in a long time, she doesn't want to be alone. The kid programs her address into his cell phone, and they're off.

The sun rises above the highway. Cars clutter the on-ramp for the morning commute. It strikes Isabelle as crazy that there are people whose days are just beginning. She feels as though she's been awake for years. The radio purrs soft rock through a fizz of static. The kid drives with the windows down; the air blasting through the car smells of hot tar. The passenger seat is pulled way back to accommodate legs much longer than Isabelle's. She can't remember the last time she was a passenger, but there's a sweet comfort in allowing herself to be driven.

One of her bird-watching neighbors—the man, Horace—is sitting in a lawn chair facing the woods when they reach Isabelle's apartment. He waves a pair of binoculars as the kid helps her out of the car.

"You just missed the most remarkable tanager!"

"Darn," says the kid. He leads Isabelle up the stairs to her door, then whispers, "What's a tanager?"

"Bird," grunts Isabelle. She maneuvers the key into its lock. "Why're you being so nice to me?"

"They were my pills."

"You didn't force them down my throat."

He follows her inside. She doesn't protest. A monstrous exhaustion is creeping over her. She stops at the kitchen sink to guzzle more water. The kid turns in a circle, taking it all in: the booklets of expired coupons taped to the fridge, the dead oregano plant on the windowsill, the pantry's scuffed accordion door, the years' worth of crusted noodles and scrambled eggs jammed in the groove between counter and stove.

"It's nice," he says.

"You're joking."

"Nicer than my place."

"I moved here after I lost the house. Child support ran out when Lynn turned twenty-one." She slips, nearly falls, but the kid's got the timing of some action-movie hero. Together they amble down the hall to the bedroom. "Started taking these jobs," mutters Isabelle. "Cashier. Car wash. Parking garage."

"You like cars?"

"I like being around folks who are on their way."

She lands on the bed without drawing back the covers, her purse pinned beneath her. The kid stands by the window. Light splinters the top of the curtains, covering him in bright moving splotches as he sways on his feet. The wave of her exhaustion reaches its crest. It's poised, waiting to crash over her head. Isabelle extracts her purse from underneath her. She fumbles for his belongings and sets them one by one on the bed. He returns everything to his pockets, taking equal care with the pills and rubber bands and tissues.

"You'll be all right once you get some sleep," he says. "You'll probably have a headache when you wake up. You got something for pain?"

"Why do you do it?" asks Isabelle. "Why do you take those pills when he says such awful things?"

"Usually I only take a half."

"But you still see him."

The kid gnaws his lower lip. "I guess it's like, there's this little voice inside my head, hating on all the wrong things I've ever done. Everything I've ever regretted. But the pills—they take it outside me where I can look at it. Fight it if I want."

Isabelle curls onto her side, smothering her laughter in a pillow. She wants to ask this child what he could possibly know about regret. She wants to present to him the unsolvable riddle of love and resentment that have curdled until one is indistinguishable from the other. But she also wants to find him here when she wakes. His stupid T-shirt. His ludicrous faith.

RECOMMENDED READING

Brewer, Josh A., ed. *Writers Resist: Hoosier Writers Unite*. Chatter House Press, 2017.

Kander, Jenny, and C. E. Greer, eds. *And Know This Place: Poetry of Indiana*. Indiana Historical Society, 2011.

Love, Samuel A., ed. *The Gary Anthology*. Belt Publishing, 2020.

Martone, Michael, and Bryan Furuness, eds. *Winesburg, Indiana: A Fork River Anthology*. Break Away Books, 2015.

Minnick, Norman, ed. *The Indianapolis Anthology*. Belt Publishing, 2021.

Shoup, Barbara, ed. *Not Like the Rest of Us: An Anthology of Contemporary Indiana Writers*. INwords, 2016.

BOOKS

Adams, Michael. *In Praise of Profanity*. Oxford University Press, 2016.

Begnal, Michael. *Future Blues*. Salmon Poetry, 2012.

Boruch, Marianne. *Bestiary Dark*. Copper Canyon, 2021.

———. *The Little Death of Self*. University of Michigan Press, 2017.

Bowman, Catherine. *Can I Finish, Please?* Four Way, 2016.

Brown, Stacey Lynn. *The Shallows*. Persea, 2018.

Christman, Jill. *If This Were Fiction*. University of Nebraska Press, 2022.

Coleman, Patrick. *The Churchgoer*. Harper Perennial, 2019.

———. *Fire Season*. Tupelo, 2018.

Daniels, David J. *Clean*. Four Way, 2014.

Dargan, Kyle. *Anagnorisis*. TriQuarterly Books, 2018.

———. *Honest Engine.* University of Georgia Press, 2015.

Davis, Noah. *Of This River.* Michigan State University Press, 2020.

Fowler, Karen Joy. *Booth.* G. P. Putnam's Sons, 2022.

——— *We Are All Completely beside Ourselves.* G. P. Putnam's Sons, 2022.

Gay, Ross. *Be Holding.* University of Pittsburgh Press, 2020.

———. *Bringing the Shovel Down.* University of Pittsburgh Press, 2011.

———. *Catalog of Unabashed Gratitude.* University of Pittsburgh Press, 2015.

Gay, Roxane. *Difficult Women.* Grove, 2017.

Gloria, Eugene. *My Favorite Warlord.* Penguin, 2012.

———. *Sightseer in This Killing City.* Penguin, 2019.

Green, John. *The Anthropocene Reviewed.* Dutton, 2021.

———. *Turtles All the Way Down.* Penguin, 2019.

Gunty, Tess. *The Rabbit Hutch.* Knopf, 2022.

Hendrickson, Lisa. *Burning the Breeze: Three Generations of Women in the American West.* University of Nebraska Press, 2021.

Irving, Dionne. *The Islands.* Catapult, 2022.

Jackson-Brown, Angela. *House Repairs.* Negative Capability Press, 2018.

———. *The Light Always Breaks.* Harper Muse, 2022.

———. *When Stars Rain Down.* Thomas Nelson, 2021.

Johnson, Dana. *Elsewhere, California.* Counterpoint, 2012.

Kispert, Peter. *I Know You Know Who I Am.* Penguin, 2020.

Klehfoth, Elizabeth. *All These Beautiful Strangers.* William Morrow, 2018.

Krapf, Norbert. *American Dreams: Reveries and Revisitations.* Mongrel Empire, 2013.

———. *Indiana Hill Country Poems.* Dos Madres, 2019.

———. *Southwest by Midwest.* Dos Madres, 2020.

Lawson, Shayla. *This Is Major.* Harper Perennial, 2020.

Lee, Esther. *Sacrificial Metal.* Conduit Books, 2020.

Lewis, Paige. *Space Struck.* Sarabande, 2019.

Ling, Micah. *Settlement.* Sunnyoutside, 2012.

Logan, Nate. *Inside the Golden Days of Missing You.* Magic Helicopter, 2019.

Manning, Maurice. *Railsplitter.* Copper Canyon, 2019.

Matejka, Adrian. *The Big Smoke.* Penguin, 2013.

———. *Map to the Stars.* Penguin, 2017.

———. *Somebody Else Sold the World.* Penguin, 2021.

McAuliffe, Shena. *Glass Light Electricity.* University of Alaska Press, 2020.

McOmber, Adam. *Fantasy Kit.* Black Lawrence, 2022.

———. *The White Forest.* Gallery Books, 2012.

McSweeney, Joyelle. *Percussion Grenade.* Fence Books, 2012.

———. *Toxicon and Arachne.* Nightboat Books, 2020.

Miller, Alyce. *Skunk.* Reaktion Books, 2015.

———. *Sweet Love*. China Grove Press, 2015.
Orem, William. *Miss Lucy*. Gival Press, 2019.
Platt, Donald. *Man Praying*. Parlor, 2017.
Rebein, Robert. *Headlights on the Prairie*. University Press of Kansas, 2017.
Schwipps, Gregory. *What This River Keeps*. Indiana University Press, 2012.
Scranton, Roy. *War Porn*. Soho Press, 2017.
———. *We're Doomed. Now What?* Soho Press, 2018.
Skyhorse, Brando. *The Madonnas of Echo Park*. Free Press, 2011.
———. *Take This Man*. Simon & Schuster, 2014.
Sneed, Christine. *Please Be Advised*. 7.13 Books, 2022.
———. *Portraits of a Few of the People I've Made Cry*. Bloomsbury, 2013.
Speaker, Mary Austin. *The Bridge*. Shearsman Books, 2016.
———. *Ceremony*. Slope Editions, 2013.
Sullivan, Daniel "Sully." *O Body*. Haymarket Books, 2023.
Sykes, Taylor. *Many Small Disasters*. Los Galesburg Press, 2019.
Teare, Brian. *Doomstead Days*. Nightboat Books, 2019.
———. *The Empty Form Goes All the Way to Heaven*. Ahsahta, 2015.
Teitman, Ryan. *Litany for the City*. BOA Editions, Ltd., 2012.
Townsend, Jacinda. *Mother Country*. Graywolf, 2022.
Upadhyay, Samrat. *The City Son*. Soho Press, 2014.
———. *Mad Country*. Soho Press, 2017.
Whittenberg, Allison. *Carnival of Reality*. Apprentice House, 2022.
Young, Dean. *Shock by Shock*. Copper Canyon, 2017.
———. *Solar Perplexus*. Copper Canyon, 2021.
Young, Kevin. *The Book of Hours*. Knopf, 2015.
———. *The Grey Album*. Graywolf, 2012.
———. *Stones*. Knopf, 2021.
Zauner, Michelle. *Crying in H Mart*. Knopf, 2021.

CONTRIBUTOR BIOS

KAVEH AKBAR is author of *Pilgrim Bell* (Graywolf Press, 2021) and *Calling a Wolf a Wolf* (Alice James Books, 2017). He was born in Tehran, Iran, and is currently a professor at the University of Iowa and the low-residency program at Randolph College.

DASON ANDERSON was probably once a pirate and perhaps a cloven-hoofed creature too. This go-round he lives in Bloomington, near where he grew up amid the limestone quarries and the Hoosier National Forest. Dason sometimes writes, has been published here and there, and even once got paid $8 for a poem.

NOAH BALDINO's poems have appeared in *Poetry*, *New England Review*, and *Indiana Review*. A graduate of the MFA program at Purdue University, they currently live in Maine and serve as a reader for *Poetry*.

BRYCE BERKOWITZ received the AMC TV Pilot Award at the Austin Film Festival. He is author of *Bermuda Ferris Wheel*, winner of the 42 Miles Press Poetry Award, and his writing has appeared in *Best New Poets*, *The Sewanee Review*, and *The Missouri Review*.

JOE BETZ is Associate Professor of English at Ivy Tech Community College and produces electronic music as Knuckled Fruit. He earned an MFA in Creative Writing from the University of Missouri—St. Louis. He lives in Bloomington.

CALLISTA BUCHEN is author of *Look Look Look* (Black Lawrence, 2019). Winner of *DIAGRAM*'s essay contest, her work has appeared in *Puerto del Sol*, *Fourteen Hills*, and *Harpur Palate*. She is Assistant Professor of English at Franklin College.

DOUG PAUL CASE is author of *Americanitis* (Ghost City Press, 2023) and four chapbooks, including *Contemporary Aesthetics* (Seven Kitchens, 2019). He is Assistant Director of Creative Writing at Indiana University.

STEVE CASTRO resides in Southern Indiana where he works at a factory. His work has appeared in *Prose Online, Salamander, Dryland, The Madison Review,* and *Berkeley Fiction Review.* In July 2022 he traveled to Copenhagen and Stockholm, where he wrote some poems.

SU CHO is a poet and essayist born in South Korea and raised in Indiana. A former guest editor of *Poetry,* her debut collection, *The Symmetry of Fish* (Penguin, 2022), was a National Poetry Series selection. She is Assistant Professor of English at Clemson University.

C. L. CLARK is a BFA award-winning editor and author of Nebula-finalist *The Unbroken,* the first of the *Magic of the Lost* trilogy, and many short stories. When she's not imagining the fall of empires, she's trying not to throw her kettlebells through the walls.

TIA CLARK is a New Orleans-based writer who received their MFA in fiction from Indiana University. Their stories have appeared in *Joyland, American Short Fiction, The Offing,* and the *Kenyon Review.*

NANDI COMER is author of *American Family: A Syndrome* (Finishing Line, 2018) and *Tapping Out* (Triquarterly, 2020), which won the Society of Midland Authors Award and the Julie Suk Award. She is a Cave Canem Fellow, a Callaloo Fellow, and a Kresge Arts in Detroit Fellow. She directs the Allied Media Projects Speakers Bureau and is codirector of Detroit Lit.

PAUL CUNNINGHAM is a recipient of the 2021 Diann Blakely Poetry Prize. He is author of *Fall Garment* (Schism Press, 2022) and *The House of the Tree of Sores* (Schism Press, 2020). He lives in South Bend, Indiana, where he comanages Action Books.

MITCHELL L. H. DOUGLAS is author of *dying in the scarecrow's arms,* *blak\ \al-fə bet\,* winner of the Persea Books Lexi Rudnitsky/Editor's Choice Award, and *Cooling Board: A Long-Playing Poem,* an NAACP Image Award and Hurston/Wright Legacy Award nominee. He is Associate Professor of English at IUPUI.

M. A. DUBBS is an award-winning Mexican American and LGBT+ writer who hails from Indiana. Her poetry has been archived in Indiana's Poetry Archive (INverse), and she served as judge for the 2022 Poetry Out Loud state competition. In 2021 she published *Aerodynamic Drag,* her first collection of poetry and short fiction.

LAURA DZUBAY is a writer from Indiana with work published or forthcoming in *Mid-American Review, Electric Literature,* and *Cimarron Review.* She won the 2022 AWP Intro Prize and loves hiking, cooking, cats, and haunted places.

KELCEY PARKER ERVICK is author of *The Keeper* (Avery Books/Penguin, 2022) and *The Bitter Life of Božena Němcová* (Rose Metal Press, 2016). A recipient of grants from the Indiana Arts Commission and the Sustainable Arts Foundation, she teaches creative writing and literary collage at Indiana University South Bend.

SHREYA FADIA is a Gujarati American writer and former lawyer originally from Mumbai, India. She holds an MFA from Indiana University, where she served as editor in chief of *Indiana Review*. Her work has appeared in *Black Warrior Review*, *Cream City Review*, *Hobart*, and *The Margins*.

SAMANTHA FAIN is a writer from Indiana. Her chapbooks *Coughing Up Planets* and *sad horse music* debuted with Vegetarian Alcoholic Press and The Daily Drunk in 2021. Her work has appeared in *The Indianapolis Review*, *SWWIM*, *Peach Mag*, and *Hobart*.

SCOTT FENTON received his MFA from Indiana University in 2016. His short fiction has appeared in *Joyland*, *Split Lip*, and *Black Warrior Review*. He teaches writing at the University of Illinois Springfield.

ASHLEY C. FORD is author of the *New York Times* bestselling memoir *Somebody's Daughter* (Flatiron Books, 2021). Her work has appeared in *The Guardian*, *ELLE*, *OUT*, *Teen Vogue*, and *New York Magazine*. She lives in Indianapolis with her husband and their chocolate lab, Astro.

MEGAN GIDDINGS is author of *The Women Could Fly* (Amistand, 2022) and *Lakewood* (Amistad, 2020). A graduate of the MFA program at Indiana University, she is Assistant Professor of English at the University of Minnesota.

MAGGIE GRABER is author of *Swan Hammer: An Instructor's Guide to Mirrors* (MSU Press, 2022), winner of the 2021 Wheelbarrow Poetry Prize. A former wilderness first responder and poetry editor of *Yalobusha Review*, she lives in Oxford, where she is a PhD student at the University of Mississippi.

SILAS HANSEN's essays have appeared in *The Normal School*, *Colorado Review*, *Hayden's Ferry Review*, and *Hobart*. He is the nonfiction editor for *Waxwing* and lives in Muncie, where he teaches creative writing and literary publishing at Ball State University.

RAJPREET HEIR is an Indian from Indiana. She received her BA in Writing from DePauw University and her MFA in Creative Nonfiction from George Mason University. She is Assistant Professor of Creative Nonfiction at Ithaca College with publications in *The Atlantic*, *The New York Times*, and *Brevity*.

JOSEPH HEITHAUS is author of two books, *Poison Sonnets* and *Library of My Hands*. After earning an MFA and PhD at Indiana University, he began teaching English and writing at DePauw University in Greencastle, where he's been a professor for over twenty-five years.

B.J. HOLLARS is author of several books, including *This Is Only a Test* (2016) and *Sightings* (2013) from Indiana University Press. The recipient of the Truman Capote Prize for Literary Nonfiction and the Society of Midland Authors Award, he is Associate Professor of English at the University of Wisconsin—Eau Claire.

JAMES HUBBARD is a painter/printmaker living in Indianapolis and practicing at Thorntown Press at Sugar Creek Art Center in Thorntown, Indiana. The artist focuses on watercolors, acrylic monotypes, relief and intaglio prints of landscape, seascape, and garden subjects. The artist received his undergraduate degree in art education from Indiana University, Bloomington, and taught K–6 art in Wayne Township Indianapolis schools for thirty years, after which he launched his professional career, exhibiting work throughout the United States. James Hubbard has won many state and national awards and is a member of Indiana Artists Club, Watercolor Society of Indiana, 67th Street Printmakers (Indianapolis), Tiger Lily Press (Cincinnati), California Society of Printmakers (San Francisco), and Society of American Graphic Artists (New York City). His work can be found in the collections of Arkansas State University's Bradbury Gallery and Syracuse University Art Galleries as well as various Midwest private collections.

ALLISON JOSEPH lives in Carbondale, Illinois, where she directs the MFA Program in Creative Writing at Southern Illinois University. She is author of several poetry collections, including *Confessions of a Barefaced Woman* (Red Hen, 2018) and *My Father's Kites* (Steel Toe Books, 2010).

YALIE SAWEDA KAMARA, MFA, PhD, is a Sierra Leonean-American writer from Oakland, California. Kamara is the 2022–2023 Cincinnati and Mercantile Library Poet Laureate, author of two poetry chapbooks, and editor of *What You Need to Know about Me: Young Writers on Their Experience of Immigration* (The Hawkins Project, 2022).

CHRISTOPHER KEMPF is author of *What Though the Field Be Lost* (LSU, 2021) and *Late in the Empire of Men*, which won the 2015 Levis Prize from Four Way Books. Kempf holds a PhD in English Literature from the University of Chicago, an MFA from Cornell University, and teaches in the MFA program at the University of Illinois.

PATRICK KINDIG is author of the chapbooks *all the catholic gods* (Seven Kitchens Press 2019) and *Dry Spell* (Porkbelly Press 2016). His poems have appeared in *Colorado Review*, *Copper Nickel*, and *Washington Square Review*. He is Assistant Professor of English at Tarleton State University.

KAREN KOVACIK, a native of Lake County, was Indiana Poet Laureate 2012–2014. Professor of English at IUPUI, she's author of *Nixon and I*, *Beyond the Velvet Curtain*, and *Metropolis Burning*; the editor of *Scattering the Dark*, an anthology of

Polish women poets; and the translator of Jacek Dehnel's *Aperture*, a finalist for the 2019 PEN Award for Poetry in Translation.

KIEN LAM is author of *Extinction Theory* (UGA Press, 2022), winner of the 2021 National Poetry Series. He is a Kundiman fellow and received his MFA from Indiana University. He lives in Los Angeles and works in esports and television.

JACQUELINE JONES LAMON is author of three books of poems, including *What Water Knows* (TriQuarterly, 2021), and the novel *In the Arms of One Who Loves Me* (One World, 2002). A graduate of Mount Holyoke College and UCLA School of Law, she earned her MFA in Creative Writing from Indiana University.

KIESE LAYMON is author of the novel *Long Division* (Scribner, 2021) and the memoirs *How to Slowly Kill Yourself and Others in America* (Scribner, 2020) and *Heavy* (Scribner, 2019). A graduate of the MFA program at Indiana University, he is currently the Libby Shearn Moody Professor of Creative Writing and English at Rice University.

REBECCA LEHMANN is author of *Ringer* (University of Pittsburgh Press, 2019) and *Between the Crackups* (Salt, 2011). Her work has appeared in *Copper Nickel*, *Ploughshares*, NPR's The Slowdown with Tracy K. Smith, and the New York Library's Poem in Your Pocket program. She lives in South Bend and is the founding editor of *Couplet Poetry*.

JOHN LEO is author of *The Names of Ancient Wars* (Ghost City Press, 2021) and the chapbook *The Long Weekend is Over* (CWP Collective Press, 2018). He is the designer of the board games *Wolves of Mercia* (2019) and *Eat the Rich!* (2020). He has an MFA from Butler University.

KEITH LEONARD is author of *Ramshackle Ode* (Mainer/HarperCollins, 2016). His poems have appeared in *The Believer, New England Review,* and *Ploughshares*. Keith has received fellowships from the Bread Loaf Writers' Conference, the Sewanee Writers' Conference, and the Sustainable Arts Foundation.

BRIAN LEUNG is author of *All I Should Not Tell* (C&R, 2022), *Ivy vs. Dogg* (C&R, 2018), and *Take Me Home* (Harper, 2010). A recipient of the Asian American Literary Award and the Mary McCarthy Prize in Short Fiction, he teaches in the MFA program at Purdue University.

ANNI LIU is author of *Border Vista* (Persea, 2022). Born and raised in 西安, 陕西, then later in Bowling Green, Ohio, Liu earned a BA in Creative Writing with honors from Ohio Wesleyan University and an MFA at Indiana University. Liu works as an editor at Graywolf Press.

NANCY CHEN LONG is author of *Wider than the Sky* (Diode Editions, 2020) and *Light into Bodies* (University of Tampa Press, 2017). Her work has been supported by a National Endowment of the Arts Creative Writing Fellowship and the Poetry Society of America Robert H. Winner Award. She works at Indiana University.

ALESSANDRA LYNCH is author of *Daylily Called It a Dangerous Moment* (Alice James Books, 2017), *It was a terrible cloud at twilight* (LSU Press, 2008), and *Sails the Wind Left Behind* (Alice James Books, 2002). She received fellowships from Yaddo and The MacDowell Colony, serves as poet-in-residence at Butler University, and lives in Indianapolis.

MICHAEL MARTONE was born in Fort Wayne, Indiana, and went to the public school there, attending North Side High School during the years they took to renovate the old building. The construction went on all four years of Martone's time in high school, and the students worked around the workers who closed first one wing of rooms then the next, sending classes looking for a new space or reclaiming a room now rewired or freshly painted or floored with new terrazzo. The electricity for the master clock in the principal's office had been cut early, and all the clocks in the hallways and classrooms found their own separate times. Most stopped. Some sped up, swept ceaselessly, or stuttered in place as if it was now impossible to move to the next second or the next, sticking with each tick, mesmerizing Martone with a cruel montage of what was now becoming his lost and wasted youth. The period bells, the commencement and dismissal bells, had quit ringing months ago, and the space of time when the students changed classes was marked in gritty silence. A rudimentary PA system had been jerry-rigged, tinny speakers and exposed wires, and each morning the Guidance Counselor squeaked that the official North Side time was whatever it was. Everyone set his or her watch, regulated for the rest of the day, shuffling through the debris and drop cloths in the work-light-lit hallways. It was here Martone first studied chemistry in the fifty year old laboratories on the third floor east wing that would be the last to see repair. He still has his slide rule, Army surplus, in its leather case. The hairline cursor embedded in the sliding glass indicator, he realized, was a real hair. He learned to manipulate the contraption in the oversubscribed extra credit slide rule seminar after the regulation lab session. There, too, in the chemistry labs, he saw, for the first time, his teacher perform the Old Nassau clock reaction. He mixed the solutions in the big Pyrex beaker to first produce a pumpkin orange precipitate as a mercury compound settled out and then, after several seconds, the bright orange suddenly turned to a liquid lamp black as the excess iodine leftover transmuted to starch and turned on its color, a black, black curtain dropping instantly. The demonstration was meant to astound with its alchemy, and Martone was astounded, asking to see again the chemical logic of it, how benign soluble concoctions created a product that became a new reactant that then was ready to react. He liked both the anticipation and the rapidity of the transformations, the visual demonstration of whole moles being stewed in their own molecular juices, the quick switch and then its double-cross. It

was called a "clock" because of the predictable ticking of the bonding and unbond-
ing that timed out perfectly, a collection of ionic seconds spinning on their own
internal clocks. This led to this and that to this. The equal sign is replaced by
arrows in a chemical reaction, one thing after the other. Years later, when he was a
senior in organic chemistry, Martone asked the teacher if he could, in his spare
time, work on constructing a new clock reaction that would, this time, express
itself in North Side High School's colors, red and white, not out of any school spirit
but mainly out of an urge to tinker with the watch-works of cooked-up nuclei and
electron shells. After all, the class he was taking spent its time knitting together
long compounded chains of carbons and hydrogens and oxygens, matrices of
esters and ethers, another kind of ticking, the proteins twisted into the worsted
zipper of a gene undergoing mitosis, another two-step through time. In that lab,
too, he set a girl's hair on fire with the Bunsen burner, the flame eating up the
straight strands of her long brown hair like a fuse, another illustration of time. The
burned hair, turning to ash, flaked, crumbs of a rubber eraser, spilling to the floor
as the stink of it, the hair burning, rose in almost visible solid cartoon waves of
wavy stench, the glow of the actual burning peeling now in the nape of her neck,
the instant chemical reaction of it, giving off its own unique rainbow of bright colors. They had been performing primitive, spectral analysis, igniting unknown
compounds held in little wire loops over the lip of flame, reading the combustion's
signature through the slit of a cheap prism tube. The tip of her hair sparked as Martone tipped the burner toward what turned out to be a sulfuric something or other.
Martone damped down the crawling flicker with his hand, his fingers flouncing the
hairs that wove themselves into a now ratted cap, a nest, and for a moment it
seemed that the whole canopy would ignite, enriched by the addition of fresh air.
Martone was left holding this halo of fire, a hat from hell, a melodrama of oxida-
tion, when, just then, the teacher pulled them both into the emergency shower
where they were doused and, just as suddenly, engulfed in wet smoke and sodden
hairy ash. Martone never did find the combination of compounds to create the
clock reaction in his school colors. He remembers pouring through old manuals
his teacher gave him with pages of tables listing reactants and products and their
shades of colors, valences and radicals, ions and elements, metals and base. He
wandered through the old laboratory's closets looking for odd specimens in
ancient glass bottles stopped up with moldy cork or decaying rubber stoppers, the
forgotten chemicals undergoing their own unsupervised and unrecorded experi-
ments, reactions oxidizing into clumps of rusty rust, bleached stains, inert crystal-
line sweating salts, the paper labels foxing, the beakers mired in viscous goo, and
the wood racks gnawed at by some now long-gone acidic lick. Helping to clean out
the closets in anticipation of the renovation, Martone garnered extra credit to off-
set the disappointment and possible average grade for his disappointing independent study. In the mess, he found the apparatus used through the years to create

the famous Old Nassau clock reactions for succeeding classes—the tinctures of iodine, the compounds of starch, the granules of potassium, and the etched graduated cylinders set to deliver the proper quantities of chemical ingredients for the demonstration of time all that time ago. Years later, Martone is on the phone with his classmate from those years whose hair he set on fire during an experiment meant to identify certain chemicals by the spectrum of light they emit when set on fire. Martone has taken to looking through his past lives, has found many of his former classmates by employing the emerging electronic technologies online. He now lives far away from Fort Wayne, in Alabama, and finds it difficult to return home for the sporadic reunions, and when he does, others from back then now live even farther away or seem to have disappeared altogether. He thinks of it as a reconstitution, as hydration, this telephoning, and admits that his efforts redoubled after the collapse of the towers in 2001. That collapse seemed to be a kind of boundary, a membrane, a demarcation as narrow and fine as the hair fused in glass on his slide rule, of before and after. He found her, the woman whose hair he set on fire in his high school chemistry lab, living in New York teaching organic chemistry, of all things, at Columbia University there. The irony was not lost on them. She explained to him that she now was attempting to isolate low-molecular-weight chromium-binding substance in human urine. It had something to do with diabetes and insulin and iron in the blood. It was late at night, and they had been talking on the phone for a while about the past and chemistry and what they had both been doing separately at the same time during all those years when suddenly Martone heard band music. It was past midnight. The music, even diminished by the telephone, was distinctively brassy and rhythmic, shrill and thumping. Martone identified it as "The Horse," a favorite of their own high school's pep band years before. "Oh that," she said. "It's Columbia's marching band. A tradition. They spontaneously appear on the night before the orgo final and march around the Upper West Side." No one will believe this, Martone thinks. After all these years, no one will believe such coincidences of time and space. He learned long ago in the sciences classes of his high school that there were these things called constants. Gravity was one. The speed of light, he remembered. And time—time was constant too.

ORLANDO RICARDO MENES, a National Endowment for the Arts Fellow, is Professor of English at the University of Notre Dame and Poetry Editor of the *Notre Dame Review*. He is author of *Memoria* (LSU Press, 2019), *Heresies* (UNM Press, 2015), and *Furia* (Milkweed, 2005).

KYLE MINOR is author of *Praying Drunk* (Sarabande Books, 2014), winner of the 2015 Story Prize Spotlight Award. His work has appeared in *Esquire, The Atlantic, Salon,* the *New York Times Book Review,* and in three volumes of Houghton Mifflin Harcourt's *Best American* series. He is Director of Creative Writing at IUPUI.

MICHAEL MLEKODAY is author of *All Earthly Bodies* (University of Arkansas Press, 2022) and *The Dead Eat Everything* (The Kent State University Press, 2014). They hold degrees from the University of Minnesota, Kansas State University, and Indiana University, and are currently a PhD candidate at the University of California, Davis.

KATIE MOULTON is author of *Dead Dad Club* (Audible, 2022). Her essays appear in *New England Review, The Believer, Oxford American,* and *Sewanee Review.* Her work has been supported by MacDowell, Bread Loaf, Art Omi, Djerassi, Tin House, and Indiana University, where she earned her MFA and edited *Indiana Review.*

XAVIER NAVARRO AQUINO was born and raised in Puerto Rico. He is author of the novel *Velorio* (HarperCollins, 2022). He has been awarded scholarships from Bread Loaf, the Sewanee Writers' Conference, MacDowell, and an ACLS Emerging Voices Fellowship. Navarro Aquino is Assistant Professor of English at the University of Notre Dame.

SUSAN NEVILLE is author of *The Town of Whispering Dolls* (Fiction Collective 2, 2020), winner of the Catherine Doctorow Prize for Innovative Fiction, and *Fabrication: Essays on Making Things and Making Meaning* (MacMurray & Beck, 2001). She lives in Indianapolis and teaches at Butler University and in the Warren Wilson MFA Program for Writers.

DANNI QUINTOS is author of *Two Brown Dots* (BOA Editions, 2022), winner of the twentieth A. Poulin Jr. Prize, and *PYTHON* (Argus House, 2017), an ekphrastic chapbook featuring photography by her sister, Shelli Quintos. She is a Kentuckian, a mom, an educator, and an Affrilachian Poet.

SAM ROSS's debut collection of poetry, *Company,* was selected by Carl Phillips for the Four Way Books Levis Prize in Poetry and received the 2020 Thom Gunn Award for Gay Poetry from the Publishing Triangle. He is also a painter.

SCOTT RUSSELL SANDERS is author of more than twenty books, including *Small Marvels* (2022), *A Conservationist Manifesto* (2009), and *Writing from the Center* (1997), with Indiana University Press. He and his wife, Ruth, a biochemist, raised their two children in their hometown of Bloomington, where he is Professor Emeritus of English at Indiana University.

JASMINE SAWERS is a Kundiman fiction fellow whose work has won the *Ploughshares* Emerging Writers' Contest and the NANO Prize. Their debut collection, *The Anchored World,* is available from Rose Metal Press. They serve as an associate fiction editor for *Fairy Tale Review.*

BRUCE SNIDER is author of *Fruit* (University of Wisconsin Press, Spring 2020); *Paradise, Indiana* (Pleiades Press, 2013); and *The Year We Studied Women*

(University of Wisconsin Press, 2003). He is Associate Professor of English at the University of San Francisco.

LANA SPENDL is author of the chapbook *We Cradled Each Other in the Air*. Her work has appeared in *The Rumpus, The Greensboro Review, New Ohio Review*, and *Zone 3*. She is from Bosnia, and her childhood was divided between Bosnia and Spain due to the Bosnian War.

MAURA STANTON has published six books of poetry, including *Snow on Snow*, which won the Yale Younger Poets Award. She has also published a novel and three collections of short stories. She is Professor Emeritus at Indiana University.

PABLO PIÑERO STILLMANN is author of *Our Brains and the Brains of Miniature Sharks* (Moon City Press, 2020) and *Temblador* (Conaculta, 2014). A graduate of the MFA Program at Indiana University, his work has appeared in *Ninth Letter, Bennington Review*, and the *Notre Dame Review*.

JACOB SUNDERLIN is author of *This We in the Back of the House* (Saturnalia Books, 2022), winner of the Saturnalia Editors' Prize. He's received fellowships from the National Endowment for the Arts, the Fine Arts Work Center in Provincetown, and the Djerassi Resident Artists Program. Educated at public schools, he teaches high school at one in Indiana.

GIN FAITH THOMAS holds an MFA in Poetry from Indiana University in Bloomington, where she still lives, writes, and occasionally teaches. Her work has appeared in *[PANK], Hobart, Flying Island*, and *Bluestem*. She is currently seeking a publisher for her collection of poems about grief, social strictures, werewolves, and the perceived monstrosity of teen girl bodies.

CHUCK WAGNER lives in Westfield with his wife, Shari. He is presently retired after a teaching career in English and Creative Writing, primarily at Brebeuf Jesuit. He has been the recipient of a Creative Renewal Fellowship, and his work has appeared in *And Know This Place: Poetry of Indiana*.

SHARI WAGNER, Indiana's fifth Poet Laureate (2016–2017), is author of *The Farm Wife's Almanac, The Harmonist at Nightfall: Poems of Indiana*, and *Evening Chore*. Her poems have appeared in *North American Review, Shenandoah, The Writer's Almanac*, and the anthology *An Indiana Christmas*.

ALEXANDER WEINSTEIN is author of *Universal Love* (Henry Holt, 2020) and *Children of the New World* (Picador, 2016), which was a *New York Times* Notable Book of the Year. He is Director of the Martha's Vineyard Institute of Creative Writing and Professor of Creative Writing at Siena Heights University.

MARCUS WICKER is author of *Silencer* (Houghton Mifflin Harcourt, 2017), winner of the Society of Midland Authors Award, and *Maybe the Saddest Thing* (Harper

Perennial, 2012), selected by D. A. Powell for the National Poetry Series. He is Poetry Editor of *Southern Indiana Review* and Associate Professor of English at the University of Memphis.

TESSA YANG is author of *The Runaway Restaurant* (7.13 Books, 2022) and Assistant Professor of English at Hartwick College. She received her MFA from Indiana University, where she served as Editor of *Indiana Review*.

BRANDON YOUNG is a PhD student in creative writing at the University of Utah, where he is Poetry Editor of *Quarterly West*. He holds a BA from Indiana University and an MFA from Virginia Commonwealth University. His work has appeared in *RHINO* and *Poet Lore*.

PERMISSIONS

Akbar, Kaveh: "Orchids Are Sprouting from the Floorboards" from *Calling a Wolf a Wolf*. Copyright © 2017 by Kaveh Akbar. Reprinted by permission of the author.

Anderson, Dason: "Looking for Mushrooms" originally appeared in *Word Riot*. Reprinted by permission of the author.

Baldino, Noah: "The Creator Takes the Stand" originally appeared in *The Iowa Review*. Reprinted by permission of the author.

Berkowitz, Bryce: "Atmosphere in Our Bullshit Little Town" originally appeared in *The Normal School*. Reprinted by permission of the author.

Betz, Joe: "Red-Winged Blackbird" originally appeared in *Ninth Letter*. Reprinted by permission of the author.

Buchen, Callista: "Pretend" from *Look Look Look*. Copyright © 2019 by Callisa Buchen. Reprinted by permission of Black Lawrence Press.

Castro, Steve: "Deer Whisperer" originally appeared in *Slice Magazine*. Reprinted by permission of the author.

Cho, Su: "Hello, My Parents Don't Speak English Well, How Can I Help You?" from *The Symmetry of Fish*. Copyright © 2022 by Su Cho. Reprinted by permission of the author and Penguin Books.

Clark, C. L.: "You Perfect, Broken Thing" originally appeared in *Uncanny Magazine*. Reprinted by permission of the author.

Clark, Tia: "Insults for Ugly Girls" originally appeared in *Five Chapters*. Reprinted by permission of the author.

Comer, Nandi: "Ode to the Tongue" from *Tapping Out*. Copyright © 2020 by Nandi Comer. Reprinted by permission of Northwestern University Press.

Cunningham, Paul: "Feast Green and Stained" originally appeared in the Academy of American Poets' Poem-a-Day. Reprinted by permission of the author.

For Indiana University Press
Lesley Bolton, Project Manager/Editor
Brian Carroll, Rights Manager
Dan Crissman, Trade and Regional Acquisitions Editor
Samantha Heffner, Trade Acquisitions Assistant
Brenna Hosman, Production Coordinator
Katie Huggins, Production Manager
Dan Pyle, Online Publishing Manager
Rachel Rosolina, Marketing and Publicity Manager
Jennifer Witzke, Senior Artist and Book Designer